Decoding the TOEFL® iBT

Basic

LISTENING

INTRODUCTION

For many learners of English, the TOEFL® iBT will be the most important standardized test they ever take. Unfortunately for a large number of these individuals, the material covered on the TOEFL® iBT remains a mystery to them, so they are unable to do well on the test. We hope that by using the *Decoding the TOEFL® iBT* series, individuals who take the TOEFL® iBT will be able to excel on the test and, in the process of using the book, may unravel the mysteries of the test and therefore make the material covered on the TOEFL® iBT more familiar to themselves.

The TOEFL® iBT covers the four main skills that a person must learn when studying any foreign language: reading, listening, speaking, and writing. The *Decoding the TOEFL® iBT* series contains books that cover all four of these skills. The *Decoding the TOEFL® iBT* series contains books with three separate levels for all four of the topics, and it also contains the *Decoding the TOEFL® iBT Actual Test* books. These books contain several actual tests that learners can utilize to help them become better prepared to take the TOEFL® iBT. This book, *Decoding the TOEFL® iBT Listening Basic*, covers the listening aspect of the test. Finally, the TOEFL® iBT underwent a number of changes in August 2019. This book—and the others in the series—takes those changes into account and incorporates them in the texts and questions, so readers of this second edition can be assured that they have up-to-date knowledge of the test.

Decoding the TOEFL® iBT Listening Basic can be used by learners who are taking classes and also by individuals who are studying by themselves. It contains eight chapters, each of which focuses on a different listening question, and one actual test at the end of the book. Each chapter contains explanations of the questions and how to answer them correctly. It also contains passages of varying lengths, and it focuses on asking the types of questions that are covered in the chapter. The passages and question types in *Decoding the TOEFL® iBT Listening Basic* are lower levels than those found on the TOEFL® iBT. Individuals who use *Decoding the TOEFL® iBT Listening Basic* will therefore be able to prepare themselves not only to take the TOEFL® iBT but also to perform well on the test.

We hope that everyone who uses *Decoding the TOEFL® iBT Listening Basic* will be able to become more familiar with the TOEFL® iBT and will additionally improve his or her score on the test. As the title of the book implies, we hope that learners can use it to crack the code on the TOEFL® iBT, to make the test itself less mysterious and confusing, and to get the highest score possible. Finally, we hope that both learners and instructors can use this book to its full potential. We wish all of you the best of luck as you study English and prepare for the TOEFL® iBT, and we hope that *Decoding the TOEFL® iBT Listening Basic* can provide you with assistance during the course of your studies.

Michael A. Putlack
Stephen Poirier
Maximilian Tolochko

TABLE
OF
CONTENTS

ABOUT THE TOEFL® iBT LISTENING SECTION

Changes in the Listening Section

TOEFL® underwent many changes in August of 2019. The following is an explanation of some of the changes that have been made to the Listening section.

Format

The Listening section contains either two or three parts. Before August 2019, each part had one conversation and two lectures. However, since the changes in August 2019, each part can have either one conversation and one lecture or one conversation and two lectures. In total, two conversations and three lectures (in two parts) or three conversations and four lectures (in three parts) can appear. The possible formats of the Listening section include the following:

Number of Parts	First Part	Second Part	Third Part
2	1 Conversation + 1 Lecture	1 Conversation + 2 Lectures	
	1 Conversation + 2 Lectures	1 Conversation + 1 Lecture	
3	1 Conversation + 1 Lecture	1 Conversation + 1 Lecture	1 Conversation + 2 Lectures
	1 Conversation + 1 Lecture	1 Conversation + 2 Lectures	1 Conversation + 1 Lecture
	1 Conversation + 2 Lectures	1 Conversation + 1 Lecture	1 Conversation + 1 Lecture

The time given for the Listening section has been reduced from 60-90 minutes to 41-57 minutes.

Passages and Questions

The lengths of the conversations and the lectures remain the same as before. The length of each conversation and lecture is 3 to 6 minutes.

It has been reported that some conversations have academic discussions that are of high difficulty levels, making them almost similar to lectures. For example, some questions might ask about academic information discussed between a student and a professor in the conversation. In addition, questions for both the conversations and the lectures tend to ask for more detailed information than before.

The numbers of questions remain the same. The test taker is given five questions after each conversation and six questions after each lecture. The time given for answering each set of questions is either 6.5 or 10 minutes.

Each conversation or lecture is heard only once. The test taker can take notes while listening to the passage and refer to them when answering the questions.

Question Types

TYPE 1 Gist-Content Questions

Gist-Content questions cover the test taker's basic comprehension of the listening passage. While they are typically asked after lectures, they are sometimes asked after conversations as well. These questions check to see if the test taker has understood the gist of the passage. They focus on the passage as a whole, so it is important to recognize what the main point of the lecture is or why the two people in the conversation are having a particular discussion. The test taker should therefore be able to recognize the theme of the lecture or conversation in order to answer this question correctly.

TYPE 2 Gist-Purpose Questions

Gist-Purpose questions cover the underlying theme of the passage. While they are typically asked after conversations, they are sometimes asked after lectures as well. Because these questions focus on the purpose or theme of the conversation or lecture, they begin with the word "why." They focus on the conversation or lecture as a whole, but they are not concerned with details; instead, they are concerned with why the student is speaking with the professor or employee or why the professor is covering a specific topic.

TYPE 3 Detail Questions

Detail questions cover the test taker's ability to understand facts and data that are mentioned in the listening passage. These questions appear after both conversations and lectures. Detail questions require the test taker to listen for and remember details from the passage. The majority of these questions concern major details that are related to the main topic of the lecture or conversation rather than minor ones. However, in some cases where there is a long digression that is not clearly related to the main idea, there may be a question about the details of the digression.

TYPE 4 Making Inferences Questions

Making Inferences questions cover the test taker's ability to understand implications made in the passage and to come to a conclusion about what these implications mean. These questions appear after both conversations and lectures. These questions require the test taker to hear the information being presented and then to make conclusions about what the information means or what is going to happen as a result of that information.

TYPE 5 · Understanding Function Questions

Understanding Function questions cover the test taker's ability to determine the underlying meaning of what has been said in the passage. This question type often involves replaying a portion of the listening passage. There are two types of these questions. Some ask the test taker to infer the meaning of a phrase or a sentence. Thus the test taker needs to determine the implication—not the literal meaning—of the sentence. Other questions ask the test taker to infer the purpose of a statement made by one of the speakers. These questions specifically ask about the intended effect of a particular statement on the listener.

TYPE 6 · Understanding Attitude Questions

Understanding Attitude questions cover the speaker's attitude or opinion toward something. These questions may appear after both lectures and conversations. This question type often involves replaying a portion of the listening passage. There are two types of these questions. Some ask about one of the speakers' feelings concerning something. These questions may check to see whether the test taker understands how a speaker feels about a particular topic, if a speaker likes or dislikes something, or why a speaker might feel anxiety or amusement. The other category asks about one of the speaker's opinions. These questions may inquire about a speaker's degree of certainty. Others may ask what a speaker thinks or implies about a topic, person, thing, or idea.

TYPE 7 · Understanding Organization Questions

Understanding Organization questions cover the test taker's ability to determine the overall organization of the passage. These questions almost always appear after lectures. They rarely appear after conversations. These questions require the test taker to pay attention to two factors. The first is the way that the professor has organized the lecture and how he or she presents the information to the class. The second is how individual information given in the lecture relates to the lecture as a whole. To answer these questions correctly, test takers should focus more on the presentation and the professor's purpose in mentioning the facts rather than the facts themselves.

TYPE 8 · Connecting Content Questions

Connecting Content questions almost exclusively appear after lectures, not after conversations. These questions measure the test taker's ability to understand how the ideas in the lecture relate to one another. These relationships may be explicitly stated, or you may have to infer them from the words you hear. The majority of these questions concern major relationships in the passage. These questions also commonly appear in passages where a number of different themes, ideas, objects, or individuals are being discussed.

HOW TO USE THIS BOOK

Decoding the TOEFL® iBT Listening Basic is designed to be used either as a textbook in a classroom environment or as a study guide for individual learners. There are 8 chapters in this book. Each chapter provides comprehensive information about one type of listening question. There are 6 sections in each chapter, which enable you to build up your skills on a particular listening question. At the end of the book, there is one actual test of the Listening section of the TOEFL® iBT.

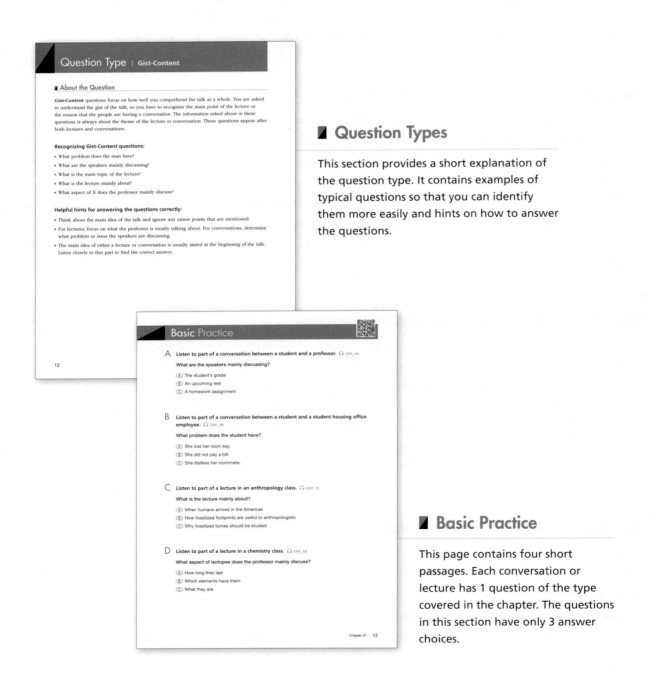

■ Question Types

This section provides a short explanation of the question type. It contains examples of typical questions so that you can identify them more easily and hints on how to answer the questions.

■ Basic Practice

This page contains four short passages. Each conversation or lecture has 1 question of the type covered in the chapter. The questions in this section have only 3 answer choices.

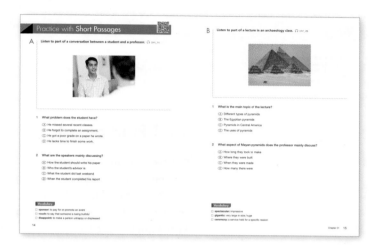

▮ Practice with Short Passages

The section contains 2 passages. There are usually 1 conversation between 150 and 200 words long and 1 lecture between 250 and 300 words long. However, depending on the question type, there may be 2 conversations or 2 lectures. Each passage contains 2 questions of the type covered in the chapter and has a short vocabulary section.

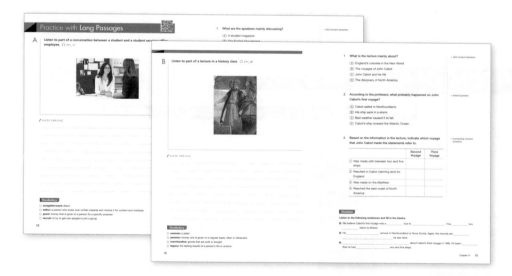

▮ Practice with Long Passages

This section contains 2 passages. There are normally 1 conversation between 250 and 300 words long and 1 lecture between 350 and 400 words long. However, depending on the question type, there may be either 2 conversations or 2 lectures. There is at least 1 question about the type of question covered in the chapter. The other questions are of various types. There are also a short vocabulary section and a dictation section to practice your listening skills.

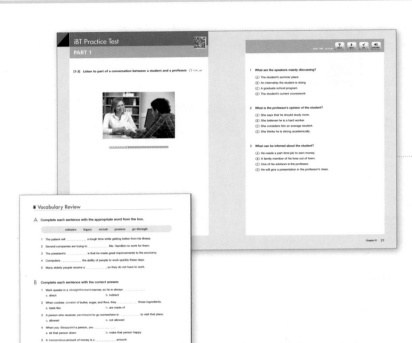

iBT Practice Test

This section has 2 conversations between 400 and 450 words long with 3 questions and 3 lectures between 550 and 600 words long with 4 questions each.

Vocabulary Review

This section has two vocabulary exercises using words that appear in the passages in the chapter.

Actual Test (at the end of the book)

This section has 1 full-length listening test, which contains 2 full-length conversations with 5 questions and 3 full-length lectures with 6 questions.

Chapter **01**

Gist-Content

◪ About the Question

Gist-Content questions focus on how well you comprehend the talk as a whole. You are asked to understand the gist of the talk, so you have to recognize the main point of the lecture or the reason that the people are having a conversation. The information asked about in these questions is always about the theme of the lecture or conversation. These questions appear after both lectures and conversations.

Recognizing Gist-Content questions:

- What problem does the man have?
- What are the speakers mainly discussing?
- What is the main topic of the lecture?
- What is the lecture mainly about?
- What aspect of X does the professor mainly discuss?

Helpful hints for answering the questions correctly:

- Think about the main idea of the talk and ignore any minor points that are mentioned.
- For lectures, focus on what the professor is mostly talking about. For conversations, determine what problem or issue the speakers are discussing.
- The main idea of either a lecture or conversation is usually stated at the beginning of the talk. Listen closely to this part to find the correct answer.

Basic Practice

A **Listen to part of a conversation between a student and a professor.** 🎧 CH1_1A

What are the speakers mainly discussing?

(A) The student's grade

(B) An upcoming test

(C) A homework assignment

B **Listen to part of a conversation between a student and a student housing office employee.** 🎧 CH1_1B

What problem does the student have?

(A) She lost her room key.

(B) She did not pay a bill.

(C) She dislikes her roommate.

C **Listen to part of a lecture in an anthropology class.** 🎧 CH1_1C

What is the lecture mainly about?

(A) When humans arrived in the Americas

(B) How fossilized footprints are useful to anthropologists

(C) Why fossilized bones should be studied

D **Listen to part of a lecture in a chemistry class.** 🎧 CH1_1D

What aspect of isotopes does the professor mainly discuss?

(A) How long they last

(B) Which elements have them

(C) What they are

A **Listen to part of a conversation between a student and a professor.** 🎧 CH1_2A

1 **What problem does the student have?**

Ⓐ He missed several recent classes.

Ⓑ He forgot to complete an assignment.

Ⓒ He got a poor grade on a paper he wrote.

Ⓓ He lacks time to finish some work.

2 **What are the speakers mainly discussing?**

Ⓐ How the student should write his paper

Ⓑ Who the student's advisor is

Ⓒ What the student did last weekend

Ⓓ When the student completed his report

Vocabulary

☐ **sponsor**: to pay for or promote an event

☐ **vouch**: to say that someone is being truthful

☐ **disappoint**: to make a person unhappy or displeased

Listen to part of a lecture in an archaeology class. 🎧 CH1_2B

1   **What is the main topic of the lecture?**

Ⓐ Different types of pyramids

Ⓑ The Egyptian pyramids

Ⓒ Pyramids in Central America

Ⓓ The uses of pyramids

2   **What aspect of Mayan pyramids does the professor mainly discuss?**

Ⓐ How long they took to make

Ⓑ Where they were built

Ⓒ When they were made

Ⓓ How many there were

Vocabulary

☐ **spectacular:** impressive

☐ **gigantic:** very large in size; huge

☐ **ceremony:** a service held for a specific reason

A | **Listen to part of a conversation between a student and a student services office employee.** 🎧 CH1_3A

✏ NOTE-TAKING

....

....

....

....

....

....

....

....

Vocabulary

☐ **straightforward:** direct

☐ **editor:** a person who looks over written material and checks it for content and mistakes

☐ **grant:** money that is given to a person for a specific purpose

☐ **recruit:** to try to get new people to join a group

1 What are the speakers mainly discussing?

← Gist-Content Question

  Ⓐ A student magazine

  Ⓑ The English Department

  Ⓒ The student newspaper

  Ⓓ A new advisor

2 What is the likely outcome of the employee speaking with Professor Martin?

← Connecting Content Question

  Ⓐ She will learn about a source of funding.

  Ⓑ She will talk about the student newspaper.

  Ⓒ She will approve a request to sell ads.

  Ⓓ She will learn about the English Department.

3 What will the student probably do next?

← Making Inferences Question

  Ⓐ Speak with her advisor

  Ⓑ Submit a written proposal

  Ⓒ Give the employee a phone number

  Ⓓ Introduce some of her writers

Dictation

Listen to part of the conversation again and fill in the blanks.

W1: Hello. I'm Henrietta Reynolds. You're Ms. Lucent, right? I talked to you _____ _____ _____ this morning.

W2: Oh, hello. It's nice to meet you _____ _____. You're here about the student magazine, aren't you?

W1: _____ _____. Did you understand everything I told you over the phone?

W2: Uh . . . _____ _____. Why don't you _____ _____ _____? That way, I can _____ _____ I know what you want to do.

W1: Sure, I can do that. _____ _____ _____ . . .

B | Listen to part of a lecture in a history class. 🎧 CH1_3B

✏️ NOTE-TAKING

....

....

....

....

....

....

....

....

Vocabulary

☐ **seaman:** a sailor

☐ **pension:** money one is given on a regular basis, often in retirement

☐ **merchandise:** goods that are sold or bought

☐ **legacy:** the lasting results of a person's life or actions

1   **What is the lecture mainly about?**

← Gist-Content Question

   Ⓐ England's colonies in the New World

   Ⓑ The voyages of John Cabot

   Ⓒ John Cabot and his life

   Ⓓ The discovery of North America

2   **According to the professor, what probably happened on John Cabot's first voyage?**

← Detail Question

   Ⓐ Cabot sailed to Newfoundland.

   Ⓑ His ship sank in a storm.

   Ⓒ Bad weather caused it to fail.

   Ⓓ Cabot's ship crossed the Atlantic Ocean.

3   **Based on the information in the lecture, indicate which voyage that John Cabot made the statements refer to.**

← Connecting Content Question

	Second Voyage	Third Voyage
① Was made with between two and five ships		
② Resulted in Cabot claiming land for England		
③ Was made on the *Matthew*		
④ Reached the east coast of North America		

Dictation

Listen to the following sentences and fill in the blanks.

❶ We believe Cabot's first voyage was a _____ due to _____ _____ . This _____ him _____ return to Bristol.

❷ He _____ _____ arrived in Newfoundland or Nova Scotia. Again, the records are _____ _____ _____ _____ he saw land.

❸ _____ _____ _____ _____ _____ about Cabot's third voyage in 1498. It's been _____ that he had _____ _____ two and five ships.

[1-3]   Listen to part of a conversation between a student and a professor. 🎧 CH1_4A

1 **What are the speakers mainly discussing?**

Ⓐ The student's summer plans

Ⓑ An internship the student is doing

Ⓒ A graduate school program

Ⓓ The student's current coursework

2 **What is the professor's opinion of the student?**

Ⓐ She says that he should study more.

Ⓑ She believes he is a hard worker.

Ⓒ She considers him an average student.

Ⓓ She thinks he is strong academically.

3 **What can be inferred about the student?**

Ⓐ He needs a part-time job to earn money.

Ⓑ A family member of his lives out of town.

Ⓒ One of his advisors is the professor.

Ⓓ He will give a presentation in the professor's class.

[4-7] **Listen to part of a lecture in a botany class.** 🎧 CH1_4B

Botany

4   What is the lecture mainly about?

    Ⓐ The life cycles of flowering plants

    Ⓑ The ways flowering plants can get pollinated

    Ⓒ The requirements flowers need to survive

    Ⓓ The best places for flowers to grow

5   Why does the professor mention birds and bees?

    Ⓐ To talk about why they like flowers

    Ⓑ To show how they can transport seeds

    Ⓒ To explain their role in pollination

    Ⓓ To name which flowers they prefer

6   What will the professor probably do next?

    Ⓐ Test the students on the information

    Ⓑ Let the students take a break

    Ⓒ Continue lecturing to the students

    Ⓓ Show the students a short video

7   Listen again to part of the lecture. Then answer the question.
       What does the professor mean when she says this: 🎧

    Ⓐ She has time to discuss photosynthesis now.

    Ⓑ She hopes the students understand a topic.

    Ⓒ She will not talk more about a topic today.

    Ⓓ She believes photosynthesis is easy to understand.

[8-11] Listen to part of a lecture in an astronomy class. 🎧 CH1_4C

Astronomy

8 In the lecture, the professor describes a number of facts about the inner planets. Indicate whether each of the following is a fact or not.

Click in the correct box for each statement.

	Fact	Not a Fact
1 They are rocky planets.		
2 Some of them have ring systems.		
3 Not all of them have moons.		
4 Their atmospheres are made of gases.		

9 What aspect of the Kuiper Belt does the professor mainly discuss?

Ⓐ Its distance from the sun

Ⓑ Its appearance

Ⓒ The objects located in it

Ⓓ The asteroid belt in it

10 What can be inferred about the Oort Cloud?

Ⓐ Several main dwarf planets are in it.

Ⓑ Humans hope to travel there someday.

Ⓒ Very little is known about it today.

Ⓓ It is located beside the outer planets.

11 Listen again to part of the lecture. Then answer the question.
What does the professor imply when he says this: 🎧

Ⓐ Most of Jupiter's moons are merely small asteroids.

Ⓑ It is possible there is life on some of Jupiter's moons.

Ⓒ Astronomers believe some of the objects are not really moons.

Ⓓ More moons may be discovered around Jupiter one day.

[1-3] Listen to part of a conversation between a student and a student services office employee. 🎧 CH1_4D

1   **What problem does the student have?**

    Ⓐ He is doing poorly in some of his classes.

    Ⓑ He lacks permission to study in a special area.

    Ⓒ He has a heavy course load this semester.

    Ⓓ He has not started writing his thesis yet.

2   **What can be inferred about the student?**

    Ⓐ He gets along well with his roommate.

    Ⓑ He is doing well in his classes.

    Ⓒ He has an apartment far from campus.

    Ⓓ He has a part-time job.

3   **Why does the student need to return to his dormitory?**

    Ⓐ To show the seminar paper he is writing

    Ⓑ To find his student identification card

    Ⓒ To get a copy of his class schedule

    Ⓓ To get a note from his residential assistant

[4-7] Listen to part of a lecture in a cinematography class. 🎧 CH1_4E

4 What aspect of *Russian Ark* does the professor mainly discuss?

Ⓐ What happens in it

Ⓑ How it was filmed

Ⓒ When it was filmed

Ⓓ Why it was filmed

5 What role did Alexander Sokurov have in *Russian Ark*?

Click on 2 answers.

1 He filmed the movie.

2 He was the European.

3 He voiced the narrator.

4 He directed the film.

6 Why does the professor tell the students about the European?

Ⓐ To say he provided financial backing

Ⓑ To point out that he does not speak Russian

Ⓒ To state that his parts were deleted from *Russian Ark*

Ⓓ To explain his role in *Russian Ark*

7 What will the professor probably do next?

Ⓐ Screen a film for the students

Ⓑ Answer some questions

Ⓒ Continue explaining the story in *Russian Ark*

Ⓓ Take a short break

◢ Vocabulary Review

A **Complete each sentence with the appropriate word from the box.**

| enhance | legacy | recruit | pension | go through |

1 The patient will _____ a tough time while getting better from his illness.

2 Several companies are trying to _____ Ms. Hamilton to work for them.

3 The president's _____ is that he made great improvements to the economy.

4 Computers _____ the ability of people to work quickly these days.

5 Many elderly people receive a _____, so they do not have to work.

B **Complete each sentence with the correct answer.**

1 Mark speaks in a **straightforward** manner, so he is always _____.
   a. direct   b. indirect

2 When cookies **consist of** butter, sugar, and flour, they _____ those ingredients.
   a. taste like   b. are made of

3 A person who receives **permission** to go somewhere is _____ to visit that place.
   a. allowed   b. not allowed

4 When you **disappoint** a person, you _____.
   a. let that person down   b. make that person happy

5 A **tremendous** amount of money is a _____ amount.
   a. very small   b. very large

6 A manufacturing **process** is the _____ that things get made.
   a. way   b. style

7 A **gigantic** animal is one that is _____ than normal.
   a. much smaller   b. much larger

8 The wall that **surrounds** the city _____.
   a. goes all around it   b. is very high

9 Because Helen has a lot of **potential**, she can be _____ in the future.
   a. healthy   b. successful

Chapter **02**

Gist-Purpose

About the Question

Gist-Purpose questions focus on the theme of the talk. You must determine why the conversation is taking place or why the professor is lecturing about a specific topic. These questions begin with "why." They do not ask about details. Instead, they ask about why the talk is taking place. These questions sometimes follow lectures but are more common after conversations.

Recognizing Gist-Purpose questions:

- Why does the student visit the professor?
- Why does the student visit the Registrar's office?
- Why did the professor ask to see the student?
- Why does the professor explain X?

Helpful hints for answering the questions correctly:

- Think about why the lecture or conversation is happening.
- For conversations, listen closely to the description of the problem the student has as well as the solution. Knowing both of them can help you determine why the student is speaking with the professor or visiting a certain office.
- In many instances, the student explains the reason he or she is visiting the professor or office at the beginning of the conversation. Always listen carefully to this part.
- In other instances, the student sums up the conversation at the end and therefore provides the answer to the question.

Basic Practice

A **Listen to part of a conversation between a student and a cafeteria employee.** 🎧 CH2_1A

Why did the man ask to see the student?

Ⓐ To change her working hours

Ⓑ To rate her job performance

Ⓒ To give her a promotion

B **Listen to part of a conversation between a student and a professor.** 🎧 CH2_1B

Why does the student visit the professor?

Ⓐ To inform her of an absence

Ⓑ To submit a paper

Ⓒ To inquire about an assignment

C **Listen to part of a conversation between a student and a school newspaper employee.** 🎧 CH2_1C

Why does the student visit the school newspaper office?

Ⓐ To comment on an article

Ⓑ To apply for a job

Ⓒ To place an advertisement

D **Listen to part of a lecture in an art history class.** 🎧 CH2_1D

Why does the professor explain what illuminated manuscripts are?

Ⓐ Some students may not know about them.

Ⓑ She wants to point out that they are art.

Ⓒ Their history is important for the class.

A   **Listen to part of a conversation between a student and a professor.** 🎧 CH2_2A

1   Why does the student visit the professor?

Ⓐ To ask about her grade

Ⓑ To talk about an assignment

Ⓒ To discuss which class to take

Ⓓ To mention changing her major

2   Why does the student explain her summer plans?

Ⓐ To say why she changed her mind

Ⓑ To express her desire to graduate early

Ⓒ To inquire about doing an internship

Ⓓ To state that she needs to find a job

B Listen to part of a conversation between a student and a student activities office employee. 🎧 CH2_2B

1 Why does the student visit the student activities office?

ⓐ To reschedule a club meeting

ⓑ To ask about membership in a club

ⓒ To try to learn about a new club

ⓓ To find out when a club has its first meeting

2 Why does the woman explain about Professor Johnson's class?

ⓐ To say there is still space left in it

ⓑ To suggest the student enroll in it

ⓒ To mention the time it will be held

ⓓ To say why a room is available

Vocabulary

☐ **on behalf of:** for; in support of

☐ **reschedule:** to change the time or date when an event will take place

☐ **cancel:** to decide that a planned event will not take place

A **Listen to part of a conversation between a student and a professor.** 🎧 CH2_3A

✏ NOTE-TAKING

....

....

....

....

....

....

....

....

....

Vocabulary

☐ **catch up:** to get back to a normal state after falling behind

☐ **load:** an amount of work a person must do

☐ **incomplete:** unfinished

☐ **paperwork:** written work that is often required, such as official documents

1   **Why does the student visit the professor?**

← Gist-Purpose Question

    Ⓐ To ask about a homework assignment

    Ⓑ To find out how to finish her work

    Ⓒ To get some hints for an exam

    Ⓓ To say that she is dropping out of his class

2   **What is the professor's attitude toward the student's situation?**

← Understanding Attitude Question

    Ⓐ He thinks her situation is not important.

    Ⓑ He is unsure about her problem.

    Ⓒ He is sympathetic toward her.

    Ⓓ He believes that she is working hard.

3   **Listen again to part of the conversation. Then answer the question. Why does the professor say this:** 🎧

← Understanding Function Question

    Ⓐ To remind the student of her class time

    Ⓑ To find out when the student's next class is

    Ⓒ To indicate the student should get the form today

    Ⓓ To let the student know he is busy this afternoon

Dictation

Listen to part of the conversation again and fill in the blanks.

M: Okay, _____ _____ _____ . . . How are you doing in your other classes? Are you going to _____ _____ _____ _____ or not?

W: I'm _____ _____ _____ in two of them. I think I can finish one more on time. But I _____ _____ your work or my work for Professor Powell or Professor Kennedy.

M: All right. _____ _____ _____ _____ you an incomplete grade? Then, you can finish the work for me _____ _____ _____ . Oh, you're going to _____ _____ _____ _____ , aren't you?

W: Yes, I'll be taking it. And your _____ sounds great. I _____ _____ _____ .

B | Listen to part of a lecture in an anthropology class. 🎧 CH2_3B

✏ NOTE-TAKING

....

....

....

....

....

....

....

....

....

1 How does the professor organize the information about the Incan classes that she presents to the class?

← Understanding Organization Question

    Ⓐ By focusing only on the upper classes

    Ⓑ By going from the top of the hierarchy to the bottom

    Ⓒ By stressing the importance of the lower classes

    Ⓓ By discussing how many people belonged to each class

2 Why does the professor explain a duty of the governors?

← Gist-Purpose Question

    Ⓐ To say they had to maintain the roads

    Ⓑ To mention that they collected *mita*

    Ⓒ To explain their role in Incan religion

    Ⓓ To discuss the distribution of food

3 According to the professor, what was *allyu*?

← Detail Question

    Ⓐ A government tax

    Ⓑ The Incan name of the emperor

    Ⓒ A large group of families

    Ⓓ The Incan high priest

Dictation

Listen to the following sentences and fill in the blanks.

❶ The people _____ the emperor a _____ of their sun god, so they _____ him _____ a god.

❷ The empire was large and often _____ _____ _____ its neighbors. It _____ _____ _____ four parts.

❸ _____ , the Incans had almost no merchants. _____ _____ _____ _____ the government controlled the collection and distribution of food and other goods.

[1-3] Listen to part of a conversation between a student and a librarian. CH2_4A

1 Why does the student visit the librarian?

Ⓐ To return an overdue book

Ⓑ To inquire about some missing items

Ⓒ To find out where the rare book collection is

Ⓓ To learn to use the computer system

2 What does the student ask the librarian to let him do?

Ⓐ Look through some boxes

Ⓑ Borrow some reference books

Ⓒ Make photocopies of documents

Ⓓ Check out books without a library card

3 Listen again to part of the conversation. Then answer the question. What does the student imply when he says this: 🎧

Ⓐ The library's collection of books is poor.

Ⓑ He needs to borrow many books.

Ⓒ A large number of books are missing.

Ⓓ He needs some books immediately.

[4-7] Listen to part of a lecture in a geology class. 🎧 CH2_4B

Geology

4   Based on the information in the lecture, indicate which type of crater lake the statements refer to.

Click in the correct box for each statement.

	Collapsed Crater Lake	Explosive Crater Lake
① Results from a very violent eruption		
② Can happen when magma departs a chamber underground		
③ Is the type of lake that Lake Toba is		
④ May occur when the roof of a magma chamber has no internal support		

5   **Why does the professor explain the formation of Crater Lake in Oregon?**

   Ⓐ To respond to a student's request

   Ⓑ To show how unusual it was

   Ⓒ To describe it as an explosive crater lake

   Ⓓ To point out exactly when it happened

6   **Why does the professor tell the students to look in their textbooks?**

   Ⓐ To see a diagram of a magma chamber

   Ⓑ To check out a list of some crater lakes

   Ⓒ To look at some pictures of crater lakes

   Ⓓ To read a passage on crater lake formation

7   **What comparison does the professor make between Crater Lake and Lake Toba?**

   Ⓐ The sizes of the eruptions that formed them

   Ⓑ Their depths

   Ⓒ Their altitudes above sea level

   Ⓓ The ways they filled with water

[8-11] Listen to part of a lecture in a marine biology class. 🎧 CH2_4C

Marine Biology

8   What aspect of whale sounds does the professor mainly discuss?

Click on 2 answers.

   ☐1   Why they are made

   ☐2   How they are produced

   ☐3   How they sound to humans

   ☐4   What animals can hear them

9   What is the professor's opinion of whale songs?

   Ⓐ She finds them pleasant to hear.

   Ⓑ She thinks they serve no purpose.

   Ⓒ She likes them better than music.

   Ⓓ She does not enjoy listening to them.

10   Why does the professor explain the sounds male humpback whales make?

   Ⓐ To discuss their possible purposes

   Ⓑ To compare them with sounds made by females

   Ⓒ To argue that they only make feeding calls

   Ⓓ To mention how old they are when they make sounds

11   What will the professor probably do next?

   Ⓐ Play a recording

   Ⓑ Take a break

   Ⓒ Assign some work

   Ⓓ Review the material

[1-3] Listen to part of a conversation between a student and a student activities office employee. 🎧 CH2_4D

HIDE TIME 00:06:30 HELP NEXT OK VOLUME

1 **Why does the student visit the student activities office?**

Ⓐ To drop off some posters

Ⓑ To pick up some items

Ⓒ To make a request

Ⓓ To pay an application fee

2 **What does the man give the student?**

Ⓐ A stamp

Ⓑ An application form

Ⓒ A campus map

Ⓓ A permission slip

3 **According to the man, where can the student put the posters?**

Click on 2 answers.

[1] On sidewalks

[2] On bulletin boards

[3] On lampposts

[4] Inside buildings

[4-7] **Listen to part of a lecture in a zoology class.** 🎧 CH2_4E

Zoology

the meerkat

4   **What aspect of the meerkat does the professor mainly discuss?**

     (A) Its burrowing habits

     (B) Its special warning system

     (C) Its feeding methods

     (D) Its size and shape

5   **According to the professor, why does the meerkat live underground?**

Click on 2 answers.

     ☐1 To let it store food more easily

     ☐2 To hide itself from animals hunting it

     ☐3 To provide places to raise its young

     ☐4 To get away from hot temperatures

6   **Why does the professor explain the sounds the meerkat makes?**

     (A) To prove it is capable of communicating

     (B) To state how scientists learned the sounds' meanings

     (C) To show how it warns others of danger

     (D) To note that it makes sounds when hunting

7   **Listen again to part of the lecture. Then answer the question.**
      What does the student imply when he says this: 🎧

     (A) He thinks that meerkats can kill snakes.

     (B) He cannot believe that snakes hunt meerkats.

     (C) He wants the professor to prove meerkats hunts snakes.

     (D) He expected meerkats to be scared of snakes.

◪ Vocabulary Review

A Complete each sentence with the appropriate word from the box.

on behalf of	impact	application	remove	rely on

1 Most experts believe that the _____ of the law will be minor.

2 Many people _____ their families to help them during difficult times.

3 Jane attended the event last night _____ her supervisor.

4 Thomas filled out an _____ to apply for a job at the company.

5 It was necessary to _____ the posters before painting the walls.

B Complete each sentence with the correct answer.

1 A truck carrying a large **load** has _____ in the back.

   a. expensive goods   b. many items

2 Whenever an animal **forages for** food, it _____ some food.

   a. looks for   b. eats

3 Someone with **extensive** knowledge of history knows _____ about it.

   a. very little   b. a great deal

4 A person who **alters** an electric motor _____ it.

   a. repairs   b. changes

5 When Eric **collapsed** in the hospital, he _____.

   a. fell onto the floor   b. vomited everywhere

6 **Carnivores** are animals that only eat _____.

   a. vegetation   b. meat

7 Because Allen is a **descendant** of a Native American tribe, he is _____ people in that tribe.

   a. related to   b. unaware of

8 An **incomplete** report is one that is _____.

   a. not finished   b. well written

9 A company with **multiple** departments has _____ of them.

   a. only a few   b. a large number

Chapter **03**

Detail

■ About the Question

Detail questions focus on your ability to understand the facts that are mentioned in a talk. You must listen closely to the details and remember them. These questions cover major details, not minor ones. However, if a speaker talks about something not related to the main topic for a while, there may be a question about the details covered in it. These questions appear after both lectures and conversations.

Recognizing Detail questions:

1 Most Detail questions have four answer choices and one correct answer. These questions appear on the test like this:

- According to the professor, what is one way that X can affect Y?

- What are X?

- What resulted from the invention of the X?

- According to the professor, what is the main problem with the X theory?

2 Other detail questions have two or more correct answers though. These questions will either require you to click on two answer choices or will ask you to check if several statements are true or not. These questions appear on the test like this:

- According to the professor, how did prehistoric humans get to Australia?
  [Click on 2 answers.]

- In the lecture, the professor describes a number of facts about earthquakes. Indicate whether each of the following is a fact about earthquakes.
  [Click in the correct box for each statement.]

Helpful hints for answering the questions correctly:

- Be sure to recognize the main idea or topic of the talk. Then, focus on any facts mentioned that are related to it. If you are not sure about the correct answer, select the answer choice closest to the main idea or topic of the talk.

- Ignore facts about minor details in the talk.

- The correct answers to these questions are often paraphrased from the talk. Be careful of answer choices that use the exact words from the talk. These are sometimes purposely misleading.

A **Listen to part of a conversation between a student and a transportation office employee.** 🎧 CH3_1A

According to the student, what qualification does he have?

(A) He passed a professional exam.

(B) He can speak a foreign language.

(C) He did similar work in the past.

B **Listen to part of a conversation between a student and a professor.** 🎧 CH3_1B

Why does the student need a handout?

(A) She gave hers to another student.

(B) The teaching assistant did not give her one.

(C) She did not attend the day's class.

C **Listen to part of a lecture in a zoology class.** 🎧 CH3_1C

According to the professor, how do people use reindeer?

(A) To train horses to pull sleds

(B) To use their skin to make items

(C) To make objects with their antlers

D **Listen to part of a lecture in an archaeology class.** 🎧 CH3_1D

In the lecture, the professor describes a number of facts about the Dead Sea Scrolls. Indicate whether each of the following is a fact or not.

	Fact	Not a Fact
1 They are all written in the same language.		
2 They contain works from the Bible and other sources.		
3 They were found in several different places.		

Practice with Short Passages

A **Listen to part of a conversation between a student and a mailroom employee.**

🎧 CH3_2A

1 **When did the student get an email from the online retailer?**

    Ⓐ Last week

    Ⓑ On Monday

    Ⓒ Yesterday

    Ⓓ This morning

2 **What does the man say that he will do?**

    Ⓐ Try to find the package

    Ⓑ Send the student an email

    Ⓒ Let the student look for the item

    Ⓓ Contact the online retailer

Vocabulary

☐ **retailer:** a store that sells goods, often in small quantities

☐ **understaffed:** lacking enough workers

☐ **priority:** urgent; of great importance

Listen to part of a lecture in an art class. 🎧 CH3_2B

1 Why should people avoid putting oil paintings in glass frames?

    (A) The paint can get smudged.

    (B) The paintings may become difficult to see.

    (C) The frames can get dirty.

    (D) The paintings need exposure to air.

2 According to the professor, how can a person remove dust from a painting?

    (A) By using linseed oil

    (B) By using a brush

    (C) By using a damp cloth

    (D) By using soap and water

Vocabulary

☐ **fade:** to lose color

☐ **smudge:** to smear

☐ **mar:** to damage in some manner

A **Listen to part of a conversation between a student and a professor.** 🎧 CH3_3A

✏ NOTE-TAKING

....

....

....

....

....

....

....

....

....

Vocabulary

☐ **comprehend:** to understand

☐ **disband:** to break up a group

☐ **outlaw:** a criminal; a person who has broken the law

☐ **civil war:** a war between two or more groups belonging to the same country or nation

1 What problem does the student have?

← Gist-Content Question

   Ⓐ She cannot think of a topic for her paper.

   Ⓑ She missed several classes.

   Ⓒ She got a poor grade on a test.

   Ⓓ She did not understand a lecture.

2 According to the professor, why was Julius Caesar's action important?

← Detail Question

   Ⓐ It encouraged some enemies.

   Ⓑ It started a war.

   Ⓒ It abolished the Senate.

   Ⓓ It established an army.

3 What can be inferred about the professor?

← Making Inferences Question

   Ⓐ He has been teaching history for many years.

   Ⓑ He assigns papers for his students to write.

   Ⓒ He has enough time to answer another question.

   Ⓓ He will speak more about Julius Caesar in class.

Dictation

Listen to part of the conversation again and fill in the blanks.

M: What can I do for you today?

W: Thank you, sir. I have a _____ _____ questions about today's lecture. I'm, um, I'm _____ _____ _____ I understood everything properly. There were, um, two things _____ _____ _____.

M: That's perfectly _____. Today's lecture was one of _____ _____ _____ of the year for many students. _____ _____ _____ _____ your questions, please.

W: Thank you.

B | Listen to part of a lecture in a biology class. 🎧 CH3_3B

✏ NOTE-TAKING

....

....

....

....

....

....

....

....

....

Vocabulary

☐ **niche:** a small area that is suitable for someone or something

☐ **offspring:** children; babies

☐ **outcompete:** to do better than another in a contest

☐ **partition:** to divide into different parts

1 In the lecture, the professor describes a number of facts about ecological niches. Indicate whether each of the following is a fact or not.

← Detail Question

	Fact	Not a Fact
① They help species avoid competing against one another.		
② They are related to the acquiring of food.		
③ They prevent animals from sharing resources.		
④ They can be occupied by subspecies of animals.		

2 What does the professor say about the competition exclusion principle?

← Detail Question

(A) It is useful for understanding the anole lizard.

(B) It is a relatively new theory.

(C) It is not always accurate.

(D) It is effective for animals in tropical areas.

3 Listen again to part of the lecture. Then answer the question. What can be inferred about the professor when he says this: 🎧

← Understanding Attitude Question

(A) He hopes the students read the handout he gave them.

(B) He thinks the students do not understand the material.

(C) He wants the students to ask him some questions.

(D) He intends to show the students a short video soon.

Dictation

Listen to the following sentences and fill in the blanks.

❶ All life needs certain things _____ _____. Food and water are two _____. Yet species _____ _____ _____ _____ for these resources.

❷ The main factor in an ecological niche is _____ _____ _____ _____. This behavior mostly _____ _____ _____ _____ enemies and acquiring food.

❸ _____ _____ _____ they can't defend their territory?

[1-3] **Listen to part of a conversation between a student and a resident assistant.**

🎧 CH3_4A

1   According to the resident assistant, what do the students have to do?

    (A) Be quiet during the exam period

    (B) Stop making noise late at night

    (C) Return to their rooms before midnight

    (D) Make less noise when someone complains

2   What is the likely outcome of a student getting fined six times?

    (A) The student will be expelled from school.

    (B) The student will have to meet the dean of students.

    (C) The student will have to move out of the dormitory.

    (D) The student will be transferred to another room.

3   Listen again to part of the conversation. Then answer the question.
What can be inferred about the student when he says this: 🎧

    (A) He gets along well with his roommate.

    (B) His roommate gets upset easily.

    (C) He does not know his roommate very well.

    (D) His roommate plays a musical instrument.

[4-7] Listen to part of a lecture in a geology class. 🎧 CH3_4B

Geology

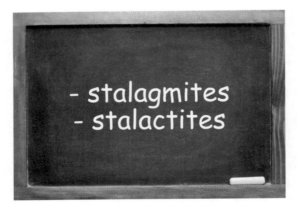

4   **What is the main topic of the lecture?**

Ⓐ Cave sizes

Ⓑ Cave formation

Ⓒ Cave exploring

Ⓓ Cave depth

5   **In the lecture, the professor describes a number of facts about caves formed by water erosion. Indicate whether each of the following is a fact or not.**

Click in the correct box for each statement.

	Fact	Not a Fact
① They have stalagmites in them.		
② They form because of acid in the water.		
③ They are created very quickly.		
④ They often form in very hard rock.		

6   **According to the professor, which types of caves often collapse?**

Ⓐ Volcanic caves

Ⓑ Ice caves

Ⓒ Caves formed in soil

Ⓓ Caves formed in soft rocks

7   **Listen again to part of the lecture. Then answer the question.**
Why does the professor say this: 🎧

Ⓐ To indicate he does not want to discuss a topic

Ⓑ To ask the students to research a topic

Ⓒ To show his interest in the student's question

Ⓓ To say he will talk about something later

[8-11] Listen to part of a lecture in an economics class. 🎧 CH3_4C

Economics

8 **Why does the professor discuss Batavia and Galle?**

    Ⓐ To show how the Dutch acquired them

    Ⓑ To mention how wealthy they became

    Ⓒ To point out their importance as hubs

    Ⓓ To claim they were the first Dutch colonies

9 **According to the professor, how did the Dutch obtain various trade goods?**

Click on 2 answers.

    1 By winning them in battles

    2 By paying for them with silver

    3 By stealing them from natives

    4 By bartering for various items

10 **What does the professor imply about spices?**

    Ⓐ They were more expensive than gold.

    Ⓑ They were only available in India.

    Ⓒ They were frequently traded for tea.

    Ⓓ They were highly desired in Europe.

11 **What resulted from the establishment of the Dutch East India Company?**

    Ⓐ The Dutch people gained a lot of power.

    Ⓑ Holland fought several wars in Europe.

    Ⓒ India became a colony belonging to Holland.

    Ⓓ The Dutch discovered several places in Asia.

[1-3] **Listen to part of a conversation between a student and a librarian.** 🎧 CH3_4D

1 According to the librarian, what kind of music should the student avoid?

   (A) Music that is subtle

   (B) Music that is quiet

   (C) Music with fanfare

   (D) Music which is upbeat

2 Which composer does the librarian suggest to the student?

   (A) Tchaikovsky

   (B) Debussy

   (C) Holst

   (D) Copland

3 What will the student probably do next?

   (A) Listen to some music

   (B) Borrow some CDs

   (C) Show the librarian his presentation

   (D) Watch a musical performance on video

Listen to part of a lecture in an astronomy class. 🎧 CH3_4E

Astronomy

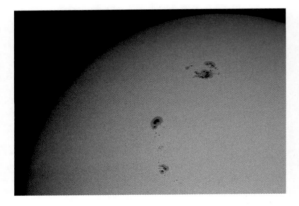

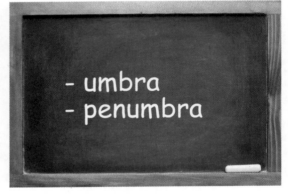

- umbra
- penumbra

the Carrington Event

the Little Ice Age

4 What is an umbra?

    Ⓐ The outer area of a sunspot

    Ⓑ The magnetic field of a sunspot

    Ⓒ The center of a sunspot

    Ⓓ The heat of a sunspot

5 Why does the professor mention the Carrington Event?

    Ⓐ To discuss the astronomer who named it

    Ⓑ To identify it as an electromagnetic storm

    Ⓒ To say it was caused by an enormous sunspot

    Ⓓ To note how dangerous it was to the Earth

6 What was a possible cause of the Little Ice Age?

Click on 2 answers.

    1️⃣ The tilting of the Earth's axis

    2️⃣ Increased sunspot activity

    3️⃣ The slowing of ocean currents

    4️⃣ Large eruptions of volcanoes

7 Listen again to part of the lecture. Then answer the question.
What does the professor imply when he says this: 🎧

    Ⓐ Most sunspots have relatively small diameters.

    Ⓑ It can be difficult to see some smaller sunspots.

    Ⓒ The Earth is one of the bigger planets in the solar system.

    Ⓓ Sunspots can be several times larger than the Earth.

◼ Vocabulary Review

A Complete each sentence with the appropriate word from the box.

> features   partitioned   offspring   commodities   outlaw

1 Smartphones have _____ such as cameras and microphones.

2 Most reptiles do not care for their _____ once they hatch from eggs.

3 The government is going to _____ several corrupt business practices.

4 The teacher _____ the students into two separate groups.

5 Sugar and flour are _____ that people frequently buy.

B Complete each sentence with the correct answer.

1 If a person **comprehends** some instructions, that person _____ them.

   a. remembers   b. understands

2 When an individual **establishes** a new organization, that person _____ it.

   a. starts   b. joins

3 Because the box is **hollow**, there is _____ in its center.

   a. something   b. nothing

4 A **priority** work assignment is one that must be completed _____.

   a. immediately   b. later

5 If a submarine goes to the ocean's **surface**, it _____.

   a. goes down to the bottom   b. rises to the top

6 When prices rise **dramatically**, they go up _____.

   a. slightly   b. a large amount

7 An **appealing** offer from a store is one that makes people _____ something.

   a. want to buy   b. uninterested in buying

8 A **restriction** on how people can act _____ their behavior.

   a. puts limits on   b. makes comments about

9 When the colors on a painting begin to **fade**, they _____.

   a. become easier to see   b. become harder to see

Chapter **04**

Making Inferences

Question Type | Making Inferences

◢ About the Question

Making Inferences questions focus on your ability to understand the implications that are made in a talk. You are asked to determine the meanings of these implications. These are sometimes replay questions, or you may simply need to make a conclusion based on the information in a talk. These questions appear after both lectures and conversations.

Recognizing Making Inferences questions:

- What does the professor imply about X?

- What will the student probably do next?

- What can be inferred about X?

- What does the professor imply when he says this: (replay)

Helpful hints for answering the questions correctly:

- Learn how to read between the lines to understand what implications speakers are making. Don't focus on the literal meanings of some sentences.

- For replay questions, listen to all of the excerpted sentences since they often provide context clues and hints that can help you find the correct answer.

- Pay close attention to the end of a talk. That is when the student or professor often mentions what is going to happen next.

Basic Practice

A   **Listen to part of a conversation between a student and a student employment office employee.** 🎧 CH4_1A

What will the student probably do next?

Ⓐ Give the employee her bankbook

Ⓑ Sign her paycheck

Ⓒ Deposit some money

B   **Listen to part of a lecture in an environmental science class.** 🎧 CH4_1B

What can be inferred about Niagara Falls?

Ⓐ It has become higher over time

Ⓑ It continues to change its location.

Ⓒ It is the world's highest waterfall.

C   **Listen to part of a lecture in a botany class.** 🎧 CH4_1C

What does the professor imply about plant diseases?

Ⓐ They are easy for people to prevent.

Ⓑ They can affect every part of a plant.

Ⓒ They are the most dangerous in winter.

D   **Listen to part of a lecture in a geology class.** 🎧 CH4_1D

Listen again to part of the lecture. Then answer the question.
What does the professor imply when he says this: 🎧

Ⓐ He already answered the student's question.

Ⓑ Some fjords were not formed by glaciers.

Ⓒ He plans to discuss glacier formation in his lecture.

Practice with Short Passages

A

Listen to part of a conversation between a student and an Economics Department office secretary. 🎧 CH4_2A

1   **What does the woman imply about Professor Nelson?**

   (A) He is somewhere nearby.

   (B) He is teaching class now.

   (C) He has an appointment with the dean.

   (D) He will not teach Economics 18.

2   **What will the student probably do next?**

   (A) Send an email to Professor Nelson

   (B) Go to his classroom

   (C) Call Professor Nelson on the phone

   (D) Ask the woman another question

Vocabulary

☐ **requirement:** something that is necessary

☐ **step out:** to go outside; to leave the place where one should be for a short time

☐ **consider:** to think about

B **Listen to part of a lecture in an education class.** 🎧 CH4_2B

1 What can be inferred about gymnasia?

Ⓐ Visitors paid a fee to enter them.

Ⓑ People visited them for different reasons.

Ⓒ They were the largest buildings in Greek cities.

Ⓓ The Romans had them in their cities.

2 What will the professor probably do next?

Ⓐ Show some pictures of gymnasia

Ⓑ Give the students a quiz on Plato

Ⓒ Let the students take a break

Ⓓ Answer a question from a student

Vocabulary

☐ **engage in:** to participate in; to do

☐ **armor:** protective gear often worn by soldiers

☐ **mentally:** relating to the mind

A **Listen to part of a conversation between a student and a professor.** 🎧 CH4_3A

✏ NOTE-TAKING

....

....

....

....

....

....

....

....

....

Vocabulary

☐ **promptly:** very fast; at once

☐ **salary:** a regular amount of money a person gets for doing work

☐ **summarize:** to describe the overall content of something; to provide a recap

☐ **translate:** to change from one language to another

1 Why did the professor ask to see the student?

← Gist-Purpose Question

 Ⓐ To offer her a job

 Ⓑ To discuss her grade

 Ⓒ To find out her interest in teaching

 Ⓓ To talk about a research topic

2 In the conversation, the professor describes a number of facts about the position. Indicate whether each of the following is a fact or not.

← Detail Question

	Fact	Not a Fact
1 It does not pay a salary.		
2 It requires the student to do research.		
3 The student will have to travel.		
4 The student will do some teaching.		

3 What can be inferred about the student?

← Making Inferences Question

 Ⓐ She is fluent in a foreign language.

 Ⓑ She has never been to Toronto.

 Ⓒ She will graduate at the end of the semester.

 Ⓓ She is writing a paper for the professor.

Dictation

Listen to part of the conversation again and fill in the blanks.

M: Excellent. _____ _____ _____ _____ to work for me?

W: That _____ _____ . But, um . . . doing what? Uh, wait a minute. You don't want me to teach a class, _____ _____ ? I don't think I _____ _____ _____ .

M: Oh, no. It's not a teaching position. I need a _____ _____ for some work I'm doing this summer.

B | Listen to part of a lecture in an astronomy class. 🎧 CH4_3B

✎ NOTE-TAKING

....

....

....

....

....

....

....

....

....

| Vocabulary |

☐ **countless:** great in number; limitless

☐ **habitable:** able to be lived in

☐ **sustain:** to support; to make it possible to live

☐ **exoplanet:** a planet orbiting a star that is not the Earth's sun

1 Why does the professor explain the importance of stars?

    Ⓐ To show where life can get energy from

    Ⓑ To stress how much light they produce

    Ⓒ To argue that some of them do not live very long

    Ⓓ To point out that they produce little radiation

← Gist-Purpose Question

2 What is the professor's opinion of life on other planets?

    Ⓐ It does not exist anywhere else.

    Ⓑ It could exist under the right conditions.

    Ⓒ It likely exists on most planets.

    Ⓓ It exists on other planets in the solar system.

← Understanding Attitude Question

3 What will the professor probably do next?

    Ⓐ Continue his lecture

    Ⓑ Take a short break

    Ⓒ Hand back some exams

    Ⓓ Give the students an assignment

← Making Inferences Question

Dictation

Listen to the following sentences and fill in the blanks.

❶ We know _____ _____ _____ _____ on the Earth. But we don't _____ _____ the same rules _____ elsewhere.

❷ _____ _____ _____ we know, most life needs liquid water. _____, it's _____ _____ that life forms on other planets don't need it. We have _____ _____ _____ _____ right now.

❸ In the past _____ _____ _____, powerful telescopes _____ _____ many exoplanets in habitable zones around distant stars. Yet that _____ _____ _____ that those planets have life.

[1-3] **Listen to part of a conversation between a student and a professor.**

🎧 CH4_4A

1   Why does the professor tell the student about a newspaper article?

   (A) To criticize him for the quality of his work

   (B) To check his knowledge of local events

   (C) To encourage him to do better research

   (D) To advise him to alter his paper topic

2   What is the professor's attitude toward the student?

   (A) She is eager to help him with his paper.

   (B) She thinks he put little effort into his topic.

   (C) She believes he needs to try harder in class.

   (D) She considers him the best student in her class.

3   What can be inferred about the professor?

   (A) She is a member of the local tribe.

   (B) She knows Professor Red Eagle personally.

   (C) She has visited some local dig sites.

   (D) She specializes in the history of the local tribe.

[4-7] **Listen to part of a lecture in a history class.** 🎧 CH4_4B

History

4   What aspect of Greek farming does the professor mainly discuss?

   (A) The lifestyles that Greek farmers lived

   (B) The crops grown and animals raised on the farms

   (C) The difficulties that Greek farmers had

   (D) The ways crops were planted and grown in fields

5   What type of food did the Greeks mainly consume?

   (A) Grains

   (B) Dairy products

   (C) Fish

   (D) Meat

6   In the lecture, the professor describes a number of facts about Greek farming.
    Indicate whether each of the following is a fact or not.

    Click in the correct box for each statement.

	Fact	Not a Fact
1 Crop rotation was practiced by all farmers.		
2 Most Greek farms were small in size.		
3 Slave labor was utilized by most farmers.		
4 Many farmers grew vegetables and had fruit trees.		

7   What will the professor probably do next?

   (A) Have the students submit their homework

   (B) Show some pictures to the students

   (C) Continue lecturing on farming methods

   (D) Have the students read from the book

[8-11] Listen to part of a lecture in a physiology class. 🎧 CH4_4C

Physiology

zygote

8   **What is the lecture mainly about?**

    Ⓐ The differences between two types of twins

    Ⓑ The reasons that twins are born

    Ⓒ The personalities of various twins

    Ⓓ The medical issues some twins face

9   **According to the professor, what is always different about twins?**

    Ⓐ Their weights

    Ⓑ Their fingerprints

    Ⓒ Their eye colors

    Ⓓ Their personalities

10   **What does the professor imply about twins?**

    Ⓐ They usually act in identical manners.

    Ⓑ It is likely that their children will also be twins.

    Ⓒ Their DNA makes them valuable for scientific studies.

    Ⓓ Many of them get Alzheimer's disease later in life.

11   **Based on the information in the lecture, indicate which type of twins the statements refer to.**

Click in the correct box for each statement.

	Fraternal Twins	Identical Twins
1 Are typically the same sex		
2 Happen when two eggs are fertilized by two different sperm		
3 Are more likely to have the same medical problems		
4 Share fifty percent of their DNA		

[1-3]   Listen to part of a conversation between a student and a professor. 🎧 CH4_4D

1   **What problem does the student have?**

     Ⓐ A class he wants to take will not be offered.

     Ⓑ He does not have enough credits to graduate yet.

     Ⓒ An assignment for a class is too hard for him.

     Ⓓ He does not understand some material in a class.

2   **What does the professor imply about the student?**

     Ⓐ He has good study habits.

     Ⓑ He is getting high grades.

     Ⓒ He is in his freshman year.

     Ⓓ He is majoring in History.

3   **Listen again to part of the conversation. Then answer the question.**
    What can be inferred from the student's response to the professor? 🎧

     Ⓐ He wants to work on a project with the professor.

     Ⓑ He already knows about the program.

     Ⓒ He is interested in going to Lakeview College.

     Ⓓ He does not have time to take more classes.

[4-7] Listen to part of a lecture in an environmental science class. 🎧 CH4_4E

Environmental
Science

4   What is the main topic of the lecture?

    Ⓐ Drawbacks of bacteria in the air

    Ⓑ The benefits of *P. syringae*

    Ⓒ The formation of bioprecipitation

    Ⓓ The water cycle

5   Why does the professor show the students a chart?

    Ⓐ To focus on the steps in the water cycle

    Ⓑ To explain a mathematical formula

    Ⓒ To help explain the bioprecipitation cycle

    Ⓓ To show the chemical formulas of some molecules

6   In the lecture, the professor describes a number of facts about *P. syringae*. Indicate whether each of the following is a fact or not.

Click in the correct box for each statement.

	Fact	Not a Fact
① It can cause harm to various plants.		
② It can only be found in Antarctica.		
③ It stops ice from forming at temperatures below freezing.		
④ It has its own way of binding water molecules to itself.		

7   What will the professor probably do next?

    Ⓐ Continue lecturing on the topic

    Ⓑ Begin a class discussion

    Ⓒ Give the students a short quiz

    Ⓓ Answer the student's question

◢ Vocabulary Review

A   Complete each sentence with the appropriate word from the box.

| harvest | sustain | personality | requirement | mentally |

1   Thanks to greenhouses, farmers can _____ crops all year long in many places.

2   Alice has a pleasant _____, which results in her having lots of friends.

3   Having experience is a common _____ for many jobs.

4   People who are _____ ill may need to see a doctor.

5   The arch can _____ a great amount of weight on it.

B   Complete each sentence with the correct answer.

1   Birds that **migrate** fly _____, often in search of food.
    a. to distant places   b. to nearby places

2   People who **consider** other people's ideas _____ them.
    a. think about   b. ignore

3   When water **evaporates**, it turns into a _____.
    a. solid   b. gas

4   If you **summarize** a book, you _____ it.
    a. highlight the main parts of   b. describe the characters in

5   People who complete their work **promptly** do it _____.
    a. slowly   b. at once

6   Steve and Doug are **identical** twins, so they look _____.
    a. alike   b. different

7   **Surplus** items are those items which _____.
    a. are needed immediately   b. are left over

8   If you must **infer** what a person desires, that individual _____ what he wants.
    a. does not say   b. explains exactly

9   Because there are **countless** stars in the sky, there are _____ of them.
    a. very many   b. very few

Chapter 05

Understanding Function

◢ About the Question

Understanding Function questions focus on your ability to understand the underlying meaning of what the speakers are saying in the talk. You are asked to infer the meaning of a phrase or sentence said by a person in the talk. Or you are asked to determine why a speaker brings up a particular topic or discusses some matter. These questions appear after both lectures and conversations.

Recognizing Understanding Function questions:

1   Some Understanding Function questions ask about what the speaker is inferring. These are often replay questions. They may appear like this:

- What does the professor imply when he says this: (replay)

- What can be inferred from the professor's response to the student? (replay)

2   Other Understanding Function questions ask about the purpose of a statement or a topic in the talk. These may be regular questions or replay questions. They may appear like this:

- What is the purpose of the woman's response? (replay)

- Why does the student say this: (replay)

- Why does the professor ask the student about his grades?

- Why does the man tell the student about the library?

Helpful hints for answering the questions correctly:

- Do not think about the literal meaning of what is being said. Instead, try to read between the lines to determine the real meaning by understanding what people are implying. Think about what the effect of a particular statement is on the listener.

- When professors interact with students in lectures, pay close attention to what is being said. This dialog is often used for replay questions.

- While replay questions ask about one sentence in particular, there are usually three or four sentences excerpted for them. Listen carefully to all of the sentences since they can provide context clues that will enable you to find the correct answer.

Basic Practice

A **Listen to part of a conversation between a student and a student activities office employee.** 🎧 CH5_1A

Listen again to part of the conversation. Then answer the question.
What does the student imply when she says this: 🎧

  Ⓐ She will join a different type of club.

  Ⓑ She will call the man to schedule an appointment.

  Ⓒ She will attempt to recruit more members.

B **Listen to part of a lecture in a zoology class.** 🎧 CH5_1B

Listen again to part of the lecture. Then answer the question.
What is the purpose of the professor's response? 🎧

  Ⓐ To prove he knows her name

  Ⓑ To ask her to guess again

  Ⓒ To indicate she is correct

C **Listen to part of a lecture in an art class.** 🎧 CH5_1C

Why does the professor tell the students to knead the clay?

  Ⓐ To make it soft

  Ⓑ To get the air out of it

  Ⓒ To remove the cracks

D **Listen to part of a lecture in a history class.** 🎧 CH5_1D

Listen again to part of the lecture. Then answer the question.
What does the professor imply when he says this: 🎧

  Ⓐ Using stagecoaches to send mail was too slow.

  Ⓑ Few stagecoaches went to the west.

  Ⓒ It was expensive to send mail by stagecoach.

A Listen to part of a conversation between a student and a professor. 🎧 CH5_2A

1 Why does the student ask the professor about equipment?

Ⓐ To find out what he needs to bring

Ⓑ To ask where he can purchase it

Ⓒ To learn what they will be using

Ⓓ To determine where it is located

2 Listen again to part of the conversation. Then answer the question.
What can be inferred from the student's response to the professor? 🎧

Ⓐ He cannot recall the departure time.

Ⓑ He will help set up the equipment.

Ⓒ He is willing to help the professor.

Ⓓ He is ready to leave at once.

Vocabulary

☐ **field trip:** a trip taken by students for educational purposes

☐ **fossil:** the preserved remains of an animal or plant

☐ **hunt:** to search for something

Listen to part of a lecture in an astronomy class. 🎧 CH5_2B

1 **Why does the professor tell the students about the sun?**

- Ⓐ To mention when it is likely to use its energy
- Ⓑ To name a star likely to become a white dwarf
- Ⓒ To compare it with black dwarf stars
- Ⓓ To explain why it may not become a supernova

2 **Listen again to part of the lecture. Then answer the question.**
Why does the professor say this: 🎧

- Ⓐ To show his certainty in a statement
- Ⓑ To ask the students what their thoughts are
- Ⓒ To say he knows what is going to happen
- Ⓓ To indicate his next comment is a guess

Vocabulary

☐ **exhaust:** to use up
☐ **engulf:** to absorb; to swallow
☐ **binary system:** a star system in which two stars revolve around each other

A | **Listen to part of a conversation between a student and a student center employee.**

🎧 CH5_3A

✏️ NOTE-TAKING

....

....

....

....

....

....

....

....

Vocabulary

☐ **confirmation:** the act of providing proof or evidence of something

☐ **maintenance:** care for something such as equipment

☐ **booking:** a reservation

☐ **exception:** something that goes against a general rule or policy

1 Why does the student visit the student center?

← Gist-Purpose Question

  (A) To file a complaint

  (B) To report a website is not working

  (C) To inquire about a reservation

  (D) To book a room

2 Why does the man tell the student about the website maintenance?

← Understanding Function Question

  (A) To explain why a website was not working

  (B) To ask her to assist with the process

  (C) To tell her that a website will be unavailable

  (D) To apologize for the slowness of a website

3 Listen again to part of the conversation. Then answer the question.

What does the man imply when he says this: 🎧

← Understanding Function Question

  (A) The student has to pay a fee now.

  (B) The student can use his computer.

  (C) The student does not need to go online.

  (D) The student should submit some information.

Dictation

Listen to part of the conversation again and fill in the blanks.

M: _____ _____ _____ _____ that you made the reservation?

W: Three days ago. So _____ _____ _____, uh, Saturday night.

M: Okay, _____ _____ _____. The website was _____ _____ _____ during parts of the weekend.

W: Yeah, I _____ that. It was pretty hard for me to log on. I even _____ _____ _____ the website a couple of times before I _____ _____ make the booking.

B Listen to part of a lecture in a history of technology class. 🎧 CH5_3B

✎ NOTE-TAKING

....

....

....

....

....

....

....

....

....

Vocabulary

☐ **steer:** to move in various directions

☐ **propel:** to cause to move forward

☐ **aloft:** in the air

☐ **rigid:** stiff; unable to move

1 How is the lecture organized?

← Understanding Organization Question

   Ⓐ The airships are mentioned according to their importance.

   Ⓑ The lives of the inventors are covered in detail.

   Ⓒ The inventions are described in chronological order.

   Ⓓ The uses of the machines are compared and contrasted.

2 Based on the information in the lecture, indicate which type of airship the statements refer to.

← Connecting Content Question

	Le France	Zeppelin
☐1 Was made for the military		
☐2 Was inspired by the work of David Schwarz		
☐3 Had cabins underneath its frame		
☐4 Could take off and land in the same spot		

3 Listen again to part of the lecture. Then answer the question. What is the purpose of the professor's response? 🎧

← Understanding Function Question

   Ⓐ To point out a mistake

   Ⓑ To describe an advantage of an airship

   Ⓒ To stress the slowness of the vehicle

   Ⓓ To disagree with the student

Dictation

Listen to the following sentences and fill in the blanks.

❶ The first airships _____ _____ in France in the late eighteenth century. These early designs _____ _____ human power for energy.

❷ _____ _____ the speeds we can reach today, it was _____ _____ . However, for the time, it was _____ _____ _____ achievement.

❸ Zeppelin _____ the design. In 1900, he flew his first airship, _____ _____ _____ _____ himself.

[1-3] **Listen to part of a conversation between a student and a professor.** 🎧 CH5_4A

1   According to the professor, what information did the student include on her résumé?
Click on 2 answers.

    ☐1   Her work experience
    ☐2   Her objective
    ☐3   Her education
    ☐4   Her volunteer work

2   What comparison does the professor make between the academic world and the business world?

    Ⓐ The amount of effort people make
    Ⓑ The salaries people receive in them
    Ⓒ The lengths of works written for them
    Ⓓ The type of work people do in them

3   Listen again to part of the conversation. Then answer the question.
Why does the professor say this: 🎧

    Ⓐ To ask the student when she has some free time
    Ⓑ To stress the importance of writing better
    Ⓒ To tell the student she needs to rewrite her term paper
    Ⓓ To indicate his desire to look at the student's work

[4-7] Listen to part of a lecture in a music class. 🎧 CH5_4B

Music

Franz Joseph
Haydn

4   Why does the professor tell the students about their papers?

Ⓐ To encourage the students to submit them

Ⓑ To say she has almost finished grading them

Ⓒ To express her pleasure in their quality

Ⓓ To mention that they are due next week

5   What is the professor's attitude toward Franz Joseph Haydn?

Ⓐ He needed more professional training.

Ⓑ He wasted a lot of time working for his patron.

Ⓒ He was an important person in classical music.

Ⓓ He wrote better music than Mozart and Bach.

6   According to the professor, why do some people believe Franz Joseph Haydn had a unique style?

Ⓐ He wanted to create a new type of music.

Ⓑ He was isolated from most other composers.

Ⓒ He was trained in several musical instruments.

Ⓓ He was influenced by his major patron.

7   In the lecture, the professor talks about the events in Franz Joseph Haydn's life. Put the events in the correct order.

1	
2	
3	
4	

Ⓐ He became friends with Mozart.

Ⓑ He sang in the choir at St. Stephen's Cathedral.

Ⓒ He served as Beethoven's teacher.

Ⓓ He served as the court composer for the Esterhazy family.

[8-11] Listen to part of a lecture in an economics class. 🎧 CH5_4C

Economics

8 What aspect of marketing does the professor mainly discuss?

    (A) The effects it has on consumers

    (B) The various types of it

    (C) The most efficient way to do it

    (D) The reasons companies need it

9 How does the professor organize the information about word of mouth that he presents to the class?

    (A) By comparing it with social media

    (B) By explaining how much he likes it

    (C) By giving examples of some companies that use it

    (D) By talking about the positive and negative points

10 Listen again to part of the lecture. Then answer the question.
   What can be inferred about the professor when he says this: 🎧

    (A) He believes more companies should advertise in newspapers.

    (B) He thinks newspapers are less important than TV.

    (C) He has not read a newspaper in a long time.

    (D) He has a subscription to the local newspaper.

11 Listen again to part of the lecture. Then answer the question.
   Why does the professor say this: 🎧

    (A) To encourage the students to do more research

    (B) To repeat a point to avoid confusing the students

    (C) To make sure that the students are listening

    (D) To emphasize the point that he is making

[1-3] **Listen to part of a conversation between a student and a professor.** 🎧 CH5_4D

1   Why does the student visit the professor?

    (A) To find out about an upcoming exam

    (B) To have him check her research paper

    (C) To complain about a class assignment

    (D) To inquire about a recent lecture

2   According to the professor, which part of the airplane has an effect on lift?

    (A) The engines

    (B) The wings

    (C) The tail

    (D) The nose

3   Why does the professor tell the student about the video?

    (A) To point out that it is available in the library

    (B) To mention that she must watch it for an assignment

    (C) To say that it can improve her understanding

    (D) To tell her to write a report on the information in it

[4-7] **Listen to part of a lecture in a zoology class.** 🎧 CH5_4E

Zoology

brood chamber

pheromone

4   **What is a brood chamber?**

   Ⓐ A place where eggs are laid

   Ⓑ A place where food is stored

   Ⓒ A place where ants eat food

   Ⓓ A place where soldier ants stay

5   **Why does the professor discuss the three types of ants?**

   Ⓐ To discuss their mutualistic relationships

   Ⓑ To describe their lifespans

   Ⓒ To talk about their duties

   Ⓓ To show how they use pheromones

6   **How do ants use pheromones?**

Click on 2 answers.

   ☐ 1   To obtain food

   ☐ 2   To find new homes

   ☐ 3   To fight battles

   ☐ 4   To defend their colonies

7   **Listen again to part of the lecture. Then answer the question.**
What does the professor imply when she says this: 🎧

   Ⓐ More ant species will be discovered one day.

   Ⓑ Scientists know how ants work together now.

   Ⓒ Little is known about many kinds of ants.

   Ⓓ Ants have been observed working together.

■ Vocabulary Review

A Complete each sentence with the appropriate word from the box.

fossils	released	propel	colonies	influenced

1 Picasso _____ a large number of artists in modern times.

2 The hospital _____ the patient after he had completely recovered.

3 The engine of the spaceship can _____ it forward at great speeds.

4 The paleontologists found several dinosaur _____ in the field.

5 Many European countries once had _____ in Asia, Africa, and the Americas.

B Complete each sentence with the correct answer.

1 A person who makes a **booking** at a hotel _____.

   a. cancels a reservation   b. makes a reservation

2 When a problem is **widespread**, it is _____.

   a. in a single place   b. in many places

3 An **apprentice** goes to work for an artisan in order to _____.

   a. learn a trade   b. make money

4 When a metal pole is **rigid**, it is _____.

   a. easy to break   b. hard to bend

5 When an engine **exhausts** its fuel supply, it _____ fuel.

   a. runs out of   b. gets more

6 The **downside** of an agreement refers to its _____.

   a. benefits   b. disadvantages

7 A **replacement** worker is a person who _____.

   a. works in place of another   b. received a promotion

8 Information that is **relevant** to a discussion is _____.

   a. useless   b. important

9 Doing **maintenance** on machines stops them from _____.

   a. breaking down   b. using more fuel

Chapter **06**

Understanding Attitude

◼ About the Question

Understanding Attitude questions focus on your ability to recognize the attitudes or opinions of speakers. You are asked to recognize how speakers feel about particular topics, to determine if speakers like or dislike something, or to understand why speakers are experiencing particular emotions. You are also asked to recognize speakers' opinions regarding various topics. These questions appear after both lectures and conversations.

Recognizing Understanding Attitude questions:

1 Some Understanding Attitude questions ask about speakers' feelings. These may be regular questions or replay questions. They may appear like this:

- What is the professor's attitude toward X?
- What is the professor's opinion of X?
- What does the woman mean when she says this: (replay)

2 Other Understanding Attitude questions ask about speakers' opinions. These may be regular questions or replay questions. They may appear like this:

- What can be inferred about the student?
- What can be inferred about the student when she says this: (replay)
- What does the professor imply about the student's paper?

Helpful hints for answering the questions correctly:

- The tone of voice that a speaker uses can be helpful in finding the correct answer.
- When speakers give their opinions on topics, pay close attention. Be sure to differentiate between the facts and opinions of speakers.
- You may need to read between the lines for these questions. The literal meanings of sentences may not be their actual meanings.
- When there are replay questions, pay close attention to all of the excerpted sentences rather than only the sentence that the question asks about. The excerpted sentences provide context clues and hints that can help you find the correct answer.

A **Listen to part of a conversation between a student and a Registrar's office employee.** 🎧 CH6_1A

What is the student's opinion of the rule at the Registrar's office?

(A) She dislikes it.

(B) She understands it.

(C) She approves of it.

B **Listen to part of a conversation between a student and a professor.** 🎧 CH6_1B

Listen again to part of the conversation. Then answer the question.
What can be inferred about the student when he says this: 🎧

(A) He appreciates the professor's help.

(B) He is still not sure what to do.

(C) He needs more time to complete the work.

C **Listen to part of a lecture in a chemistry class.** 🎧 CH6_1C

What is the professor's opinion of William T.G. Morton?

(A) His medical methods were not effective.

(B) He is important to the history of medicine.

(C) His work is appreciated be many people.

D **Listen to part of a lecture in a music class.** 🎧 CH6_1D

Listen again to part of the lecture. Then answer the question.
What does the professor mean when he says this: 🎧

(A) The student gave an incorrect answer.

(B) The student knows a lot about music.

(C) The student should try again.

A

Listen to part of a conversation between a student and a study abroad office employee. 🎧 CH6_2A

1   Listen again to part of the conversation. Then answer the question.

What does the man mean when he says this: 🎧

(A) He can answer the student's questions.

(B) He knows what the student wants.

(C) He has been in the office all day long.

(D) He came to visit the student.

2   Listen again to part of the conversation. Then answer the question.

What can be inferred about the student when she says this: 🎧

(A) Her GPA is too low to get accepted.

(B) She intends to apply to the program.

(C) She will think of another place to go.

(D) Her grades have gone up recently.

Listen to part of a lecture in a marine biology class. 🎧 CH6_2B

1   **What is the professor's opinion of sea snakes?**

    Ⓐ They are not harmful to people.

    Ⓑ They should be hunted by people.

    Ⓒ They can be very dangerous animals.

    Ⓓ They ought to be protected.

2   **What does the professor imply about sea snakes?**

    Ⓐ They prefer deep water to shallow water.

    Ⓑ They are excellent hunters of prey.

    Ⓒ They will attack people that bother them.

    Ⓓ They spend lots of time resting on beaches.

Vocabulary

☐ **provoke:** to cause a person or animal to attack

☐ **lethal:** deadly; causing death

☐ **startle:** to surprise or suddenly frighten

A **Listen to part of a conversation between a student and a professor.** 🎧 CH6_3A

✏️ NOTE-TAKING

....

....

....

....

....

....

....

....

....

Vocabulary

☐ **option:** a choice

☐ **extra credit:** work in a class that can get bonus points

☐ **down:** sad or disappointed

☐ **careless:** done without thought

1 **What problem does the student have?**

← Gist-Content Question

  (A) He does not understand the class material.

  (B) He is getting a low grade in a class.

  (C) He has not submitted some assignments.

  (D) He failed a recent paper he wrote.

2 **What does the student want to do in the class?**

← Detail Question

  (A) Write an extra report

  (B) Submit some late homework

  (C) Give a group presentation

  (D) Take a makeup test

3 **Listen again to part of the conversation. Then answer the question.**

What can be inferred about the student when he says this: 🎧

← Understanding Attitude Question

  (A) He is sometimes late for the professor's class.

  (B) He dislikes wearing a watch most of the time.

  (C) He is looking forward to the end of the semester.

  (D) He agrees with the professor's advice.

Dictation

Listen to part of the conversation again and fill in the blanks.

M1: So, uh, anyway . . . I _____ _____ _____ there was something I could do to _____ _____ _____ .

M2: Well, studying harder and doing better on your homework _____ _____ _____ .

M1: Right. But how about writing an essay for _____ _____ ? Do you permit that?

M2: Sorry, Brian, but I don't _____ that. However, _____ _____ _____ . There are still two more tests in this class. If you do well on them, you can _____ _____ _____ _____ . And start focusing on your homework. You're losing easy points _____ _____ _____ _____ .

B Listen to part of a lecture in an anthropology class. 🎧 CH6_3B

✏ NOTE-TAKING

1 Why does the professor mention Western art?

← Understanding Organization Question

    Ⓐ To name some popular artists

    Ⓑ To make a detailed comparison

    Ⓒ To state that she does not like it

    Ⓓ To respond to a student's comment

2 Why does the professor tell the students about the spiritual aspect of *inuksuit*?

← Understanding Function Question

    Ⓐ To state one of their purposes

    Ⓑ To describe Native American society

    Ⓒ To focus on how they were built

    Ⓓ To claim that it does not exist

3 Listen again to part of the lecture. Then answer the question. What does the professor mean when she says this: 🎧

← Understanding Attitude Question

    Ⓐ There is some new research on *inuksuit*.

    Ⓑ Her analysis may be incorrect.

    Ⓒ She is going to make some guesses next.

    Ⓓ She has seen some *inuksuit* in person.

Dictation

Listen to the following sentences and fill in the blanks.

❶ _____ _____ _____ _____ this statue here . . . We _____ that an *inuksuk*. Spell it I-N-U-K-S-U-K. _____ _____ _____ _____ , it's an Inuit word.

❷ The *inuksuit* therefore _____ _____ _____ . They show travelers waypoints _____ _____ they don't get lost on their journeys.

❸ The Inuit people say that *inuksuit* _____ _____ _____ _____ the human spirit.

[1-3]   Listen to part of a conversation between a student and a Chemistry Department office secretary. 🎧 CH6_4A

1   What is the employee's attitude toward the student?

   (A) She is polite but answers few questions.

   (B) She is a bit impatient with the student.

   (C) She is not interested in assisting the student.

   (D) She helps by giving complete explanations.

2   What does the employee give the student?

   (A) A form

   (B) A brochure

   (C) A course catalog

   (D) A list of professors' names

3   What will the student probably do next?

   (A) Complete a form

   (B) Look for an instructor

   (C) Go to the Registrar's office

   (D) Speak with her advisor

[4-7]   Listen to part of a lecture in an astronomy class. 🎧 CH6_4B

Astronomy

4 Why does the professor discuss the *Voyager* space probes?

    (A) He finds the topic fascinating.

    (B) A student was curious and asked about them.

    (C) Knowledge of them is important to the class.

    (D) He wants to point out what they learned about the outer planets.

5 What is the professor's opinion of the *Voyager 1* space probe?

    (A) It did not contain enough scientific instruments.

    (B) It is more impressive than any of NASA's other accomplishments.

    (C) It used the technology of the time very well.

    (D) It has discovered more than *Voyager 2* has.

6 Based on the information in the lecture, indicate which space probe the statements refer to.

Click in the correct box for each statement.

	Voyager 1	Voyager 2
① Was the first probe to be launched		
② Passed by one of Saturn's moons		
③ Reached Jupiter first		
④ Visited Uranus and Neptune		

7 According to the professor, where are the *Voyager* space probes now?

    (A) In the Oort Cloud

    (B) Close to Pluto

    (C) Near Neptune

    (D) In interstellar space

[8-11] Listen to part of a lecture in an environmental science class. 🎧 CH6_4C

Environmental Science

forest fires

8   Why does the professor explain how forest fires clear the forest floor?

    Ⓐ To show how quickly they can burn

    Ⓑ To mention which vegetation burns the fastest

    Ⓒ To explain why forests have few dead trees

    Ⓓ To describe one benefit of forest fires

9   According to the professor, how do forest fires help forests?

Click on 2 answers.

    ☐1 By letting more sunlight reach the forest floor

    ☐2 By killing many insects

    ☐3 By increasing the amount of water in them

    ☐4 By making animals migrate elsewhere

10 What does the professor imply about the chaparral family of plants?

    Ⓐ Its seeds germinate after forest fires end.

    Ⓑ It consumes a large amount of water.

    Ⓒ It grows in places that rarely get forest fires.

    Ⓓ It is easily killed by certain tree diseases.

11 Listen again to part of the lecture. Then answer the question.

What can be inferred about the professor when she says this: 🎧

    Ⓐ She cannot believe the comment she just made.

    Ⓑ She expected her statement to surprise the students.

    Ⓒ She wanted to see if the students were listening.

    Ⓓ She hopes a student will disagree with her.

[1-3]   **Listen to part of a conversation between a student and a professor.** CH6_4D

1   Why does the student visit the professor?

    Ⓐ To ask him to sign a form

    Ⓑ To ask about her class grade

    Ⓒ To ask about double-majoring

    Ⓓ To sign up for a special program

2   What is the professor's opinion of the student?

    Ⓐ She did not always work hard in class.

    Ⓑ She is excellent at giving presentations.

    Ⓒ She was one of the best students in his class.

    Ⓓ She is the top student he has ever had.

3   What will the professor do during the next summer break?

    Ⓐ Take some students on a trip

    Ⓑ Teach a class in summer school

    Ⓒ Visit Europe on vacation

    Ⓓ Do some independent research

[4-7] **Listen to part of a lecture in an education class.** 🎧 CH6_4E

Education

Horace Mann

4 According to the professor, why did some students stop attending school for certain periods of time?

  Ⓐ They preferred to be taught by private tutors.

  Ⓑ They could not afford to pay school tuition.

  Ⓒ They had to help with chores on family farms.

  Ⓓ They were not interested in learning more.

5 Why does the professor explain the education system in the southern American states?

  Ⓐ To emphasize the role of the family in education there

  Ⓑ To say that few students there went to college

  Ⓒ To point out how many schools there were

  Ⓓ To compare it with education in the northern states

6 What is the professor's opinion of Horace Mann?

  Ⓐ He had a great effect on American education.

  Ⓑ He relied too much on Prussian methods.

  Ⓒ He was ineffective at making changes in education.

  Ⓓ He should have focused more on college education.

7 What was a likely outcome of Horace Mann becoming the Secretary of Education in Massachusetts?

  Ⓐ Massachusetts students were taught by college graduates.

  Ⓑ Massachusetts students were grouped according to their age.

  Ⓒ Massachusetts students no longer got long vacations.

  Ⓓ Massachusetts students had to pay to attend school.

◼ Vocabulary Review

A Complete each sentence with the appropriate word from the box.

methods	equipment	occur	glimpse	generates

1 This motor _____ a lot of energy while using little gasoline.

2 The scientists ordered some more _____ for their laboratory.

3 I got a _____ of the movie star in the crowd of people.

4 Earthquakes usually _____ in places where two tectonic plates meet.

5 There are many _____ of using solar power to create electricity.

B Complete each sentence with the correct answer.

1 Because transferring is not the only **option**, then Kate has _____.
   a. a choice   b. nothing to do

2 Someone who requires **assistance** is _____.
   a. able to do something alone   b. in need of help

3 A person who is **fluent** in a foreign language speaks that language _____.
   a. very well   b. a bit

4 When belonging to a study group is **mandatory**, _____ must join it.
   a. only students with low grades   b. all students

5 When a building in a city is a **landmark**, it is _____.
   a. a place most people know   b. a place in the middle of downtown

6 If a lion **startles** a zebra, then the zebra is _____.
   a. hunted   b. surprised

7 A person who **enrolls** in a course at an academy _____ it.
   a. signs up for   b. gets a grade in

8 A **careless** person is someone who _____.
   a. pays close attention to details   b. does not pay attention to details

9 When firefighters **extinguish** a fire, they _____.
   a. put it out   b. slow it down

Chapter 07

Understanding Organization

Question Type | Understanding Organization

■ About the Question

Understanding Organization questions focus on your ability to determine how a talk is organized. You are asked to notice how the professor organizes the lecture or presents certain information to the class. Or you may be asked to determine how specific information relates to the lecture as a whole. These questions almost always appear after lectures.

Recognizing Understanding Organization questions:

1 Some Understanding Organization questions ask how the material in the professor's lecture is organized. They may appear like this:

   - How does the professor organize the information about X that he presents to the class?

   - How is the discussion organized?

2 Other Understanding Organization questions ask about the information that is presented in the lecture. They may appear like this:

   - Why does the professor discuss X?

   - Why does the professor mention X?

Helpful hints for answering the questions correctly:

- Consider how the professor organizes the lecture. Common ways are by using chronological order, by providing a cause and an effect, by comparing and contrasting, by categorizing, by describing a problem and a solution, by giving examples, and by using sequence.

- The professor may explain the purpose of the lecture at its beginning or end. Pay close attention to these parts of the lecture.

- When the professor talks about something not related to the main topic of the lecture, consider why that happened.

- For specific facts, think about the professor's purpose in mentioning them.

A **Listen to part of a lecture in a history of technology class.** 🎧 CH7_1A

Why does the professor discuss ENIAC?

    Ⓐ To talk about its capabilities

    Ⓑ To explain how it was made

    Ⓒ To describe its impact on society

B **Listen to part of a lecture in an astronomy class.** 🎧 CH7_1B

How does the professor organize the information about the *Cassini* space probe that he presents to the class?

    Ⓐ By covering the information in chronological order

    Ⓑ By discussing its accomplishments

    Ⓒ By talking about its most recent actions

C **Listen to part of a lecture in an art class.** 🎧 CH7_1C

How is the lecture organized?

    Ⓐ By covering events in chronological order

    Ⓑ By talking about one side of an argument

    Ⓒ By discussing one specific event in the past

D **Listen to part of a lecture in an urban design class.** 🎧 CH7_1D

Why does the professor mention Central Park?

    Ⓐ To compare it with another park

    Ⓑ To relate it to urban heat island

    Ⓒ To call it a green space

A Listen to part of a lecture in an architecture class. 🎧 CH7_2A

1 How does the professor organize the information about Romanesque architecture that she presents to the class?

Ⓐ By showing pictures from the book and explaining them

Ⓑ By describing its characteristics and showing examples

Ⓒ By asking the students to describe its major features

Ⓓ By involving the class in a brief discussion

2 Why does the professor discuss Ripoll Monastery?

Ⓐ To compare it with St. Andrew's Church

Ⓑ To call it a work of Carolingian architecture

Ⓒ To talk about how it was constructed

Ⓓ To name it as an example of an Early Romanesque work

Vocabulary

☐ **prominent:** popular; famous; widespread

☐ **monastery:** a place where monks live and follow their religious vows

☐ **octagonal:** having eight sides

Listen to part of a lecture in an education class. CH7_2B

1 How is the lecture organized?

   Ⓐ The professor discusses everything in chronological order.

   Ⓑ The professor talks about facts in alphabetical order.

   Ⓒ The professor gives several examples to prove her point.

   Ⓓ The professor does an experiment and then talks about it.

2 Why does the professor mention critical thinking skills?

   Ⓐ To say rote learning does not teach them

   Ⓑ To claim they are the most important learning skill

   Ⓒ To argue that most students lack them

   Ⓓ To discuss how they can be taught to students

Vocabulary

☐ **memorize:** to remember something exactly

☐ **alphabet:** all of the letters in a written language

☐ **drawback:** a disadvantage; a problem

A | Listen to part of a lecture in a meteorology class. 🎧 CH7_3A

✏️ NOTE-TAKING

....

....

....

....

....

....

....

....

Vocabulary

☐ **mountain chain:** a large group of mountains near one another

☐ **collide:** to hit or run into someone or something

☐ **condense:** to change from a gas to a liquid

☐ **downdraft:** air that is moving downward

1 Why does the professor discuss how warm air rises above cooler air?

← Understanding Organization Question

    Ⓐ To show how warm air can create tornadoes

    Ⓑ To describe why thunderstorms drop so much rain

    Ⓒ To say that it rarely happens over the oceans

    Ⓓ To explain a condition for thunderstorms to form

2 What comparison does the professor make between farmland and cities?

← Connecting Content Question

    Ⓐ The amount of direct sunlight they get

    Ⓑ The average temperature in each place

    Ⓒ The number of thunderstorms they get

    Ⓓ The amount of rain that falls on them

3 According to the professor, how can a super cell form?

← Detail Question

    Ⓐ Many cumulus clouds suddenly appear.

    Ⓑ Lightning flashes with regularity.

    Ⓒ Winds make clouds join together.

    Ⓓ Rain falls for several hours.

Dictation

Listen to the following sentences and fill in the blanks.

❶ _____ a thunderstorm to form, there _____ _____ _____ lots of moisture in the air.

❷ It's _____ . But it _____ _____ over large areas of open land, uh, _____ _____ farmland.

❸ _____ _____ _____ the downdrafts of cool air are _____ _____ _____ the updrafts of warm air. So no new raindrops can _____ _____ clouds.

B Listen to part of a lecture in a geology class. 🎧 CH7_3B

✎ NOTE-TAKING

Vocabulary

☐ **harsh:** severe

☐ **fluctuate:** to change constantly

☐ **transform:** to change from one form into another

☐ **carnivore:** an animal that eats meat

1 How does the professor organize the information about the ice caps that he presents to the class?

← Understanding Organization Question

Ⓐ By discussing how they are slowly melting

Ⓑ By focusing on the animals living in each place

Ⓒ By showing pictures and then describing them

Ⓓ By describing their similarities and differences

2 Listen again to part of the lecture. Then answer the question. Why does the professor say this: 🎧

← Understanding Function Question

Ⓐ To respond to a student's question

Ⓑ To indicate that he spoke correctly

Ⓒ To provide a detailed analysis

Ⓓ To apologize for making a mistake

3 Listen again to part of the lecture. Then answer the question. What can be inferred about the professor when he says this: 🎧

← Making Inferences Question

Ⓐ He will no longer lecture to the class.

Ⓑ He is ready to let the students leave.

Ⓒ He wants the students to turn in their papers.

Ⓓ He would like to discuss an upcoming exam.

Dictation

Listen to the following sentences and fill in the blanks.

❶ Both poles formed _____ _____ their location _____ _____ _____ the sun.

❷ I consider that _____ _____. While there's some melting during summer, the ice caps are _____ _____ _____ _____ entirely. They're _____ _____ _____ expand.

❸ The northern ice cap is frozen sea water _____ _____ _____ _____ more water. The southern one _____ _____ freshwater ice _____ _____ a landmass.

[1-3] **Listen to part of a conversation between a student and a professor.** 🎧 CH7_4A

1   What problem does the student have?

　　Ⓐ She cannot decide what to major in.

　　Ⓑ She dislikes a topic she chose.

　　Ⓒ She is getting a low grade in a class.

　　Ⓓ She has no time to finish her thesis.

2   Why does the professor discuss getting a W on a transcript?

　　Ⓐ To describe a result of not doing a thesis

　　Ⓑ To point out that it is better than getting an F

　　Ⓒ To convince the student to drop a class

　　Ⓓ To tell the student to change her topic

3   Listen again to part of the conversation. Then answer the question. What does the student imply when she says this: 🎧

　　Ⓐ She will apply to some graduate schools.

　　Ⓑ She will continue doing a research project.

　　Ⓒ She will submit her outline to the professor.

　　Ⓓ She will change her thesis topic.

[4-7]   Listen to part of a lecture in a history class. 🎧 CH7_4B

History

4   How is the lecture organized?

Ⓐ The professor discusses only the major events that happened.

Ⓑ The professor points out places on a map as he talks.

Ⓒ The professor describes the events in chronological order.

Ⓓ The professor answers questions that the students ask.

5   What can be inferred about John Davis?

Ⓐ Some people doubt he visited Antarctica.

Ⓑ He traveled to inland parts of Antarctica.

Ⓒ His expedition sailed before Captain Cook's.

Ⓓ It is believed that he went to the South Pole.

6   According to the professor, what did James Ross try to do in Antarctica?

Ⓐ Make a map of the continent

Ⓑ Find the south magnetic pole

Ⓒ Discover new animal species

Ⓓ Create a permanent settlement

7   Listen again to part of the lecture. Then answer the question.
    What does the professor imply when he says this: 🎧

Ⓐ The southern oceans have more ice than anywhere else.

Ⓑ Bad weather affected many ships near Antarctica.

Ⓒ Captain Cook's ship nearly sank on his journey.

Ⓓ Only Captain Cook's ship could sail through the ice.

[8-11] Listen to part of a lecture in a zoology class. 🎧 CH7_4C

Zoology

8 How does the professor organize the information about Death Valley that she presents to the class?

    Ⓐ By talking about the environment there

    Ⓑ By giving a history of the region

    Ⓒ By focusing on the animals that live there

    Ⓓ By talking exclusively about the mammals there

9 Why does the professor explain about the pupfish?

    Ⓐ To point out that the student's statement is wrong

    Ⓑ To mention how it has adapted to its environment

    Ⓒ To tell the students what its body looks like

    Ⓓ To argue that it is in danger of going extinct soon

10 What is the professor's attitude toward the student?

    Ⓐ She wants him to pay more attention in class.

    Ⓑ She is pleased with his response to her question.

    Ⓒ She believes he did not do the reading she assigned.

    Ⓓ She thinks he provided a very detailed answer.

11 According to the professor, how does the tortoise survive in Death Valley?

Click on 2 answers.

    1️⃣ By drinking water very rarely

    2️⃣ By becoming inactive in summer

    3️⃣ By staying in holes underground

    4️⃣ By getting water from the food it eats

[1-3] **Listen to part of a conversation between a student and a professor.** 🎧 CH7_4D

1   What are the speakers mainly discussing?

   (A) Taking summer school classes

   (B) Applying to do some fieldwork

   (C) Signing up for a seminar

   (D) Doing some work for extra credit

2   According to the professor, why does she have to accept senior applicants?

   (A) They are planning to attend graduate school.

   (B) They have the most experience.

   (C) They need to do some work to graduate.

   (D) They always get chosen before freshmen.

3   Listen again to part of the conversation. Then answer the question.
   What does the professor mean when she says this: 🎧

   (A) She will recommend the student to a professor.

   (B) She frequently compliments the student.

   (C) The student is a good public speaker.

   (D) The student needs to finish his application.

[4-7]   Listen to part of a lecture in an urban design class. 🎧 CH7_4E

Urban Design

the Home Insurance
Building

the Equitable Building
© Felix Lipov

the Empire State Building
© travelview

the Chrysler Building
© MISHELLA

4 **What is the lecture mainly about?**

   Ⓐ The canyon effect created by skyscrapers

   Ⓑ The most famous skyscrapers in New York City

   Ⓒ Inventions that allowed skyscrapers to be built

   Ⓓ How laws changed the way skyscrapers were made

5 **Why does the professor discuss the Equitable Building in Manhattan?**

   Ⓐ To show how it caused zoning laws to be changed

   Ⓑ To claim it was the first skyscraper in Manhattan

   Ⓒ To point out how many people building it got injured

   Ⓓ To say how much local residents liked it

6 **According to the professor, what did the 1916 reform of New York City's zoning laws do?**

Click on 2 answers.

   1️⃣ It increased the cost of building skyscrapers.

   2️⃣ It limited the total heights that buildings could be made.

   3️⃣ It caused tall buildings to have to use setbacks.

   4️⃣ It allowed more sunlight to reach the street.

7 **What can be inferred about the Empire State Building?**

   Ⓐ It was the first building to use setbacks.

   Ⓑ It is the tallest building in New York City.

   Ⓒ It was designed in the Art Deco style.

   Ⓓ It was built before the 1916 zoning law passed.

■ Vocabulary Review

A Complete each sentence with the appropriate word from the box.

> construct   voyage   harsh   prominent   dense

1 The vegetation in a rainforest can be very _____ in places.

2 One of the most _____ features of the building is its large antenna.

3 It often takes at least a year to _____ new buildings today.

4 The desert is a _____ environment that is difficult for people to live in.

5 The _____ to the island took more than three weeks to complete.

B Complete each sentence with the correct answer.

1 A **permanent** injury is one that a person will have for _____.

   a. a short period of time   b. the rest of that person's life

2 Someone who is **qualified** for a job has _____.

   a. what a company is looking for   b. no chance to get hired

3 When a tadpole **transforms**, it _____ a frog.

   a. eats   b. becomes

4 When a person **memorizes** a song, that person _____.

   a. knows all the words to it   b. can play it on a musical instrument

5 Someone who is able to **accomplish** a task _____ it.

   a. can complete   b. cannot complete

6 If a person **determines** the cause of an accident, that person _____.

   a. figures out what happened   b. cannot find out the cause

7 When food in a forest is **plentiful**, it is _____ to find.

   a. easy   b. hard

8 If two cars on a street **collide**, they _____.

   a. almost get in an accident   b. hit each other

9 People who want to **conserve** energy are interested in _____ it.

   a. using   b. saving

Chapter **08**

Connecting Content

■ About the Question

Connecting Content questions focus on your ability to recognize how ideas or topics in a talk relate to one another. You are asked to notice what their connections are. These connections may be stated overtly, or you may have to infer them. These questions usually appear in talks where different ideas, people, places, themes, or objects are discussed. These questions almost always appear after lectures.

Recognizing Connecting Content questions:

1   Many Connecting Content questions appear as charges or tables. They have four sentences or phrases, and you must match them with various themes, ideas, causes, effects, problems, solutions, objects, or individuals. They may appear like this:

• Based on the information in the lecture, indicate which . . . the statements refer to.
  [Click in the correct box for each statement.]

	X	Y
1 [sentence or phrase]		
2 [sentence or phrase]		
3 [sentence or phrase]		
4 [sentence or phrase]		

2   Other Connecting Content questions ask you to make inferences based on the relationships mentioned in the talk. They may appear like this:

• What is the likely outcome of doing procedure X before procedure Y?
• What can be inferred about X?
• What does the professor imply about X?
• What comparison does the professor make between X and Y?

Helpful hints for answering the questions correctly:

• When a professor discusses multiple individuals, themes, places, ideas, or objects in a lecture, it is likely that a chart question will appear. Pay attention to the important details the professor mentions.

• Pay close attention when a professor makes comparisons in a lecture.

• Think about possible future results of events or actions that the professor describes. You may sometimes need to predict a future result, come to a conclusion, or determine the effect of some cause.

Basic Practice

A **Listen to part of a conversation between a student and a professor.** 🎧 CH8_1A

What is the likely outcome of the student attending summer school?

- Ⓐ He will graduate one semester early.
- Ⓑ He will take a seminar in the fall.
- Ⓒ He will get a job next semester.

B **Listen to part of a lecture in an anthropology class.** 🎧 CH8_1B

What is the likely result of ancient farmers practicing crop rotation?

- Ⓐ Their fields produced more crops.
- Ⓑ Important nutrients were lost.
- Ⓒ Legumes grew very well.

C **Listen to part of a lecture in a psychology class.** 🎧 CH8_1C

Based on the information in the lecture, indicate which psychologist the statements refer to.

	Sigmund Freud	Carl Jung
1 Was influenced by Buddhism and Hinduism		
2 Thought the mind was based on the id, the ego, and the superego		
3 Believed dreams could have various meanings		

D **Listen to part of a lecture in an environmental science class.** 🎧 CH8_1D

What comparison does the professor make between the United States and Ireland?

- Ⓐ What the temperature dropped to in the summer of 1816
- Ⓑ How much snow fell during 1816 in both places
- Ⓒ What the weather was like in the summer of 1816

A Listen to part of a conversation between a student and a professor. 🎧 CH8_2A

1 What comparison does the professor make between day classes and night classes?

- Ⓐ The lengths
- Ⓑ The quality
- Ⓒ The workload
- Ⓓ The assignments

2 Based on the information in the conversation, indicate which school the statements refer to.

	Day School	Night School
① Does not offer every class		
② Has higher attendance		
③ Can have students get more attention from professors		
④ Lets students speak more in class		

Vocabulary

- ☐ **quality:** how good or bad something is
- ☐ **advantage:** a benefit; something that helps a person
- ☐ **shift:** a period of time during which a person works

Listen to part of a lecture in a geology class. 🎧 CH8_2B

1   What does the professor imply about deserts?

    Ⓐ They are hot nearly all year long.

    Ⓑ Deserts are bigger than other land ecosystems.

    Ⓒ Most of them have rivers flowing in some places.

    Ⓓ The sand in most of them used to be fertile soil.

2   Based on the information in the lecture, indicate which desert landform the statements refer to.

	Dune	Wadi
1 Is also called an arroyo		
2 Tends to change shape over time		
3 Is made up of sand		
4 Can be dangerous during a rainstorm		

Vocabulary

☐ **crescent:** having the shape of a half moon

☐ **dry up:** to lose all of the water or other moisture in a place or thing

☐ **flashflood:** a sudden, often violent, flood

A Listen to part of a lecture in a literature class. 🎧 CH8_3A

✏️ NOTE-TAKING

....

....

....

....

....

....

....

....

....

Vocabulary

☐ **masterpiece:** a great work of literature or art

☐ **orphan:** a child with no parents

☐ **serialize:** to publish a long work as several shorter pieces

☐ **redemption:** the act of being renewed or forgiven for one's past actions

1 What is the main topic of the lecture?

← Gist-Content Question

    Ⓐ The life of Charles Dickens

    Ⓑ The success of Charles Dickens

    Ⓒ The works of Charles Dickens

    Ⓓ The most famous characters of Charles Dickens

2 What does the professor imply about Oliver Twist?

← Connecting Content Question

    Ⓐ It is Dickens's best novel.

    Ⓑ It is shorter than *A Christmas Carol*.

    Ⓒ It was Dickens's favorite work.

    Ⓓ It was later published as a book.

3 Based on the information in the lecture, indicate which work by Charles Dickens the statements refer to.

← Connecting Content Question

	Oliver Twist	A Christmas Carol
① Features several ghosts in the story		
② Was first published as a book		
③ Focuses on the lives of orphans		
④ First appeared in print in a magazine		

Dictation

Listen to the following sentences and fill in the blanks.

❶ Charles Dickens was _____ _____ _____ British writer of the nineteenth century. Many works of his _____ _____ _____ of literature.

❷ Much of the novel _____ _____ the plight of orphans and other social problems _____ _____ _____. Dickens also _____ _____ _____ _____ about criminal life in Britain.

❸ _____ _____, serialization was _____ and _____ than printing a book that might not sell. _____, when a serialized story was successful, it was _____ published in book form later.

Listen to part of a lecture in an economics class. 🎧 CH8_3B

✏ NOTE-TAKING

....

....

....

....

....

....

....

....

....

....

Vocabulary

☐ **shockwave:** the results caused by a sudden event

☐ **caravan:** a group of people, such as merchants, who travel together

☐ **panic:** a time of great fear

☐ **depositor:** a person who saves money in a bank

1 What is the professor's opinion of the financial crisis of 33 A.D.?

← Understanding Attitude Question

  Ⓐ It could not be stopped by the emperor.

  Ⓑ It was a major problem for the Roman Empire.

  Ⓒ It let Roman banks become more influential.

  Ⓓ It only affected a few banks in Rome.

2 Based on the information in the lecture, indicate whether the statements refer to causes or effects of the financial crisis of 33 A.D.

← Connecting Content Question

	Cause	Effect
① An agriculture law was passed.		
② Some merchant houses in Egypt and Phoenicia went bankrupt.		
③ The emperor lent millions of sesterces to banks.		
④ Roman senators were obliged to purchase land.		

3 Listen again to part of the lecture. Then answer the question. Why does the professor say this: 🎧

← Understanding Function Question

  Ⓐ To make a comparison

  Ⓑ To provide detailed information

  Ⓒ To suggest a problem

  Ⓓ To discuss a result

Dictation

Listen to the following sentences and fill in the blanks.

❶ Events in one place _____ _____ faraway places. This was _____ _____ _____ _____ during the financial crisis of 33 A.D.

❷ The crisis _____ _____ _____ a new agriculture law.

❸ Tiberius finally _____ _____ to stop the panic. He _____ the most _____ banks one hundred million sesterces.

[1-3] **Listen to part of a conversation between a student and a dormitory manager.**

🎧 CH8_4A

1 According to the student, what does his roommate do?

Click on 2 answers.

1. ☐ He gets up very early in the morning.

2. ☐ He plays a musical instrument in the room.

3. ☐ He studies in the room all the time.

4. ☐ He eats food that is not his own.

2 What is the likely outcome of the student going to the student housing office?

Ⓐ He will get a new dormitory room.

Ⓑ He will pay a reduced price.

Ⓒ He will have his fine waived.

Ⓓ He will be allowed to move off campus.

3 What can be inferred about the woman?

Ⓐ She has worked as the dormitory manager for years.

Ⓑ She has dealt with similar problems in the past.

Ⓒ She has never met the student's roommate before.

Ⓓ She can think of no way to solve the student's problem.

4 **What is the main topic of the lecture?**

    Ⓐ Excavation work on Sumerian cities

    Ⓑ Problems with digging up ancient places

    Ⓒ The history of ancient Sumer

    Ⓓ The establishment of the city of Ur

5   What can be inferred about Ur?

    Ⓐ It was located near some oil fields.

    Ⓑ Several wars were fought around it.

    Ⓒ It was once the capital of Sumer.

    Ⓓ Almost a million people once lived in it.

6   Based on the information in the lecture, indicate which Sumerian city the statements refer to.

Click in the correct box for each statement.

	Ur	Lagash
① Has some examples of cuneiform writing		
② Contains a very famous ziggurat		
③ Is believed to be the world's oldest city		
④ Is presently being protected by guards		

7   Listen again to part of the lecture. Then answer the question.
What does the professor mean when he says this: 🎧

    Ⓐ Buildings have been constructed on some dig sites.

    Ⓑ Excavating places takes a lot of time.

    Ⓒ It is hard to find some ancient sites.

    Ⓓ Dig sites often get robbed.

[8-11] Listen to part of a lecture in a musicology class. 🎧 CH8_4C

Musicology

Prince Colloredo

King Ludwig II of Bavaria

Nadezhda von Meck

8 According to the professor, what was a disadvantage of a composer who lived with his patron?

Click on 2 answers.

☐1 He had to write his works very quickly.

☐2 He was unable to meet other composers.

☐3 He was not able to perform the works he wrote.

☐4 He could not be very creative.

9 What does the professor imply about Wolfgang Amadeus Mozart?

Ⓐ He did not get along well with Prince Colloredo.

Ⓑ He traveled throughout Europe when he had a patron.

Ⓒ He wrote his best pieces at the court in Salzburg.

Ⓓ He had his first patron when he was a young man.

10 Why does the professor tell the students about King Ludwig II of Bavaria?

Ⓐ To mention some music that he sponsored

Ⓑ To say how he influenced Richard Wagner's work

Ⓒ To show how he acted when he was a patron

Ⓓ To describe the performances that he attended

11 What can be inferred about Nadezhda von Meck?

Ⓐ She only supported Peter Tchaikovsky with funds.

Ⓑ She frequently attended performances by orchestras.

Ⓒ She traveled through Europe with a composer.

Ⓓ She met Richard Wagner on several occasions.

[1-3] Listen to part of a conversation between a student and an audio-visual services office employee. 🎧 CH8_4D

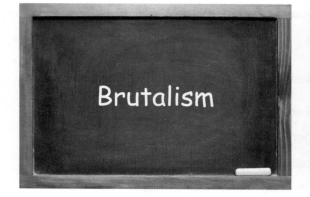

1   Why does the student visit the audio-visual services office?

   Ⓐ To borrow some equipment

   Ⓑ To create a video

   Ⓒ To listen to some recorded material

   Ⓓ To take a class on filming

2   What does the employee give the student?

   Ⓐ A user's manual

   Ⓑ Her ID card

   Ⓒ Several books

   Ⓓ Some camera film

3   What can be inferred about Maxwell Hall?

   Ⓐ It will be featured in a student-run magazine.

   Ⓑ It is used by engineering students.

   Ⓒ It is the newest building on campus.

   Ⓓ It is a work of Neoclassical architecture.

Engineering

embedded
healing agents

vascular
systems

shape-memory
materials

reversible
polymer

4   What is the main topic of the lecture?

    Ⓐ Traditional building methods

    Ⓑ Failures in some building materials

    Ⓒ Ways to construct buildings quickly

    Ⓓ Materials that can repair themselves

5   What is the likely result of a large crack developing quickly in a material using a vascular system?

    Ⓐ The material will suffer a catastrophic failure.

    Ⓑ The crack will not be repaired.

    Ⓒ Pressure will make the crack bigger.

    Ⓓ The tubes will fix the crack.

6   What is the professor's opinion of shape-memory materials?

    Ⓐ He believes they are mostly ineffective.

    Ⓑ He thinks more work needs to be done on them.

    Ⓒ He is interested in learning more about them.

    Ⓓ He is impressed with their level of technology.

7   According to the professor, what do reversible polymers need to work?

    Ⓐ Light from a laser

    Ⓑ Tubes smaller than human hair

    Ⓒ Some kind of a heat source

    Ⓓ A bonding agent such as glue

◼ Vocabulary Review

A Complete each sentence with the appropriate word from the box.

dry up	article	panic	materials	caravan

1 Some of the _____ used to make this item are very expensive.

2 The merchants formed a(n) _____ to protect themselves from bandits.

3 The lake will usually _____ during months when there is no rain.

4 The reporter wrote a(n) _____ for the student newspaper.

5 People started to _____ when a fire started in the building.

B Complete each sentence with the correct answer.

1 A country that is **independent** is _____.

   a. free from rule by another country   b. a colony of a larger country

2 Since the effects of her injury are **reversible**, then she _____.

   a. will suffer for the rest of her life   b. can get better

3 A relic that is **ancient** is considered _____.

   a. very old   b. valuable

4 Because Jeff was an **orphan**, he had _____.

   a. no parents   b. no brothers or sisters

5 A job that has a lot of **prestige** is one that people _____.

   a. want to avoid   b. want to do

6 The artist's **masterpiece** is frequently considered his _____.

   a. greatest work   b. first work

7 Because this diet has several **advantages**, it can _____ people who are on it.

   a. benefit   b. harm

8 When two words are **opposites** of each other, they have _____.

   a. the same meaning   b. different meanings

9 Archaeologists plan to **excavate** the area by _____ the old temple.

   a. digging up   b. discovering

Actual Test

Listening Section Directions

This section measures your ability to understand conversations and lectures in English.

The Listening section is divided into separately timed parts. In each part, you will listen to 1 conversation and 1 or 2 lectures. You will hear each conversation or lecture only one time.

After each conversation or lecture, you will answer some questions about it. The questions typically ask about the main idea and supporting details. Some questions ask about a speaker's purpose or attitude. Answer the questions based on what is stated or implied by the speakers.

You may take notes while you listen. You may use your notes to help you answer the questions. Your notes will not be scored.

If you need to change the volume while you listen, click on the **VOLUME ICON** at the top of the screen.

In some questions, you will see this icon: 🎧 This means that you will hear, but not see, part of the question.

Some of the questions have special directions. These directions appear in a gray box on the screen.

Most questions are worth 1 point. If a question is worth more than 1 point, it will have special directions that indicate how many points you can receive.

A clock at the top of the screen will show you how much time is remaining. The clock will not count down while you are listening. The clock will count down only while you are answering the questions.

1   **Why did the professor ask to see the student?**

   (A) To advise her to speak with the dean of students

   (B) To tell her to submit a paper

   (C) To ask about her progress on an assignment

   (D) To find out why her grades are low

2   **What kind of problem does the student have?**

   (A) She has a family problem.

   (B) She has an academic problem.

   (C) She has a health problem.

   (D) She has a problem with her roommate.

3   **Why does the professor tell the student about a leave of absence?**

   (A) To suggest a solution to her problem

   (B) To explain how to avoid losing her scholarship

   (C) To tell the student to avoid doing that

   (D) To advise the student not to transfer

4 What can be inferred about the professor?

   Ⓐ She has rarely spoken with the student.

   Ⓑ She is interested in the student's well-being.

   Ⓒ The student is in her class this semester.

   Ⓓ The student received an A from her before.

5 Listen again to part of the conversation. Then answer the question.

What does the professor mean when she says this:

   Ⓐ She believes the student is making a bad decision.

   Ⓑ She is satisfied with the student's comment.

   Ⓒ She thinks she has made a fair offer.

   Ⓓ She wants the student to tell her everything now.

AT02

Environmental
Science

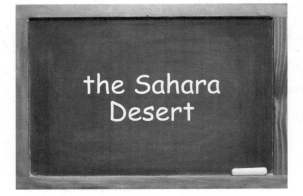

the Sahara
Desert

the Intertropical
Convergence
Zone

6 What aspect of the Sahara Desert does the professor mainly discuss?

    Ⓐ Its land formations

    Ⓑ The countries it is found in

    Ⓒ Its creation in the past

    Ⓓ The rivers that flowed in it

7 According to the professor, what caused the Sahara to turn into a desert?

Click on 2 answers.

    ☐1 The actions of humans

    ☐2 Winds from the east

    ☐3 Changes in the Earth's orbit

    ☐4 An increase in the sun's heat

8 What is the likely result of the Intertropical Convergence Zone moving to the north?

    Ⓐ More rain will fall in Southern Africa.

    Ⓑ The wind will begin to blow more strongly.

    Ⓒ Dry riverbeds and lakebeds will fill with water.

    Ⓓ The Sahara Desert will become smaller.

9   Why does the professor discuss a feedback loop?

    Ⓐ To explain how the Sahara Desert became larger

    Ⓑ To respond to the student's question

    Ⓒ To point out why the Sahara Desert is so hot

    Ⓓ To argue that humans can grow crops in the Sahara Desert

10   What does the professor imply about China and Mongolia?

    Ⓐ The Sahara Desert is in parts of them.

    Ⓑ Hot, dry winds blow in them.

    Ⓒ Parts of them have become deserts.

    Ⓓ They receive small amounts of rain.

11   Listen again to part of the lecture. Then answer the question.
    What can be inferred about the student when he says this: 🎧

    Ⓐ He is skeptical of the professor's explanation.

    Ⓑ He wants the professor to provide another example.

    Ⓒ He does not understand the professor's point.

    Ⓓ He would like to state his own opinion.

AT03

Economics

guilds

12 What is the main topic of the lecture?

(A) The early history of guilds in America

(B) Guilds in Europe in the Middle Ages

(C) The decline of guilds in Europe and America

(D) The ways guilds helped workers

13 What was a journeyman?

(A) A traveling worker

(B) A master craftsman

(C) A skilled worker

(D) An apprentice

14 What can be inferred about guilds in Europe?

(A) They were more powerful than banks.

(B) They were only found in cities.

(C) They still exist in modern times.

(D) They harmed the economy.

15   Why does the professor explain slavery in the southern American colonies?

    (A)   To show why guilds were not needed in them

    (B)   To claim that it harmed many people

    (C)   To say that some slaves joined guilds

    (D)   To mention how slaves became apprentices

16   Based on the information in the lecture, indicate which guilds the statements refer to.

Click in the correct box for each statement.

	Guilds in Europe	Guilds in the American Colonies
1 Were loosely organized		
2 Were extremely important to the economy		
3 Were found in almost all cities and towns		
4 Became workers' associations over time		

17   Listen again to part of the lecture. Then answer the question.
What is the purpose of the professor's response? 🎧

    (A)   To indicate he will discuss a topic soon

    (B)   To ask the student to restate her question

    (C)   To say he will go into detail right now

    (D)   To comment that the student is incorrect

1   Why does the student visit the radio station manager?

Click on 2 answers.

☐1   To make a complaint

☐2   To respond to an advertisement

☐3   To apply for a position

☐4   To make a recommendation

2   In the conversation, the speakers describe a number of facts about Ken O'Brien's radio program. Indicate whether each of the following is a fact or not.

Click in the correct box for each statement.

	Fact	Not a Fact
☐1 It lasts for two hours a night.		
☐2 It features pop music.		
☐3 It sometimes has interviews.		
☐4 It has been on the air for two years.		

3   According to the student, what type of experience does he have?

Ⓐ He worked at a radio station for several years.

Ⓑ He is currently the host of a radio program.

Ⓒ He interned at a local radio station.

Ⓓ He has never worked in radio before.

4   What will the student probably do next?

    Ⓐ Speak with Ken O'Brien

    Ⓑ Complete some forms

    Ⓒ Take a written test

    Ⓓ Broadcast on the air

5   Listen again to part of the conversation. Then answer the question.
    What can be inferred from the student's response to the woman? 🎧

    Ⓐ He will come back again later.

    Ⓑ He is willing to host a radio show.

    Ⓒ He enjoys listening to the radio.

    Ⓓ He has little free time this semester.

AT05

History

Athens

the Delian League

6   How is the lecture organized?

   (A) By using chronological order

   (B) By following an outline

   (C) By focusing on famous individuals

   (D) By covering major battles

7   What is the professor's opinion of the Dorians?

   (A) They contributed very much to Athens.

   (B) They caused serious problems for Athens.

   (C) They were the strongest culture in ancient times.

   (D) They had a minor influence on Greek history.

8   According to the professor, how did Athens become wealthy?

   (A) By farming the land

   (B) By fighting wars of conquest

   (C) By establishing colonies

   (D) By engaging in trade

9　In the lecture, the professor describes a number of facts about the Persians. Indicate whether each of the following is a fact or not.

Click in the correct box for each statement.

	Fact	Not a Fact
1 Attacked Greece on several occasions		
2 Lost a sea battle against Athens		
3 Defeated the Greeks in the Delian League		
4 Won the Battle of Plataea against the Greeks		

10　Why does the professor tell the students about the Delian League?

　　Ⓐ To state that Sparta should have joined it

　　Ⓑ To argue that it successfully protected Greece

　　Ⓒ To remark that it was not planned well

　　Ⓓ To explain how Athens used it to gain power

11　What will the professor probably do next?

　　Ⓐ Talk about Sparta and Athens

　　Ⓑ Cover more Persian history

　　Ⓒ Assign the students a paper

　　Ⓓ Dismiss the class for the day

Authors

Michael A. Putlack

- MA in History, Tufts University, Medford, MA, USA
- Expert test developer of TOEFL, TOEIC, and TEPS
- Main author of the Darakwon *How to Master Skills for the TOEFL® iBT* series and *TOEFL® MAP* series

Stephen Poirier

- Candidate for PhD in History, University of Western Ontario, Canada
- Certificate of Professional Technical Writing, Carleton University, Canada
- Co-author of the Darakwon *How to Master Skills for the TOEFL® iBT* series and *TOEFL® MAP* series

Maximilian Tolochko

- BA in History and Education, University of Oklahoma, USA
- MS in Procurement and Contract Management, Florida Institute of Technology, USA
- Co-author of the Darakwon *TOEFL® MAP* series

Decoding the **TOEFL**® iBT
LISTENING Basic NEW TOEFL® EDITION

Publisher Chung Kyudo
Editors Kim Minju
Authors Michael A. Putlack, Stephen Poirier, Maximilian Tolochko
Proofreader Michael A. Putlack
Designers Koo Soojung, Park Sunyoung

First published in June 2020
By Darakwon, Inc.
Darakwon Bldg., 211, Munbal-ro, Paju-si, Gyeonggi-do 10881
Republic of Korea
Tel: 82-2-736-2031 (Ext. 250)
Fax: 82-2-732-2037

ISBN 978-89-277-0877-3 14740
        978-89-277-0875-9 14740 (set)

www.darakwon.co.kr

Photo Credits
Felix Lipov (p. 148), travelview (p. 148), MISHELLA (p. 148) /
Shutterstock.com

Components Student Book / Answer Book
11 10 9 8 7 6 5   24 25 26 27 28

Decoding the
TOEFL® iBT

Answers
Scripts
Explanations

Basic

Decoding the TOEFL® iBT

Basic

LISTENING

Answers
Scripts
Explanations

| Basic Practice

p. 13

| Answers | A Ⓑ | B Ⓐ | C Ⓑ | D Ⓒ |

| Script |

A

Listen to part of a conversation between a student and a professor.

M Student: Professor Thomas, I have a question about this Thursday's test. Uh . . . what exactly do we need to study?

W Professor: Well, it's going to cover the material in units ten to fifteen. So you should review all of those units. And don't forget to study the notes you took in class.

M: I will. What about the handouts you gave us?

W: You're responsible for them as well. Basically, if we studied it in class, you need to know it.

M: Great. Thanks for letting me know. I appreciate it.

Answer Explanation

Ⓑ The student asks the professor, "What exactly do we need to study?" The professor then gives the student an answer.

B

Listen to part of a conversation between a student and a student housing office employee.

W Student: Good afternoon. I'm here about a key for my dorm room.

M Student Housing Office Employee: You didn't get one? Every student should have one by now.

W: Actually, er . . . I received one. But I, uh, I already lost it. I can't believe I did that on the second day of school. So how do I get a new one?

M: First, fill out this form. Then, we'll replace the lock on your room. After that, we'll give you a new key.

W: That's going to cost a lot, isn't it?

M: It will be $50. And the work won't start until about three hours from now.

Answer Explanation

Ⓐ About her dorm room key, the student tells the man, "I received one. But I, uh, I already lost it."

C

Listen to part of a lecture in an anthropology class.

W Professor: As you know, there are numerous ways that we anthropologists study humans from the past. One of them is by examining fossils. Of course, we can study the bones of ancient humans. But we can also study their footprints. That's right. There are fossilized human footprints in some places.

M Student: I'm sorry, but what could we possibly learn from footprints? I don't get it.

W: Well, think about it . . . The presence of footprints means there were humans in a certain area at a specific time. We can date these footprints, you know. Why is that important? Well, there's an ongoing debate about when the first humans arrived in the Americas. Some say it happened around 12,000 years ago. But others think humans were here even earlier. Why do they think that way? It's simple. Some fossilized footprints dating to an earlier period were found. Here, uh, take a look at these pictures.

Answer Explanation

Ⓑ The professor mostly lectures on how anthropologists find fossilized footprints useful.

D

Listen to part of a lecture in a chemistry class.

M Professor: I'm sure you've all heard of isotopes, but do you know what they are . . . ? Does anybody want to guess . . . ? Okay, uh, I guess not. Well, as you know, elements have a standard number of protons. For example, hydrogen has one . . . Oxygen has eight . . . And gold has seventy-nine. These numbers never change. Now, uh, in the nucleus of an atom, in addition to protons, there are also neutrons. Unlike the number of protons, the number of neutrons can change. This creates isotopes. Each isotope of an atom has a different atomic weight. Basically, isotopes are different forms of elements.

Of the eighty-one stable elements, there are 275 isotopes. However, there are more than 800 radioactive isotopes. Okay, uh . . . Some of you look confused. Hmm . . . I should give you an example. You all have heard of carbon-14 dating, right . . . ? Well, carbon-14 is a radioactive isotope. Let me explain how it and carbon-12 are different.

Answer Explanation

Ⓒ In the lecture, the professor mostly discusses what isotopes are.

A

| Script |

Listen to part of a conversation between a student and a professor.

M Student: Good afternoon, Professor Longman. I need to speak with you about the paper we're supposed to turn in tomorrow. I, uh, I haven't finished it yet.

W Professor: And why not, Greg? It's only a five-page paper. Plus, I told you about it last week.

M: Yes, ma'am, I know that. The problem is, uh, I was at a conference all weekend. So I couldn't work on it then.

W: Conference? What conference?

M: The conference sponsored by the National Economics Council. I went to St. Louis with some students from the Economics Department. My advisor, Professor Samuels, was there, too. So, uh, he can vouch for me.

W: You were out of the state then?

M: That's right. We left on Thursday night and returned late last night. That's why I don't think I can finish by tomorrow.

W: Okay . . . I'll give you until Thursday. That's two extra days. But . . . if you're late, you'll lose twenty points.

M: I won't be late. Thanks so much, Professor Longman. I appreciate it. I'll make sure my work doesn't disappoint you.

W: I'm looking forward to reading your paper.

Answer Explanation

1 Ⓓ The student says that he was out of the state, so he was unable to finish a paper. Thus he lacks time to finish some work.

2 Ⓒ The conversation is mostly about the student's activities at the conference last weekend.

B

| Script |

Listen to part of a lecture in an archaeology class.

M Professor: Okay, we're very busy this afternoon. So, uh, please take your seats so that we can get started now. Okay, let's begin. I'm going to talk about pyramids today. As you should know, pyramids are tall structures which are quite wide at the bottom. However, as they get higher,

they become narrower. Many pyramids are more than 100 meters in height. Egypt, of course, has the most famous and spectacular pyramids. But people in ancient civilizations around the world also built pyramids.

First, uh, Egypt. There are at least 135 pyramids built during the time of ancient Egypt. There may be even more buried beneath the sand. The Egyptian pyramids were erected thousands of years ago for a single purpose: to provide the pharaohs with final resting places. These gigantic tombs were filled with the pharaohs' mummies as well as various items and treasures. The Egyptians thought the pharaohs would need them in the afterlife. Some Egyptian pyramids were step pyramids. They had large ledges, which resembled giant steps. Other pyramids had smooth, sloping sides.

Now, uh, what about pyramids in other places? Well, the Mayans and Aztecs in Central America also constructed them. Interestingly, there are more pyramids in Central America than there are in Egypt. Really. It's true. For instance, El Mirador was an ancient Mayan city. It contained more than thirty pyramids. That's right. Thirty pyramids in a single place. One of them was 172 meters high while another was 145 meters high. The Mayans and Aztecs often used their pyramids for religious ceremonies. The priests conducted special services on them while people watched from down below.

Answer Explanation

1 Ⓐ The lecture is mostly about different types of pyramids.

2 Ⓓ The professor mostly talks about how many Mayan pyramids there were.

A

| Script |

Listen to part of a conversation between a student and a student services office employee.

W1 Student: Hello. I'm Henrietta Reynolds. You're Ms. Lucent, right? I talked to you on the phone this morning.

W2 Student Services Office Employee: Oh, hello. It's nice to meet you in person. You're here about the student magazine, aren't you?

W1: That's correct. Did you understand everything I told you over the phone?

W2: Uh . . . Not everything. Why don't you start over again?

That way, I can make sure I know what you want to do.

W1: Sure, I can do that. Let me see . . . Uh, basically, I want to start a new student magazine. It would be based on life here on campus. I hope to publish it once a month during each semester.

W2: Okay. That sounds straightforward. But, um . . . that's going to be really expensive. And you'll need several writers and editors.

W1: Yes, I've thought about both of those issues. I talked to Professor Martin in the English Department. He believes that he can arrange a grant to provide some funding. Plus, we intend to sell ads in the magazine.

W2: What about the writers and editors?

W1: There are six other people interested in this project so far. Everyone has experience with the school newspaper here. We also plan to make an announcement. So, uh, we'll try to recruit some more people.

W2: Hmm . . . It sounds possible. But I need to see a written proposal. I also need to talk to the professor. Uh . . . what was his name again?

W1: Martin. Stephen Martin. I can give you his extension. I've got it here on my phone. And I'll write a proposal for you over the weekend.

W2: Excellent. I'm looking forward to reading it.

Answer Explanation

1 Ⓐ Most of the conversation is about a student magazine the student would like to establish.

2 Ⓐ The student says, "I talked to Professor Martin in the English Department. He believes that he can arrange a grant to provide some funding." The employee asks for Professor Martin's name. If she speaks with him, she will likely learn about a source of funding.

3 Ⓒ The student says, "I can give you his extension. I've got it here on my phone," so she will probably give the employee a phone number next.

Dictation

W1: Hello. I'm Henrietta Reynolds. You're Ms. Lucent, right? I talked to you on the phone this morning.

W2: Oh, hello. It's nice to meet you in person. You're here about the student magazine, aren't you?

W1: That's correct. Did you understand everything I told you over the phone?

W2: Uh . . . Not everything. Why don't you start over again? That way, I can make sure I know what you want to do.

W1: Sure, I can do that. Let me see . . .

B

| Script |

Listen to part of a lecture in a history class.

M Professor: John Cabot was one of the first people to explore the New World. In 1497, he discovered the coast of North America. Like Christopher Columbus, Cabot was Italian. He was a merchant seaman from Venice but, uh, wasn't very successful. He and his family departed Venice in 1488 because he was in debt. By 1495, they found themselves living in England. There, Cabot tried to raise funds for an expedition to the New World. In 1496, King Henry VII gave Cabot the right to explore the area for England. Cabot would eventually make three voyages.

Cabot was based in Bristol on England's west coast. He had one small ship, um, the *Matthew*, and a small crew of around twenty men. We believe Cabot's first voyage was a failure due to bad weather. This forced him to return to Bristol.

W Student: Believe? We don't know for sure?

M: There aren't many records about Cabot's expeditions. And the few that exist often have contrasting information. We really just, uh, we don't know what happened. Well, he didn't get to the New World on his first try. We know that for sure.

Cabot's second voyage in 1497 was his most famous. After a voyage of many weeks, the *Matthew* reached the east coast of North America in late June. He most likely arrived in Newfoundland or Nova Scotia. Again, the records are unclear when and where he saw land. The *Matthew* mainly sailed along the coast. It landed once so that the crew could obtain fresh water. Cabot also made sure to claim the land for England then. By early August, the *Matthew* was back in England. Cabot reported on his voyage to the king, who granted him a small pension for his efforts.

Even less is known about Cabot's third voyage in 1498. It's been reported that he had anywhere between two and five ships. They were all loaded with merchandise for trade. Some historians claim the ships were lost at sea. Other records have Cabot living into the 1500s.

W: It seems odd that we don't know much about him.

M: You have to remember that they didn't keep perfect records centuries ago. Anyway, Cabot's legacy was that his voyages let England claim part of the New World. This set the stage for the conflicts England and France fought in the next few centuries.

1 Ⓑ The professor lectures to the class on the voyages of John Cabot.

2 Ⓒ The professor states, "We believe Cabot's first voyage was a failure due to bad weather. This forced him to return to Bristol."

3 Second Voyage: ②, ③, ④   Third Voyage: ①
About the second voyage of John Cabot, the professor states, "Cabot's second voyage in 1497 was his most famous. After a voyage of many weeks, the *Matthew* reached the east coast of North America in late June. He most likely arrived in Newfoundland or Nova Scotia. Again, the records are unclear when and where he saw land. The *Matthew* mainly sailed along the coast. It landed once so that the crew could obtain fresh water. Cabot also made sure to claim the land for England then." Regarding the third voyage, the professor comments, "Even less is known about Cabot's third voyage in 1498. It's been reported that he had anywhere between two and five ships."

Dictation

❶ We believe Cabot's first voyage was a <u>failure</u> due to <u>bad weather</u>. This <u>forced</u> him <u>to</u> return to Bristol.

❷ He <u>most likely</u> arrived in Newfoundland or Nova Scotia. Again, the records are <u>unclear when and where</u> he saw land.

❸ <u>Even less is known</u> about Cabot's third voyage in 1498. It's been <u>reported</u> that he had <u>anywhere between</u> two and five ships.

iBT Practice Test
p. 20

Answers

PART 1

1 Ⓐ	2 Ⓓ	3 Ⓑ	4 Ⓐ	5 Ⓒ
6 Ⓐ	7 Ⓒ	8 Fact: ①, ③, ④ Not a Fact: ②		
9 Ⓒ	10 Ⓒ	11 Ⓓ		

PART 2

1 Ⓑ	2 Ⓐ	3 Ⓒ	4 Ⓑ	5 ③, ④
6 Ⓓ	7 Ⓐ			

PART 1

[1-3] Conversation

| Script |

Listen to part of a conversation between a student and a professor.

M Student: Good afternoon, Professor Candide. Can I speak with you for a moment? There's something on my mind I need to discuss.

W Professor: Sure, Robert. Do you need some tips for the upcoming test? It's only three days from now. And it's going to be pretty tough.

M: Oh, no. I'm not here about that. I think I know the material pretty well. I'm not particularly worried about the test.

W: That's great news. I remember you got an A+ on the first test. I was pleased with your performance. Okay, so you're not here to discuss schoolwork. In that case, uh, what do you want to talk about?

M: I'm thinking about doing an internship next year in the summer. But, uh . . . I don't know which one I should apply for.

W: All right. Let's start with an easy question . . . What kind of work do you have in mind?

M: I'd like to intern at an engineering firm. There are a couple of opportunities I know about. One's here in the city. The other is in Pittsburgh.

W: Pittsburgh? Why there? Do you know anyone there?

M: Actually, yes. My older brother lives there. He said I could stay with him for the summer if I get the position.

W: That's great news. Not all internships are paid, so it's good you have a potential place to stay.

M: So, uh . . . which one do you think I should apply for? I don't know what to do.

W: Both of them. Robert, you should probably apply to more than just two. Internships are highly competitive these days. There are probably going to be fifty or, uh, even a hundred students applying for each position. You have good grades, but I'm sure the other applicants do, too.

M: Oh . . . So you don't think I'll get accepted to either program?

W: Don't misunderstand. I have no idea about that. You're highly qualified, but I'm sure that other highly qualified individuals will also apply. Why don't you apply to those two? And why don't you search for more opportunities? Then, you can apply to those programs as well. Doing so will increase your chances of getting accepted.

M: But what if two or more programs accept me? What am I supposed to do if that happens?

W: That would be perfect. Just choose the one you prefer and turn down the others. The ones you reject will offer the positions to someone else. You need to think of yourself, Robert. Apply to as many programs as possible. And do it quickly because I'm sure there are deadlines coming up.

1 Gist-Content Question

(A) They are talking about the student's intentions to get an internship for the summer.

2 Understanding Attitude Question

(D) The professor says, "I remember you got an A+ on the first test. I was pleased with your performance." She also says that the student is "highly qualified," so she thinks he is strong academically.

3 Making Inferences Question

(B) The professor is surprised when the student mentions Pittsburgh. He also says that his older brother lives there. Since Pittsburgh is out of town, it can be inferred that the student has a family member who lives out of town.

[4-7] Lecture #1

| Script |

Listen to part of a lecture in a botany class.

W Professor: Just like people and animals, plants go through stages in life. There are different kinds of plants, so I'm going to speak about flowering plants right now. Flowering plants start their lives as seeds. Then, they grow into plants, make flowers, produce seeds, and die. How long this takes depends on the type of plant it is. Annuals live for a single year. Biennials live for two years. They sprout and grow during the first year. They produce flowers and seeds in the second year. As for perennials, um, they live for many years.

The first stage is the seed. Depending on the type of plant, a seed can remain dormant for years or sprout quickly. The conditions needed for growth also tend to vary. Among them are, um, the amount of water present, the type of soil, and the temperature. But seeds have some common characteristics. Let's see . . . They have a hard outer cover which protects them. Inside the cover is the embryo of a new plant. When the conditions are right, it germinates. So it starts to grow by bursting out of the seed.

The next stage is plant growth. The plant begins growing both up and down. It develops roots, which dig into the soil. The roots gather water and nutrients to help the plant grow. Upward, the plant grows a stem and branches with leaves. 🎧7 The stem supports the plant's weight. And the leaves contain chlorophyll, which is needed for the process of photosynthesis. **That's the primary way plants get food, but it's not something I intend to discuss until another lecture.**

Finally, the plant produces flowers. Inside each flower are the parts necessary for seed growth. The stamen is the male part, and the pistil is the female part. On the stamen is the anther, which produces pollen. On the pistil is the stigma, which collects pollen. Pollen is needed to produce seeds. In most flowering plants, the anther and the stigma are located far apart. Help is therefore needed to move the pollen from the stamen to the pistil. This help, by the way, is called pollination. Some plants can self-pollinate, but most cannot.

M Student: How do they get pollinated then?

W: I was just about to explain. Some get pollinated through the action of the wind. Others are pollinated when birds and bees suck nectar from flowers. Pollen gets stuck to them, and as they move from flower to flower, it rubs off onto another flower's stigma. We call this cross-pollination.

M Student: What time of the year does this take place?

W: Mostly in spring. But that depends on the plant species as well as some other factors. So it's impossible to get a definite answer. Now, uh, once pollination occurs, the seed starts growing inside the pistil. After a while, it will be big enough, um, and heavy enough to drop from the flower to the ground. In other instances, it gets carried away by the wind or water. Or it could get eaten by an animal. Then, it might be purged from that particular animal's body as waste and dropped to the ground later. Once that happens, a new life cycle for a new plant begins.

Now, I'd like to look at the life cycles of some different types of plants, but I'd like to give you a short quiz on what we just studied. Let me hand it out to you right now. When everyone finishes, I can continue the lecture.

4 Gist-Content Question

(A) The professor focuses her lecture on the life cycles of flowering plants.

5 Understanding Organization Question

(C) About birds and bees, the professor says, "Others are pollinated when birds and bees suck nectar from flowers. Pollen gets stuck to them, and as they move from flower to flower, it rubs off onto another flower's stigma. We call this cross-pollination."

6 Making Inferences Question

(A) At the end of the lecture, the professor tells the students, "I'd like to give you a short quiz on what we just studied. Let me hand it out to you right now. When everyone finishes, I can continue the lecture."

7 Making Inferences Question

(C) When the professor says, "It's not something I intend to discuss until another lecture," she means that she will not talk more about a topic today. She will talk about it in another class.

| Script |

Listen to part of a lecture in an astronomy class.

M Professor: The solar system formed between four and five billion years ago. It was created from the dust and gases surrounding the star we call the sun. The sun is a medium-sized star that creates heat and light through inner nuclear fusion reactions. Its gravity field holds the rest of the solar system together. Moving outward from the sun, we can divide the rest of the solar system into three basic regions. They are the inner planets, the outer planets, and the region beyond the outer planets. Included in the solar system are the eight main planets, several dwarf planets, and many smaller bodies such as moons, asteroids, and comets.

The inner planets are Mercury, Venus, Earth, and Mars. They all share some characteristics. First, they're small and rocky, especially in comparison to the outer planets. They have a solid core made mostly of iron and nickel. It's surrounded by a less solid layer called the mantle. On top, there is a rocky crust. Each inner planet also has an atmosphere of gases. It's thick on Venus and Earth but very thin on Mercury and Mars. The inner planets have few moons compared to the outer planets. Mercury and Venus have none. Earth has one, and Mars, uh, Mars has two.

Between the inner and outer planets is the asteroid belt. It contains millions of rocks orbiting the sun. Some are quite large, but most are small. They're believed to be the remains of what could have become another planet but didn't. It never formed because the strong gravity of nearby Jupiter kept the individual pieces from coming together.

There are four outer planets as well. They are Jupiter, Saturn, Uranus, and Neptune. They are . . . Yes, do you have a question?

W Student: Yes, sir. What about Pluto? I learned that it's an outer planet.

M: Well, it used to be considered a major planet, but that has changed. Nowadays, it's classified as a dwarf planet. I'll talk about it in just a moment. Now, uh, back to the outer planets. They're huge and consist mainly of gases. Their outer layers are mainly gaseous, but high pressure makes their inner layers more solid. They might have a tiny, rocky core, but we aren't sure about that. One of their most obvious features is the visible rings surrounding them. Billions of ice and rock particles make up these rings. Saturn has the most extensive ring system, but each gas giant has some rings as well. 🎧11 They also, um, have many moons. **So far, we've discovered sixty-nine orbiting Jupiter.** There are sixty-two orbiting Saturn, twenty-seven orbiting Uranus, and fourteen orbiting Neptune.

Beyond the outer planets are many other bodies lying in a region called the Kuiper Belt. The main bodies in it are dwarf planets. Pluto is the largest. As I mentioned, it used to be considered a major planet. But the world's astronomers downgraded it to a dwarf planet in 2006. They did that since its characteristics are similar to those of other dwarf planets. There are five main dwarf planets and many smaller ones. We anticipate discovering more in the future. They're all small, rocky, very cold, and far from the sun. Oh, the exception is Ceres, the smallest main dwarf planet. It's found in the asteroid belt.

Now, far beyond the Kuiper Belt is the last region, which is called the Oort Cloud. It contains countless objects made of rock and ice. Most are comets. No one knows how many objects are there. There could be billions or even trillions of them. Imagine that.

Answer Explanation

8 Detail Question

Fact: 1, 3, 4   Not a Fact: 2

About the inner planets, the professor states, "The inner planets are Mercury, Venus, Earth, and Mars. They all share some characteristics. First, they're small and rocky, especially in comparison to the outer planets. They have a solid core made mostly of iron and nickel. It's surrounded by a less solid layer called the mantle. On top, there is a rocky crust. Each inner planet also has an atmosphere of gases. It's thick on Venus and Earth but very thin on Mercury and Mars. The inner planets have few moons compared to the outer planets. Mercury and Venus have none. Earth has one, and Mars, uh, Mars has two." None of them, however, has ring systems. Only the outer planets have rings.

9 Gist-Content Question

ⓒ About the Kuiper Belt, the professor mostly discusses the objects located in it.

10 Making Inferences Question

ⓒ About the Oort Cloud, the professor remarks, "No one knows how many objects are there. There could be billions or even trillions of them." It can therefore be inferred that very little is known about the Oort Cloud today.

11 Understanding Function Question

ⓓ When the professor says, "So far, we've discovered sixty-nine orbiting Jupiter," he is implying that more moons may be discovered around the planet one day.

PART 2

| Script |

Listen to part of a conversation between a student and a student services office employee.

M Student: Hello. I was told I need to come here to get something done.

W Student Services Office Employee: Yes? Why did someone tell you to come here?

M: I'm here about the late-night study area. I tried to go there last night. However, the person at the door wouldn't let me in. He said I needed permission to study there. I wasn't really sure what was going on. And that guy didn't want to explain anything. But, uh, at least he told me to come here.

W: That wasn't very nice of him. Thanks for letting me know about that. I'll find out who was working last night and have a chat with him. We need our employees to be friendly and helpful to everyone. So, uh, anyway, about the room . . . Basically, it's one of the most popular places on campus. Unfortunately . . .

M: Unfortunately, what?

W: Well, too many students were going to the late-night study area but not actually studying. Some of them were just hanging out and goofing off with their friends. So we changed the rules last week. Now, there are restrictions on who is allowed to study there.

M: Like what?

W: You need to prove you have a need to be there.

M: What kinds of reasons are acceptable?

W: Writing a graduate thesis or a senior honors thesis qualifies. Being enrolled in a seminar and having to write a paper for that class qualifies, too. So does taking twenty or more hours of classes in one semester. And, uh, what else . . . ? Ah, yes, having a difficult roommate.

M: A difficult roommate? What's that supposed to mean?

W: You know, a roommate who plays music too loudly, who parties a lot, or who doesn't really care about studying. Students with roommate problems need the residential assistant on their floor in their dormitory to write them a letter.

M: Ah, I see. Well, Jeff is great, but I am taking two seminars this semester. That's why I desire access to the late-night study area.

W: Okay. All you need to do is show me your class schedule. Then, I can confirm that you're in two seminars. After that, I'll create an ID card for you that provides you with access at any time. But, uh, just so you know, you aren't guaranteed a seat. There are only 150 seats, and more than 400 students already have ID cards.

M: I see. I guess I'll just have to take my chances. I don't have my class schedule with me. Let me run back to my dorm to get it. I'll be back in a quarter of an hour or so.

W: See you soon.

1 Gist-Content Question

Ⓑ The student talks about his problem in saying, "I'm here about the late-night study area. I tried to go there last night. However, the person at the door wouldn't let me in. He said I needed permission to study there."

2 Making Inferences Question

Ⓐ When the woman talks about problem roommates, the student responds, "Well, Jeff is great." It can therefore be inferred that he gets along well with his roommate.

3 Detail Question

Ⓒ The student says, "I don't have my class schedule with me. Let me run back to my dorm to get it."

| Script |

Listen to part of a lecture in a cinematography class.

M Professor: I'd like to tell you about a unique movie called *Russian Ark*, and then we'll watch it. I doubt any of you have seen it, so let me discuss it a bit. The movie came out in 2002 and was screened at the Cannes Film Festival. It was directed by Alexander Sokurov. *Russian Ark* was shot in the old Winter Palace of the tsars in St. Petersburg, Russia. Today, the palace is a Russian state museum commonly known by its nickname, the Hermitage.

Now, I just said that *Russian Ark* is unique. Let me explain what I mean by that . . . The movie was filmed in one long take with no edits, and a Steadicam was used to shoot it. A Steadicam is a camera which can be held and moved, but the recorded images don't appear shaky. This wasn't a gimmick. You know, something like, "Hey, look at us. We're being really clever." On the contrary, the main reason it was filmed in a single take was due to the limited amount of time available. You see, the museum had to shut down to the public so that the movie could be made. And the museum directors permitted the moviemakers a single day to shoot the film. This was done on December 23, 2001. The Steadicam recorded everything to a digital hard drive. The single take lasted for ninety minutes.

To achieve this required a tremendous amount of preparation. The actors rehearsed a lot. More than 2,000 actors and crew members were involved in the making of the movie. So it wasn't a minor endeavor. In addition, three orchestras appear. All the actors had to say their lines perfectly and make the proper gestures. However, sound wasn't recorded but was added in postproduction.

W Student: Why was that?

M: The main reason was the language issue. The director only spoke Russian while the cameraman was German. So a translator was required as they moved through the museum. For that reason, sound was added later. The movie was also enhanced through digital means. However, the difficult part was getting the shot done in one take. How hard? Well, they failed three times. Each time, someone made a mistake big enough that the director had to stop the entire process.

After three failures, everyone was worried because time was running out. There was also only enough power in the Steadicam to film one more take. The cameraman was getting tired as well. That's understandable since the device is heavy. So they began a fourth time with everyone knowing it would be their last chance. But they managed to do it.

Now, before I turn on the film, let me give you some information about the story. It's a movie about Russian history. The story follows a rough chronological order by including scenes from Russian history focusing on Peter the Great, the nineteenth century, World War One, the Russian Revolution, and World War Two. A ghostly narrator, whom we never see, interacts with people from Russian history. The voice of the narrator is that of Sokurov, the director. The narrator meets a character called the European. He has a low opinion of Russia and Russian history. To show the European that he's wrong, the narrator invites him to take a tour of the museum.

And that's all I want to say about the film. I don't want to give away any more. Oh, the actors all speak Russian, but there are English subtitles. All right, if someone would turn off the lights, we can proceed with the film.

Answer Explanation

4 Gist-Content Question

ⓑ The professor mostly focuses on how the movie was filmed during his lecture.

5 Detail Question

③, ④ First, the professor says, "It was directed by Alexander Sokurov." Then, he states, "The voice of the narrator is that of Sokurov, the director."

6 Understanding Function Question

ⓓ The professor describes the European's role in *Russian Ark* in stating, "The narrator meets a character called the European. He has a low opinion of Russia and Russian history. To show the European that he's wrong, the narrator invites him to take a tour of the museum."

7 Making Inferences Question

ⓐ At the end of the lecture, the professor says, "All right, if someone would turn off the lights, we can

proceed with the film." So he will probably screen a film for the students.

∣ Vocabulary Review

p. 30

Answers

A

1	go through	2	recruit	3	legacy
4	enhance	5	pension		

B

1 a	2 b	3 a	4 a	5 b
6 a	7 b	8 a	9 b	

| Basic Practice

p. 33

Answers   A ⓒ   B Ⓐ   C ⓒ   D Ⓐ

| Script |

A

Listen to part of a conversation between a student and a cafeteria employee.

W Student: Hello, James. You wanted to see me about something?

M Cafeteria Employee: That's right, Cathy. I'm curious . . . How do you enjoy working here in the cafeteria?

W: Well, it's hard. But I enjoy it a lot. I used to work at my parents' restaurant. So this kind of work is fun for me.

M: It shows. You really seem to love the job. That's why I want to make you a manager here.

W: Seriously? But I've only been working here for six weeks.

M: That doesn't matter. So, uh, are you interested?

Answer Explanation

ⓒ The man tells the student, "That's why I want to make you a manager here," so he wants to give her a promotion.

B

Listen to part of a conversation between a student and a professor.

W Professor: Yes, Tim? You need to talk to me about something?

M Student: Yes, ma'am. I'm afraid I'm going to miss the next class. My boss is sending me on a business trip to Mexico City. I'm going to be there from Thursday to Sunday.

W: Okay, I understand. You're excused from the class. But, um, you know the paper is due on that day, right?

M: Yes. I'm going to submit it to you tomorrow. I just need to write the conclusion and proofread it.

W: Excellent. I love it when students do their work early.

Answer Explanation

Ⓐ The student tells the professor, "I'm afraid I'm going to miss the next class. My boss is sending me on a business trip to Mexico City. I'm going to be there from Thursday to Sunday."

C

Listen to part of a conversation between a student and a school newspaper employee.

M1 Student: Excuse me. Are you Marcus Franklin?

M2 School Newspaper Employee: That's correct. Are you here about an article?

M1: No, I'm not. I need to put an ad in the paper. The woman out front told me to talk to you.

M2: Yeah, sure, uh, I can handle it. May I see the ad, please?

M1: Here it is. I filled everything out according to the guidelines. This is for the Chemistry Department. The secretary said the department has an account here.

M2: That's correct. But I need to call to verify everything. Hold on one moment, please.

Answer Explanation

ⓒ The student remarks, "I need to put an ad in the paper."

D

Listen to part of a lecture in an art history class.

W Professor: We're talking about illuminated manuscripts today. This may be an unfamiliar term to some of you, so let me explain. Basically, they were handwritten books created during the Middle Ages. Remember, this was before the printing press was invented. As a result, people made books by hand. Illuminated manuscripts didn't just contain written material though. They were also decorated with artwork.

Now, uh, most illuminated manuscripts were religious works. People mainly copied the Bible or other religious texts back then. *The Book of Kells* is one famous example of a religious text. It contains some of the best-known illuminated manuscripts. You know, uh, there's a bit of a controversy in the art history community. Most people believe the pictures in illuminated manuscripts are art. But some argue that they aren't. Let me show you some pictures of a few pages of *The Book of Kells*. Then, we'll have a discussion about whether they are art or not.

Answer Explanation

Ⓐ The professor says, "We're talking about illuminated manuscripts today. This may be an unfamiliar term to some of you, so let me explain."

Practice with Short Passages

p. 34

A

Answers   1 ⓒ   2 Ⓐ

Script

Listen to part of a conversation between a student and a professor.

W1 Student: Before I leave, do you mind if I ask one more question? I've got something important to discuss.

W2 Professor: Sure, Stephanie. I have a couple more minutes to talk to you. My staff meeting doesn't begin until three thirty.

W1: Great. Thanks a lot . . . So, uh, I'm thinking about attending summer school. But I'm not exactly sure which class to take.

W2: Summer school? Why are you planning to do that? You've taken a full load of classes during your first two years. So, uh, you're on schedule to graduate. Plus, uh, I thought you were going to get a job this summer.

W1: I had intended to. But then, uh, I altered my plans. I've decided to hang out around campus to do some extra studying. But there aren't very many classes in our department this summer. In fact, uh, I've already taken the ones being offered.

W2: In that case, take something not related to your major. I remember that you mentioned you like creative writing. Professor Tillman is teaching that class this summer. You might enjoy it.

W1: Oh, hey, that's a great idea. I'll check out the class now. Thanks, Professor.

W2: It's my pleasure.

Answer Explanation

1 Ⓒ The student comments, "So, uh, I'm thinking about attending summer school. But I'm not exactly sure which class to take."

2 Ⓐ When the professor states she thought the student was getting a job in summer, the student responds, "I had intended to. But then, uh, I altered my plans. I've decided to hang out around campus to do some extra studying." So she talks about her summer plans to explain why she changed her mind.

B

Answers	1 Ⓐ	2 Ⓓ

Script

Listen to part of a conversation between a student and a student activities office employee.

M Student: Good morning. My name is Joe Thomas. I called about half an hour ago.

W Student Activities Office Employee: Ah, yes. You're here on behalf of the photography club, right?

M: That's correct. I'm the president of the club. I had

scheduled a meeting for this Thursday night. It turns out, however, that most of the members can't make it then. So, uh, I need to reschedule it.

W: That's not a problem. What day and time do you have in mind?

M: How about next Monday at six thirty? Is the same room available then?

W: Let me check the computer . . . Hold on one moment, please . . . Okay, I'd say you're in luck. The room had been reserved for a special class. But it appears that Professor Johnson canceled it last night. So I can give it to you. That's room 494 in Robertson Hall.

M: Wonderful. I really appreciate your assistance.

W: It's my pleasure. And the next time you need something, just call. You don't need to come down here in person.

Answer Explanation

1 Ⓐ The student comments, "I had scheduled a meeting for this Thursday night. It turns out, however, that most of the members can't make it then. So, uh, I need to reschedule it."

2 Ⓓ The woman states, "Okay, I'd say you're in luck. The room had been reserved for a special class. But it appears that Professor Johnson canceled it last night. So I can give it to you. That's room 494 in Robertson Hall." So she talks about Professor Johnson's class to explain why a room is available.

Practice with Long Passages   p. 36

A

Answers	1 Ⓑ	2 Ⓒ	3 Ⓒ

Script

Listen to part of a conversation between a student and a professor.

W Student: Professor Yang, I have something important to talk about. It concerns our class.

M Professor: Sure, April. Why don't you take a seat and tell me what's going on?

W: Thanks, sir. I, uh . . . I'm really sorry, but I don't think I can complete all of my classwork by the end of the semester. I've just got so much work to do.

M: Is this related to your illness earlier in the semester?

W: That's correct. Since I missed three weeks of classes, I've been trying to catch up. But there is simply too much to do. I'm, uh, I'm enrolled in six classes this semester.

M: That's a full load. Okay, let me think . . . How are you doing in your other classes? Are you going to finish them on time or not?

W: I'm fully caught up in two of them. I think I can finish one more on time. But I won't finish your work or my work for Professor Powell or Professor Kennedy.

M: All right. Why don't I give you an incomplete grade? Then, you can finish the work for me during winter break. Oh, you're going to take the final exam, aren't you?

W: Yes, I'll be taking it. And your suggestion sounds great. I really appreciate it.

M: 🎧³ You'll have to fill out some paperwork. Go to the Registrar's office and tell the person there you need an incomplete form. Then, come back here, and we can fill it out together. **I'll be in my office until three.**

W: Sure. I can do that. Thanks again, Professor.

Answer Explanation

1 Ⓑ The student says, "I'm really sorry, but I don't think I can complete all of my classwork by the end of the semester. I've just got so much work to do." Then, she talks about what she can do to finish her classwork.

2 Ⓒ First, the professor asks if the student's problem is related to her illness earlier in the semester. Then, he comes up with suggestions on how to help her. So he is clearly sympathetic toward the student.

3 Ⓒ When the professor tells the student to get a form and then states, "I'll be in my office until three," he is indicating that she should get the form today.

Dictation

M: Okay, <u>let me think</u> . . . How are you doing in your other classes? Are you going to <u>finish them on time</u> or not?

W: I'm <u>fully caught up</u> in two of them. I think I can finish one more on time. But I <u>won't finish</u> your work or my work for Professor Powell or Professor Kennedy.

M: All right. <u>Why don't I give</u> you an incomplete grade? Then, you can finish the work for me <u>during winter break</u>. Oh, you're going to <u>take the final exam</u>, aren't you?

W: Yes, I'll be taking it. And your <u>suggestion</u> sounds great. I <u>really appreciate it</u>.

B

Answers   1 Ⓑ   2 Ⓐ   3 Ⓒ

| Script |

Listen to part of a lecture in an anthropology class.

W Professor: When the Europeans arrived in South America in the 1500s, they discovered a vast empire there. I'm talking, of course, about the Incan Empire. It covered much of the land found in modern-day Peru, Bolivia, and Ecuador. It's believed that there were more than ten million Incan people at the empire's height. They lived in a hierarchical society based on classes.

The emperor, called the Sapa Inca, was at the top. And yes, we got the name of their empire from his title. The people considered the emperor a descendant of their sun god, so they worshiped him as a god. The high priest was second in importance as the Incans were a very religious people. Next in line was the royal family. This included the emperor's primary wife, who was the queen. Then . . .

M Student: Pardon me, but why did you call her the primary wife?

W: Incan emperors and nobles typically had more than one wife. The first wife was the primary wife. She ruled the other wives and children. There were, as you can imagine, often lots of children. They and the other relatives of the emperor held high positions in the Incan government.

So, uh, the nobles were the main administrators and generals. The empire was large and often fought wars against its neighbors. It was divided into four parts. Each part had a governor who answered only to the emperor. Maintaining roads was one of the major duties of the governors. There was, you see, an extensive road system in the empire. It connected the different parts to one another. Below the nobles were the minor administrators. They included, um, let's see . . . inspectors, tax collectors, educators, and record keepers.

Interestingly, the Incans had almost no merchants. The reason was that the government controlled the collection and distribution of food and other goods. The masses of common people grew food and made goods. These farmers and artisans were at the bottom of society. Each person belonged to his or her family. Each family belonged to a large group of families called an *allyu*. That's A-L-L-Y-U. This was the basic unit of the Incan lower class. Each *allyu* member had to pay government taxes, called *mita*. Uh . . . M-I-T-A. *Mita* could be paid in food, goods, or labor since the Incas had no money system.

Answer Explanation

1 Ⓑ In her lecture, the professor starts at the top of the Incan hierarchy by describing the emperor. Then, she goes down to the bottom to the common people.

2 Ⓐ The professor says, "Each part had a governor who answered only to the emperor. Maintaining roads was one of the major duties of the governors. There was, you see, an extensive road system in the empire."

3 Ⓒ The professor remarks, "Each family belonged to a large group of families called an *allyu*. That's A-L-L-Y-U. This was the basic unit of the Incan lower class."

❶ The people <u>considered</u> the emperor a <u>descendant</u> of their sun god, so they <u>worshiped</u> him <u>as</u> a god.

❷ The empire was large and often <u>fought wars against</u> its neighbors. It <u>was divided into</u> four parts.

❸ Interestingly, the Incans had almost no merchants. <u>The reason was that</u> the government controlled the collection and distribution of food and other goods.

iBT Practice Test
p. 40

Answers

PART 1

1 Ⓑ   2 Ⓐ   3 Ⓒ

4 Collapsed Crater Lake: ②, ④

Explosive Crater Lake: ①, ③

5 Ⓐ   6 Ⓒ   7 Ⓑ   8 ①, ②   9 Ⓐ

10 Ⓐ   11 Ⓐ

PART 2

1 Ⓐ   2 Ⓑ   3 ②, ④   4 Ⓑ   5 ②, ④

6 Ⓒ   7 Ⓓ

PART 1

[1–3] Conversation

| Script |

Listen to part of a conversation between a student and a librarian.

M Student: Pardon me. I'm searching for some books, but I can't seem to find them. Could you give me some assistance for a moment, please? It's really crucial that I find the items I'm looking for.

W Librarian: Sure. Why don't you try looking up the books you need on the computer system? It's easy to use. And it will tell you exactly where everything is.

M: Actually, um, I already did that. And I know where the books I need are supposed to be. I've, uh, I've gotten books from that area many times. 🎧³ But, uh . . . I just went there, and the books are all gone.

W: All gone?

M: Yes, they aren't there. **It's like someone checked out a thousand books.** I'm looking for books on solar energy. The library has a pretty good collection on alternative forms of energy. But I don't know where all of the material has gone.

W: Ah, all right, I know the problem. We're in the process of rearranging the library's collection.

M: Why are you doing that? It's the middle of the semester. It doesn't make much sense to move books around while classes are going on.

W: You're right about that, but it wasn't my decision to make. Anyway, you know that expansion project which was just completed? That has given us a lot more room for physical books. So some books are being moved to new locations.

M: Okay, uh, so you know where they are, right? Can you tell me where to go?

W: Um . . . As I recall, the books you want were originally on the second floor. And they're being moved to the sixth floor. I'm pretty sure they'll be on the eastern side of the building.

M: That's great news. Thanks. So I can go there now and get them?

W: Not yet. I don't believe it's possible at this time.

M: Huh? Why not?

W: The books were just boxed up today and taken upstairs. But they're not scheduled to be removed from the boxes until tomorrow. The workers are going to arrive at nine and start working then. So they should be on the shelves by, uh, by noon.

M: Is there any way I can go upstairs and look in some of the boxes now? I really need to get my hands on some of those books.

W: I'm afraid not. They're sealed and can only be opened by the people who are moving them.

M: I see. All right, I guess I'll just have to come back here tomorrow. Thanks for your assistance.

Answer Explanation

1 Gist-Purpose Question

Ⓑ The student remarks, "I know where the books I need are supposed to be. I've, uh, I've gotten books from that area many times. But, uh . . . I just went there, and the books are all gone."

2 Detail Question

Ⓐ The student asks, "Is there any way I can go upstairs and look in some of the boxes now?"

3 Understanding Function Question

Ⓒ When the student comments, "It's like someone checked out a thousand books," he is implying that a large number of books are missing.

| Script |

Listen to part of a lecture in a geology class.

M Professor: The next type of lake we're examining today is called a crater lake. It usually forms when a volcano erupts. Many eruptions leave behind a depression in the ground called a caldera. Over time, the caldera fills with water. This water can come from rain, underground water sources, or melting snow and ice. There are two ways a volcano can form a caldera and then, uh, a crater lake. Let me tell you about them.

First, there is the collapsed crater lake. It forms when an empty magma chamber collapses. As magma comes near the surface of the crust, it builds up inside an underground chamber. It may remain stable, or, uh, it could erupt. When there's a volcanic eruption, if all the magma spews from the volcano, the chamber becomes empty. Then, the roof of the chamber has no internal support. Sometimes the roof collapses inside the now-empty chamber. This forms a caldera. Another way this can happen is if the magma shifts underground. Essentially, there's no eruption, but the magma moves to a new location. Again, this results in an empty chamber and a roof with no support. This can also collapse.

The explosive crater lake is the second main type of crater lake. It forms when a volcano erupts extremely violently. The force is so powerful that much of the rocky material in the magma chamber roof is blown away. The caldera is the now-empty magma chamber.

W Student: Why do some volcanoes erupt violently while others don't?

M: Good question, Roberta. It mostly depends on the type of magma. Silica-rich magma is usually associated with violent eruptions. Why? Well, it has a higher viscosity. This means it's quite thick and flows slowly. This allows it to hold gas bubbles under high pressure deep underground. But as the magma nears the surface, the pressure lessens. So the gas bubbles burst violently from the magma, increasing the pressure on the magma chamber roof. Soon enough, there's a violent eruption which destroys the roof.

W: That sounds fascinating. Can you give us some examples, please?

M: I'd be more than glad to. Let me talk about two of them. The first is, um, the aptly named Crater Lake in the state of Oregon in the United States. It's a collapsed crater lake that formed about 7,700 years ago when the volcano Mount Mazama erupted. The eruption emptied the magma chamber below. Later, the roof collapsed. Centuries of rain and snow melt filled the caldera with water. Today, it's the deepest lake in the U.S. It's 594 meters deep and around ten kilometers wide. Interestingly, it forms an almost perfect circle. You can see a picture of it on page . . . page 184 in your textbooks. Please check it out. It's quite beautiful.

The second example is of an explosive crater lake. On the following page in your books is Lake Toba in Indonesia. It formed around 75,000 years ago when Mount Toba, a supervolcano, erupted in one of the greatest volcanic eruptions in history. This lake has an elongated shape. It's around 100 kilometers by thirty kilometers in size. This makes it the largest crater lake in the world. Yet it's not as deep as Crater Lake. It's only 505 meters deep.

Oh, before we move on to another type of lake, I should point out that crater lakes can form in other less common ways. One is when water fills in the site of a meteor impact. Another is when a nuclear explosion creates a surface crater that later gets filled with water. Fortunately, uh, both are quite rare.

Answer Explanation

4 Connecting Content Question

Collapsed Crater Lake: 2, 4 Explosive Crater Lake: 1, 3
About collapsed crater lakes, the professor notes, "First, there is the collapsed crater lake. It forms when an empty magma chamber collapses. As magma comes near the surface of the crust, it builds up inside an underground chamber. It may remain stable, or, uh, it could erupt. When there's a volcanic eruption, if all the magma spews from the volcano, the chamber becomes empty. Then, the roof of the chamber has no internal support. Sometimes the roof collapses inside the now-empty chamber. This forms a caldera." Regarding explosive crater lakes, the professor says, "The explosive crater lake is the second main type of crater lake. It forms when a volcano erupts extremely violently." He then adds, "The second example is of an explosive crater lake. On the following page in your books is Lake Toba in Indonesia. It formed around 75,000 years ago when Mount Toba, a supervolcano, erupted in one of the greatest volcanic eruptions in history."

5 Gist-Purpose Question

Ⓐ The student asks for some examples, so the professor explains the formation of Crater Lake in Oregon.

6 Understanding Function Question

Ⓒ While talking about Crater Lake, the professor tells the students, "You can see a picture of it on page . . . page 184 in your textbooks. Please check it out." He then adds, "The second example is of an explosive crater lake. On the following page in your books is Lake Toba in Indonesia."

7 Connecting Content Question

Ⓑ The professor mentions the depth of both Crater Lake and Lake Toba in the lecture.

| Script |

Listen to part of a lecture in a marine biology class.

W Professor: Another fascinating feature of whales is their ability to produce sounds. We sometimes call them whale sounds or whale vocalizations. It's most likely that they use them for communication. We believe whales rely heavily on sound rather than other senses, uh, such as sight and smell. Why is that? Well, it's dark underwater, so it's hard to see. And smells get scattered in water environments. But the quality of sound actually improves beneath the surface. In fact, sound travels four times faster under water than it does in air.

So . . . how do whales produce sounds? Well, that's a bit of a mystery. You see, most animals make sounds by passing air through a larynx, vocal cords, or both. We know dolphins and porpoises, which are related to whales, produce sounds. They have a structure near their blowhole that seems like a set of vocal cords. This structure moves as they make sounds. Yet whales lack a similar structure. We know whales have a larynx-like structure, but there are no vocal cords inside it. It's, um, it's uncertain what they use that structure for. We also know that they make sounds underwater when they aren't inhaling or exhaling. So the main conclusion here is that somehow, um, as air circulates inside their lungs, it produces sound. I know that's not very helpful, but that's all we know right now.

However, we do know some important things about whale sounds. Let's see . . . They can be measured. Most whale sounds fall within the ten hertz and thirty-one kilohertz frequency range. Scientists have observed whale sounds at different frequencies during the same group of sounds. Whales frequently repeat the same sounds over and over again for a few minutes. That's why it sounds like a long group of notes like, uh, like a song. Some of them sound quite beautiful by the way. I rather like them. We believe these notes are connected for a reason and are not merely separate sounds. Whales repeat these songs. Sometimes they may repeat them for thirty minutes. On other occasions, they sing these songs for hours. Occasionally, the songs are repeated for days. Interestingly, it's been observed that all the whales in a region sing the same song.

This information suggests that sounds—or songs—are used for communication. Let me talk about the humpback whale for a moment. Only male humpbacks make sounds. Nobody knows why. Now, uh, they normally make sounds during the mating season. Males have been observed making sounds while escorting females. This could be a signal to other males to back off. You know, the male is claiming that the female is his. In addition, multiple males have been observed making sounds when near a lone female. This could mean that each whale is trying to drive the other males away. Or they could be trying to attract the female with their singing. Whichever one makes the best song might be selected as her mate. Of course, I could be wrong because we simply don't know enough at this time.

Male humpback whales also make what we think is a feeding call. Male whales spend lots of time alone. But if they find a good food source, they will make sounds. These attract other nearby males of their species. Oh, by the way, other types of whales make sounds as well. The blue whale, for instance, is quite vocal. Why don't we listen to a few whale sounds now so that you can hear what they're like?

Answer Explanation

8   Gist-Content Question

① , ② During the lecture, the professor mostly discusses why whale sounds are made and how they are produced.

9   Understanding Attitude Question

Ⓐ The professor comments, "Whales frequently repeat the same sounds over and over again for a few minutes. That's why it sounds like a long group of notes like, uh, like a song. Some of them sound quite beautiful by the way. I rather like them."

10 Gist-Purpose Question

Ⓐ The professor talks about the sounds male humpback whales make to suggest some of their possible purposes.

11 Making Inferences Question

Ⓐ At the end of the lecture, the professor announces, "Why don't we listen to a few whale sounds now so that you can hear what they're like?"

PART 2

[1–3] Conversation

| Script |

Listen to part of a conversation between a student and a student activities office employee.

W Student: Good afternoon. I've got the posters for the upcoming special event for the movie club. I picked them up from the printer a few minutes ago. Where should I leave them? Should I put them over there in the corner? Is that all right?

M Student Activities Office Employee: Um . . . Excuse me? Who are you? What are you doing? And what am I supposed to do with those?

W: Um . . . hang them up around campus in different places.

M: I'm sorry, but we don't do that here. Who told you that we did?

W: One of the members of the movie club told me to come here. He said that someone at the student activities office would take care of everything.

M: Hmm . . . That person definitely doesn't know what he's talking about.

W: Oh, I'm, uh . . . How embarrassing. I'm so sorry. So, uh . . . what do I do?

M: First, do you have permission to hang up the signs on campus?

W: Permission?

M: Okay, let's start from the beginning. Let me see . . . You have already printed the signs, so they are ready to be hung up around campus. But before you can do that, you have to receive permission. Fortunately, that's a really easy process. All you have to do is fill out a form and show your signs. Once the request is granted, every sign will get stamped. That shows you have permission to put the signs up around campus. So school maintenance workers won't tear them down.

W: Sounds great. Where do I get an application form?

M: Here you are.

W: Wow, thanks. Do I have to pay any kind of fee?

M: Only if you are planning to hang up fifty or more posters on campus. How many of them do you have there?

W: I've only got twenty. We had a limited budget, so that's all we could afford.

M: Then there's no application fee. Now, uh, once the posters are stamped, you can place them around campus. There are bulletin boards near the main entrances of most of the buildings. You can put the posters there. You can also hang up the posters inside campus buildings. That includes dormitories and academic buildings. However, do not put them anywhere else. For instance, don't attach them to lampposts, recycling bins, or even the sidewalk.

W: Okay. That's fine. But, uh, out of curiosity . . . What happens if I do that?

M: Your signs will get torn down. And your club won't be allowed to hang up posters for the rest of the school year.

Answer Explanation

1 Gist-Purpose Question

   (A) At the start of the conversation, the student says, "Good afternoon. I've got the posters for the upcoming special event for the movie club. I picked them up from the printer a few minutes ago. Where should I leave them?" So she visits the office to drop off some posters.

2 Detail Question

   (B) When the student asks where she can get an application form, the man says, "Here you are." So the man gives her an application form.

3 Detail Question

   ☑2, ☑4 The man says, "There are bulletin boards near the main entrances of most of the buildings. You can put

the posters there. You can also hang up the posters inside campus buildings. That includes dormitories and academic buildings."

[4-7] Lecture

| Script |

Listen to part of a lecture in a zoology class.

W Professor: The meerkat is a small mammal which is a member of the mongoose family. It lives in parts of southern Africa and comes in three main species. It's a small animal, uh, growing only about twenty-five to thirty centimeters long from head to backside. It also has a long tail which can grow nearly as long as its body. As you can see in this picture . . . it has brown fur. Also note that its fur is nearly black around its eyes and on its ears and nose.

The meerkat is a carnivore and feeds on various small mammals, reptiles, and insects. It particularly loves scorpions. It lives in colonies that may have up to fifty members. All of them live in underground burrows. Colony members use their sharp claws to dig their burrows. There are two reasons the meerkat lives underground. First, it's very hot in Africa, so living underground lets it escape the heat. Second, underground burrows provide hiding places from predators. Both land animals and birds hunt the meerkat. Birds of prey such as eagles swoop down from the sky to grab meerkats with their claws. On the ground, jackals and snakes often stalk meerkat burrows in search of a meal.

To counter this, the meerkat has developed a special warning system. During the day, colony members forage for food. At that time, some meerkats stand guard. They stand on their hind legs and sit straight up. They constantly swivel their heads, looking for danger in the sky and on the ground. This guard duty lasts about an hour. Then, new guards take over while the old guards search for food.

M Student: What happens when a meerkat spots something dangerous?

W: It makes a noise to warn the others. Then, all the meerkats run for the burrow and hide. When the guards see something dangerous, they stare in the direction it's coming from. This lets the others know where the danger is. They just look in the same direction as the guards.

M: Do they make any sounds if there are no predators around?

W: Yes. The meerkat makes a sort of, uh, peeping sound at regular intervals. This means that all is well. But when it spots a predator, it makes different sounds. They're kind of like loud barks. But the sounds vary. If the predator is in the sky, the guard makes one sound. If it's on land, the warning sound is different. If danger is close by, the sound is more urgent. If it's far away, it sounds less urgent. Zoologists have identified six main warning sounds. Three are for aerial threats while the others are for land threats. There is one warning sound each for low danger, medium danger, and extreme danger.

For instance, the meerkat considers eagles a major threat because of their great speed. If a guard sees an eagle very close, it immediately gives the highest warning level. I guess it's saying, "Run! Hide!" So every meerkat flees at once. If a guard notices a jackal far away, it makes a less urgent sound. There's some danger, but it's not immediate. ∩7 If a guard spots a snake, there is less of a warning.

M: What? It's not scared of snakes? **That's shocking.**

W: Actually, meerkats frequently challenge snakes. They surround and attack snakes. Snake venom can kill meerkats, so they're wary of snakes. But meerkats often succeed either in driving off snakes or in killing them.

Answer Explanation

4 Gist-Content Question

Ⓑ Most of the lecture is about the special warning system the meerkat uses.

5 Detail Question

②, ④ The professor states, "There are two reasons the meerkat lives underground. First, it's very hot in Africa, so living underground lets it escape the heat. Second, underground burrows provide hiding places from predators."

6 Gist-Purpose Question

Ⓒ The professor talks about the sounds the meerkat makes to show how it warns others of dangers. She says, "But when it spots a predator, it makes different sounds. They're kind of like loud barks. But the sounds vary. If the predator is in the sky, the guard makes one sound. If it's on land, the warning sound is different. If danger is close by, the sound is more urgent. If it's far away, it sounds less urgent. Zoologists have identified six main warning sounds. Three are for aerial threats while the others are for land threats. There is one warning sound each for low danger, medium danger, and extreme danger."

7 Understanding Function Question

Ⓓ When the student says, "That's shocking," he implies that he expected meerkats to be scared of snakes.

| Vocabulary Review   p. 50

Answers

A
1 impact   2 rely on
3 on behalf of   4 application   5 remove
B
1 b   2 a   3 b   4 b   5 a
6 b   7 a   8 a   9 b

Basic Practice

p. 53

Answers

A Ⓒ   B Ⓑ   C Ⓑ

D Fact: ②, ③   Not a Fact: ①

| Script |

A

Listen to part of a conversation between a student and a transportation office employee.

M1 Student: Good afternoon. I'd like to apply for a job. I want to drive the campus shuttle bus.

M2 Transportation Office Employee: All right, you're the first applicant. Do you have any experience? That's crucial for a job like this.

M1: Yes. I worked part time as a bus driver last summer. And I'm licensed to drive all kinds of vehicles.

M2: That's wonderful news. Can you fill out this form? And let me know what hours you're willing to work.

M1: Sure. Let me find a pen, please. Hold on a second.

Answer Explanation

Ⓒ The student says, "I worked part time as a bus driver last summer." Since he is looking for a job driving the campus shuttle bus, he did similar work in the past.

B

Listen to part of a conversation between a student and a professor.

W Student: Professor Richardson, do you have a copy of the handout from today's class? I didn't get one.

M Professor: Weren't you in class? My teaching assistants handed them out to everyone this morning.

W: I was in class. But Robert ran out of copies and couldn't give them to everyone.

M: Oh, I see. That explains why two other students asked me for them.

W: Yeah. So, uh, do you have a copy for me? I'd appreciate it.

M: Yes, of course. Let me get one from my file. Hold on a moment.

Answer Explanation

Ⓑ The student says, "But Robert ran out of copies and couldn't give them to everyone."

C

Listen to part of a lecture in a zoology class.

W Professor: The only member of the deer family to be domesticated is the reindeer. We believe that this happened sometime around 3,000 years ago. Reindeer can be found in the cold northern regions in the Northern Hemisphere. There are large wild herds of them in places such as Northern Europe, Siberia, and Alaska.

Since people have domesticated these animals, they also live in herds managed by people. People use these reindeer for a number of purposes. Naturally, their meat is valued by those who raise them. In addition, their skins are used to make clothes and other items. Interestingly, reindeer can also be utilized for transportation. Some people use them to pull sleds like they are horses. Naturally, they can't fly like Santa's reindeer, but now you see how that story began. There really were people who used reindeer to take them from place to place.

Answer Explanation

Ⓑ The professor states, "In addition, their skins are used to make clothes and other items."

D

Listen to part of a lecture in an archaeology class.

W Professor: One of the most important discoveries in the history of archaeology was made between the years 1947 and 1956. I'm talking, of course, about the Dead Sea Scrolls. They were found in some caves along the shore of the Dead Sea in Israel.

Few intact manuscripts were found. Instead, around, uh, 15,000 fragments from more than 500 different texts were discovered. Mostly, the scrolls contain works from the Bible. Parts of nearly every book in the Old Testament were found. But nonbiblical works were also found in the Dead Sea Scrolls. For example, some of them contain prophesies made by Old Testament figures, including Daniel, Ezekiel, and Jeremiah. Most of the scrolls were written in Hebrew. However, some are in Aramaic.

So what makes the Dead Sea Scrolls so important? There are several things. Let me tell you about them right now.

Answer Explanation

Fact: ②, ③   Not a Fact: ①

The professor remarks, "They were found in some caves along the shore of the Dead Sea in Israel," and, "Mostly, the scrolls contain works from the Bible. Parts of nearly every book in the Old Testament were found. But nonbiblical works were also found in the Dead Sea Scrolls." However, it is not true that the Dead Sea Scrolls are all written in the same language. The professor states, "Most of the scrolls were written in Hebrew. However, some are in Aramaic."

A

Answers   1 Ⓒ   2 Ⓐ

| Script |

Listen to part of a conversation between a student and a mailroom employee.

W Student: Excuse me. I'm here about a package I haven't received yet.

M Mailroom Employee: Okay. What exactly is the problem?

W: I ordered some clothes from an online retailer last week. The store sent them on Monday. I received an emailed message yesterday telling me they'd been delivered to the mailroom. But, uh, I haven't gotten a message from here yet.

M: Could I see your student ID, please?

W: Sure, um . . . here you are.

M: Hmm . . . It doesn't look like it's in the system. But, uh, we're a bit understaffed today. We normally have five people working here. But as you can see, there are only two of us now. My guess is that we have the package. We just, uh . . . haven't found it yet.

W: So what should I do? There's an outfit in there I'd really like to wear tomorrow.

M: How about coming back after lunch? I'll put a priority search on the package. I just can't do that for another hour though.

W: That's great. My class finishes at half past one, so I'll come back then. Thanks for your help.

Answer Explanation

1 Ⓒ The student comments, "I received an emailed message yesterday telling me they'd been delivered to the mailroom."

2 Ⓐ The man tells the student, "I'll put a priority search on the package," so he is going to try to find the package.

B

Answers   1 Ⓐ   2 Ⓑ

| Script |

Listen to part of a lecture in an art class.

W Professor: Some works of art don't change much over time. Sculptures, for instance, can last for hundreds of thousands of years. Oil paintings, on the other hand, must be properly taken care of. If they aren't cared for properly, they can fade and lose a great deal of their beauty. Thus, um, museums as well as private collectors have to take good care of their paintings. This is especially true for masterworks.

Fortunately, there are a few simple steps people can take to preserve oil paintings. You've probably noticed that oil paintings are never kept in glass frames. There's a reason for that. You see, if glass touches the paintings, it can stick to the paint. The glass can also smudge the paint, thereby marring the paintings. Oil paintings should therefore be displayed in open frames. They also need to be displayed away from bright light, such as the sun. Exposure to sunlight can make them fade quickly. Both extreme heat and cold as well as humidity can damage oil paintings, too. They can cause the paint to crack.

In addition, uh, dust sometimes accumulates on paintings. Under no circumstances should you moisten a cloth and try to wipe off the dust. That would harm the painting. Instead, a special brush should be used to lightly remove any dust on the painting. Paintings get dirty at times, too. Now, uh, it is possible to use a damp cloth with some soap on it to wipe off the dirt. But I don't recommend doing that as it's easy to ruin the painting. Instead, an expert or art restorer should be consulted. The restorer may then use a mixture of linseed oil or turpentine to remove any dirt and to restore a painting to its previous appearance.

Answer Explanation

1 Ⓐ The professor says, "You've probably noticed that oil paintings are never kept in glass frames. There's a reason for that. You see, if glass touches the paintings, it can stick to the paint. The glass can also smudge the paint, thereby marring the painting."

2 Ⓑ The professor notes, "Instead, a special brush should be used to lightly remove any dust on the painting."

A

Answers   1 Ⓓ   2 Ⓑ   3 Ⓒ

| Script |

Listen to part of a conversation between a student and a professor.

W Student: Excuse me, sir. I would really like to talk to you about something. Do you mind?

M Professor: Not at all. What can I do for you today?

W: Thank you, sir. I have a couple of questions about today's lecture. I'm, um, I'm not positive that I understood everything properly. There were, um, two things I found confusing.

M: That's perfectly understandable. Today's lecture was one of the most difficult of the year for many students. Go ahead and ask your questions, please.

W: Thank you. All right, uh . . . What was the importance of Julius Caesar crossing the Rubicon River? I mean, I've heard that phrase before, but I, uh . . . I just don't see why it's important. What was the big deal?

M: Ah, it's extremely important to comprehend the importance of this event if you want to understand the history of Rome at that time. You see, uh, Caesar had been ordered by the Senate to return to Rome. He was supposed to disband his army. Armies were simply not permitted to enter Rome at any time.

W: Right. But he didn't do that. He took his army across the Rubicon and headed toward Rome.

M: Correct. And in doing so, he basically declared war upon the Roman Senate. He was making himself, uh, an outlaw . . . a traitor. That's supposedly when he said the famous words "the die is cast." Uh, in Latin, of course.

W: Oh, I get it. That's pretty much what started the civil war you talked about in class today.

M: Exactly. I'm glad you understand now. So, uh, what was the other part of the lecture you had trouble understanding?

Answer Explanation

1 Ⓓ The student tells the professor, "I have a couple of questions about today's lecture. I'm, um, I'm not positive that I understood everything properly."

2 Ⓑ After describing Julius Caesar's action, the professor notes, "And in doing so, he basically declared war upon the Roman Senate."

3 Ⓒ At the end of the conversation, the professor asks, "So, uh, what was the other part of the lecture you had trouble understanding?" By saying that, the professor implies that he has enough time to answer another question from the student.

Dictation

M: What can I do for you today?

W: Thank you, sir. I have a couple of questions about today's lecture. I'm, um, I'm not positive that I understood everything properly. There were, um, two things I found confusing.

M: That's perfectly understandable. Today's lecture was one of the most difficult of the year for many students. Go ahead and ask your questions, please.

W: Thank you.

B

Answers

1 Fact: ①, ②, ④   Not a Fact: ③   2 Ⓒ   3 Ⓑ

Script

Listen to part of a lecture in a biology class.

M Professor: All life needs certain things to survive. Food and water are two necessities. Yet species compete with one another for these resources. Think about a garden . . . Every plant in a garden is competing for the water, nutrients, and sunlight there. This is an example of interspecies competition. Basically, um, two or more different species fight for resources. Interestingly, to avoid this competition, many organisms have evolved to occupy certain ecological niches.

What's an ecological niche? Well, it's a set of conditions that fit one particular species. That species survives by staying within the limits of its niche. This helps it avoid unhealthy competition which could destroy it. The main factor in an ecological niche is how the species behaves. This behavior mostly relates to dealing with enemies and acquiring food. It can also include mating and raising offspring. Many predators, for example, place scent markers to define the territory in which they hunt. Within that area, there are food resources they depend on. These, in turn, let them mate and raise their offspring safely. If this area is invaded by other predators, they react by attacking the intruders.

W Student: What happens if they can't defend their territory?

M: They usually die. And, uh, that brings us to the competition exclusion principle. This theory states that two different species cannot occupy the same niche and both survive. According to it, eventually, one will outcompete the other.

However . . . that does not always happen. There are instances of different species living in the same ecological niche that all survive. This happens due to a process called resource partitioning. The different species in an area pretty much divide the available resources. On occasion, one of those species will have a population too great for its resources to support. Then, some of its members die. Other times, one species may evolve into several subspecies. Each subspecies then occupies a tiny specialized part of the ecological niche.

🎧³ Hmm . . . **Some of you look confused.** Okay, let me give you an example. Uh . . . Let's talk about Puerto Rican lizards. In one part of the island, eleven subspecies of the anole lizard live close together. They've all evolved to have different needs. Each subspecies occupies small areas with different types of vegetation growing at different heights. All of the areas have differences in the food supply, shade, moisture, and sunlight. Every anole lizard subspecies therefore occupies its own exclusive ecological niche.

Answer Explanation

1 Fact: 1, 2, 4　Not a Fact: 3

According to the professor, "What's an ecological niche? Well, it's a set of conditions that fit one particular species. That species survives by staying within the limits of its niche. This helps it avoid unhealthy competition which could destroy it." Then, he adds, "There are instances of different species living in the same ecological niche that all survive. This happens due to a process called resource partitioning. The different species in an area pretty much divide the available resources. On occasion, one of those species will have a population too great for its resources to support. Then, some of its members die. Other times, one species may evolve into several subspecies. Each subspecies then occupies a tiny specialized part of the ecological niche." However, the professor does not say that ecological niches prevent animals from sharing resources.

2 Ⓒ After describing the competition exclusion principle, the professor states, "However . . . that does not always happen."

3 Ⓑ When the professor says, "Some of you look confused," it can be inferred that he thinks the students do not understand the material that he is discussing.

Dictation

❶ All life needs certain things to survive. Food and water are two necessities. Yet species compete with one another for these resources.

❷ The main factor in an ecological niche is how the species behaves. This behavior mostly relates to dealing with enemies and acquiring food.

❸ What happens if they can't defend their territory?

Answers

PART 1

1 Ⓐ	2 Ⓒ	3 Ⓓ	4 Ⓑ	
5 Fact: 1, 2　Not a Fact: 3, 4		6 Ⓑ	7 Ⓐ	
8 Ⓒ	9 2, 4	10 Ⓓ	11 Ⓐ	

PART 2

1 Ⓒ	2 Ⓑ	3 Ⓐ	4 Ⓒ	5 Ⓑ
6 1, 4	7 Ⓓ			

PART 1

[1–3] Conversation

| Script |

Listen to part of a conversation between a student and a resident assistant.

M1 **Student:** Hey, Jason, I saw a flyer posted on the bulletin board downstairs. It's about some kind of quiet period we're going to have during midterm exams. Uh . . . what exactly is that?

M2 **Resident Assistant:** Ah, I didn't realize it had been posted already. I think students are going to get an email from the school describing it later today.

M1: Well, it seems like you know what's going on. So do you mind telling me about it?

M2: Not at all. Basically, the school has decided to make sure students stay quiet during the entire midterm period next week. So there will be some, uh, some restrictions on the amount of noise students can make.

M1: Restrictions? Like what? Uh, we can't play loud music or anything?

M2: Yes, that's exactly what's going to happen. Making any kind of noise which could disturb other students will not be allowed for an entire week. That means, uh . . . no loud music, no yelling, no noise from television, and stuff like that. ∩3 Oh, and no playing musical instruments in dorm rooms either.

M1: Really? **My roommate isn't going to be happy about that one.** Anyway, why is the school suddenly changing the rule? I've been here three years now, and we've never done anything like this.

M2: Basically, the administration received too many complaints from students. They were saying that other students were being too loud and disturbing their studies. That's why this quiet period is being tried. It'll be used not only for midterms but also for final exams later in December.

M1: So, um, what's the punishment if we make too much

noise? And who gets to determine if someone's being too noisy?

M2: Let me see . . . The first time you do it, you'll get a written warning. The second time you make too much noise, you'll get fined. I think the fine is fifty dollars, but I'm not positive about that. And by the way, every time you make too much noise, you'll get fined. Finally, you could get kicked out of the dorm if you get too many fines. Five is the limit. The RAs in every dorm have to hand out punishment. It's going to be a busy time for me. I'll have to study for my tests and also make sure everyone is being quiet.

M1: Wow, that doesn't sound like fun.

M2: Yeah, not really. Anyway, I believe you're going to like the change. You'll be able to study in peace and quiet. I know that some students are going to complain. But overall, most of them will be fine with this new policy.

Answer Explanation

1 **Detail Question**

Ⓐ The resident assistant states, "Basically, the school has decided to make sure students stay quiet during the entire midterm period next week. So there will be some, uh, some restrictions on the amount of noise students can make."

2 **Connecting Content Question**

Ⓒ The resident assistant comments, "Finally, you could get kicked out of the dorm if you get too many fines. Five is the limit." Therefore, a student who gets fined six times will have to move out of the dormitory.

3 **Understanding Attitude Question**

Ⓓ The resident assistant mentions that students cannot play musical instruments in their dorm rooms. The student states that his roommate won't be happy. So it can be inferred that the student's roommate plays a musical instrument.

[4–7] **Lecture #1**

| Script |

Listen to part of a lecture in a geology class.

M1 Professor: Caves are large open spaces in rock or ice that often have ways for people to enter them. They form in various ways. Many are created when acidic water erodes soft rock over time. Other caves form when the sea erodes a cliff base. Some caves form through volcanic action. Others are made by falling rocks, and some even get created beneath glaciers. We call those ice caves.

Now, um, the main way caves form is when acidic water erodes soft rock. Gypsum and limestone are two examples of rocks that are easily eroded. When there are layers of soft rocks underground between layers of harder rocks,

caves can form. Water containing even a slight amount of acidity will erode the soft rocks.

M2 Student: How does the water become acidic?

M1: Through a variety of ways. Some are caused by humans. But, of course, humans didn't create the acidic water responsible for creating numerous caves around the world. 🎧7 After all, many are hundreds of thousands—or even millions—of years old. Basically, natural processes caused the water to become acidic. **But that's not the main scope of today's lesson, so why don't we move on?**

So, uh, anyway . . . Basically, rainwater falls to the ground. Rainwater, by the way, usually has a pH level of five, which is slightly acidic. The acidic water seeps into the ground. It passes by hard rocks through cracks and pores. When it hits softer rocks, it begins eroding them. This doesn't happen quickly. Caves take a long time to form. As I said, some caves are hundreds of thousands of years old. Others are even older. A major feature of these caves is the large limestone columns found in them. These are called stalagmites and stalactites. They are formed by dripping water that contains limestone. It hardens over time, so stalagmites rise from the cave floor. Stalactites, meanwhile, hang from the ceiling. Many cave formations are simply breathtaking both in size and appearance.

Now, uh, the second way . . . Sea water can pound a cliff base. As time passes, the rock gets eroded. So there may be caves at the base of a cliff. This is especially true if the cliff rock is soft. Sometimes the water erodes so much rock that an overhang forms. Eventually, it breaks off and falls into the ocean. When large amounts of rock fall, caves can form under the rock pile. But these caves are extremely dangerous. The rocks often shift, collapsing the caves.

Okay, what about volcanoes? When a volcano erupts, the lava it spews forms various features when it cools. One of these is the lava tube. As lava flows, it cools. It normally cools on top first. As the top layer becomes rock, the lower layers are still lava, which is moving. If the lava flows out an opening until there's no more of it beneath the hard rock, then a hollow rock tube forms. This is a volcanic cave.

Now, ice caves . . . We normally find them under glaciers. They form when ice beneath a glacier melts at a faster rate than the ice above it. The melting is the result of flowing water or, uh, sometimes the heat of volcanic activity beneath the glacier. Whatever the case, the melting creates a hollow area under the glacier called an ice cave. These caves are not particularly stable. More melting can cause them to collapse. And because they're made of ice, they can fall down when the glacier moves. So I don't suggest that anyone explore ice caves.

4 Gist-Content Question

Ⓑ The professor mostly talks about cave formation in his lecture.

5 Detail Question

Fact: 1, 2 Not a Fact: 3, 4

The professor says, "The acidic water seeps into the ground. It passes by hard rocks through cracks and pores. When it hits softer rocks, it begins eroding them." He also mentions, "A major feature of these caves is the large limestone columns found in them. These are called stalagmites and stalactites." However, these caves do not form very quickly. The professor says, "This doesn't happen quickly. Caves take a long time to form. As I said, some caves are hundreds of thousands of years old. Others are even older." And they do not form in very hard rock. The professor states, "Now, um, the main way caves form is when acidic water erodes soft rock. Gypsum and limestone are two examples of rocks that are easily eroded. When there are layers of soft rocks underground between layers of harder rocks, caves can form. Water containing even a slight amount of acidity will erode the soft rocks."

6 Detail Question

Ⓑ The professor remarks, "Whatever the case, the melting creates a hollow area under the glacier called an ice cave. These caves are not particularly stable. More melting can cause them to collapse. And because they're made of ice, they can fall down when the glacier moves."

7 Understanding Function Question

Ⓐ When the professor says "But that's not the main scope of today's lesson, so why don't we move on?" he is indicating that he does not want to discuss a topic with the students.

[8–11] Lecture #2

| Script |

Listen to part of a lecture in an economics class.

W Professor: Trade was one of the primary factors involved in world exploration in the past. For centuries, most trade was done overland. But in the fifteenth century, the first large oceangoing ships were built. These helped broaden trade. Among the best explorers, navigators, and traders in that period were the Dutch. During some of their first trips to the islands of Indonesia, Dutch explorers discovered an immense wealth of spices. Eventually, this resulted in the founding of the Dutch East India Company in 1602. For the next 200 years, this company played a major role in both global trade and exploration.

Now, let me tell you a bit about the Dutch East India Company first. It was a joint-stock company. This means that private individuals owned shares in it. The government of Holland gave the company the right to trade in certain areas. It had a monopoly, so no other Dutch companies were permitted to engage in that particular trade. In return, the company carried the Dutch flag around the world. It established forts, set up trade routes, and dealt with the natives of various countries. To do these things, the company became almost a, uh, a state within a state. It had its own soldiers, naval ships, and merchant ships. It also had huge warehouses and forts around the world. The goals were to acquire wealth and to make the company and the Dutch people powerful.

These objectives were accomplished over the next few decades. At first, individual ships or groups of ships belonging to the company made the long, dangerous journey from the Far East to Holland. There was one major stopping point along the way: the Dutch colony of Cape Town in South Africa. But by 1641, the company had acquired two major bases in Asia. They were in Batavia, Indonesia, and Galle, Sri Lanka. They became hubs for the Dutch. Small ships sailed from these two places to local regions. They would return with trade goods to be stored at the hubs. Then, larger ships would be loaded with those goods. They would then transport them to Holland. The main port in Holland, by the way, was Amsterdam.

M Student: What did they trade?

W: Spices were the main commodity. But they also traded a variety of other goods. Let's see . . . From China, the company acquired porcelain, tea, sugar, silk, and precious metals. It mostly traded spices and cloth to get those items. For the most part, no cash changed hands. Trades were done on a barter basis. You know, they traded a certain amount of spices for a certain amount of silk. In some cases, however, silver was used as a trading medium. There was one major market in India where goods were sold for silver. Now, uh, what else . . . ? From India, the Dutch got cloth, silk, indigo, and pepper. Two other major markets were Arabia and Japan. The Dutch acquired coffee and silk in return for spices in Arabia. And they traded silk, spices, and porcelain for precious metals and lacquered wood in Japan.

As you can see, everything was interconnected in this trade system. Spices were the main component of trade between different places. Many of these spices went to Holland, where they flooded European markets. Holland subsequently became very wealthy. This led to the rise of Holland as a major European power. Of course, this led to the Dutch attracting enemies. So the Dutch East India Company was constantly involved in minor and major wars. Let's look at some of them now.

Answer Explanation

8 Understanding Organization Question

© The professor lectures, "But by 1641, the company had acquired two major bases in Asia. They were in Batavia, Indonesia, and Galle, Sri Lanka. They became hubs for the Dutch. Small ships sailed from these two places to local regions. They would return with trade goods to be stored at the hubs. Then, larger ships would be loaded with those goods. They would then transport them to Holland."

9 Detail Question

2, 4 The professor remarks, "For the most part, no cash changed hands. Trades were done on a barter basis. You know, they traded a certain amount of spices for a certain amount of silk. In some cases, however, silver was used as a trading medium. There was one major market in India where goods were sold for silver."

10 Making Inferences Question

Ⓓ The professor says, "Many of these spices went to Holland, where they flooded European markets. Holland subsequently became very wealthy." Since Holland became wealthy from selling spices in Europe, the professor implies that spices were highly desired there.

11 Detail Question

Ⓐ The professor states, "Spices were the main component of trade between different places. Many of these spices went to Holland, where they flooded European markets. Holland subsequently became very wealthy. This led to the rise of Holland as a major European power."

PART 2

[1–3] Conversation

| Script |

Listen to part of a conversation between a student and a librarian.

M Student: Um, hello? Is this the music library?

W Librarian: Yes, that's correct. Shall I assume you've never been here before?

M: That's correct. To be honest, I didn't even know we had a music library here until a couple of hours ago. My professor told me about it after class.

W: Yeah, we're mostly for specialists. So, uh, what can I do for you today? Are you looking for any specific books on music?

M: No, not books. I'd like to get some music itself. I heard you have CDs of music that people can check out. Is that right?

W: Yes, it is. Most of our collection is classical music and opera though. Is that what you're looking for?

M: Good question. I'm not actually sure. So, uh, maybe you can help me. I'm supposed to give a presentation in my

class next week. And I thought it might be nice to have a bit of background music playing during it. That could make my presentation more appealing to everyone.

W: Okay. What kind of music are you thinking of?

M: Well, I'd really love to get the class's attention. So I was thinking of playing something like, uh, the main theme from *Star Wars*. You know how the movie starts, don't you? That would be incredible.

W: Um . . . We do have the *Star Wars* soundtrack on CD, but . . . I'm not sure that the main theme would have the positive effect you want. You see, uh, the dramatic way the music begins would startle lots of students. Yes, it would get their attention. But it might have a negative effect on them.

M: What do you suggest then?

W: You definitely don't want anything loud. For instance, *The Planets* by Holst wouldn't be ideal. Neither would, uh, *The 1812 Overture* by Tchaikovsky nor *Fanfare for the Common Man* by Aaron Copland. Instead, you want something a bit more subtle.

M: Subtle? What do you mean?

W: You want some quiet yet upbeat music. Music with a lot of fanfare will distract your classmates. You want them to focus on your presentation, not your music. Music with a soft, steady pace that is not overbearing is exactly what you want.

M: That sounds good. I hadn't really given it too much thought. So, uh, what do you recommend?

W: I think something by Chopin, Debussy, or perhaps Saint-Saens would be perfect. But I can't give you a definite answer until you tell me more about your presentation. After that, we can listen to some music together to find the perfect choice for you.

M: Okay. Well, my presentation is for my botany class. I'm going to be talking about seed dispersal. That, uh, that refers to how seeds spread to different places.

Answer Explanation

1 Detail Question

Ⓒ The librarian states, "Music with a lot of fanfare will distract your classmates."

2 Detail Question

Ⓑ The librarian remarks, "I think something by Chopin, Debussy, or perhaps Saint-Saens would be perfect."

3 Making Inferences Question

Ⓐ The librarian tells the student, "We can listen to some music together to find the perfect choice for you."

| Script |

Listen to part of a lecture in an astronomy class.

M Professor: Sunspots are dark spots which appear on the sun's surface. People have observed them for thousands of years. We're only now beginning to understand them though. Interestingly, they may affect the Earth's climate.

Now, uh, let me give you some details first. Sunspots often occur in pairs as you can clearly see in this photograph which I'm holding . . . Sunspots also have extremely powerful magnetic fields. They're about 2,500 times stronger than the Earth's magnetic field. This is much stronger than anywhere else on the sun's surface. A sunspot appears as a dark region surrounded by a brighter area. Its center is much darker than its edges. The center is called the umbra . . . That's U-M-B-R-A. The surrounding lighter edges are called the penumbra. The reason for the dark color is that the surrounding surface is much hotter than the sunspot itself. The sunspot's high magnetic activity is what causes this. It reduces the flow of hot gases to the surface. This makes it cooler—and therefore darker—than the surrounding surface.

W Student: 🎧7 How big can sunspots get?

M: Some are huge. They can be more than 150,000 kilometers in diameter. In comparison, the Earth has a diameter of fewer than 13,000 kilometers. Some are quite small, being merely twenty kilometers in diameter. Some sunspots last a few days whereas others survive a few months. Eventually, they all fade and disappear. They move across the sun's surface. Most originate in high latitudes and then move toward the sun's equator.

Sunspot activity depends on what's called the eleven-year solar cycle. There are increasing and decreasing rates of sunspot activity over an eleven-year period. The solar maximum is when there is the most sunspot activity. The period of lowest activity is, uh, unsurprisingly, called the solar minimum. As I mentioned earlier, sunspots frequently appear in pairs. These pairs have opposite magnetic polarity. This actually has an effect on the Earth. You see, um, solar flares often happen near sunspots. Solar flares are massive ejections of solar material from the sun. They can cause powerful electromagnetic storms on the Earth. The Carrington Event in 1859 was one such storm. We don't have time to discuss it now, but I'll go over it next week. Anyway, when there are solar flares, electronic devices on the Earth get disrupted. So if your cell phone stops working for no apparent reason, it could be due to a solar flare. Naturally, low sunspot activity means few or no solar flares and electromagnetic storms.

Sunspots can also affect the Earth's temperature and climate. From 1645 to 1715, there was very low sunspot activity. This period is often referred to as the Little Ice Age. Global temperatures fell dramatically. Many regions had low crop yields or suffered total crop failures. As a result, there were famines around the world.

Despite this, there's debate on how much sunspots influence climate. Of course, uh, increased sunspot activity means increased energy output from the sun. And low sunspot activity equals low energy output. But how this influences the Earth's climate is not completely understood. After all, the climate is affected by a complex mixture of interactions between the land, the oceans, and the atmosphere. In addition, during the Little Ice Age, there were many large volcanic eruptions. Dust from these eruptions likely blocked solar radiation. The Earth's axis might have been tilted slightly more than normal as well. This means that winters were longer than usual in some places. So it was likely that a combination of factors caused the Little Ice Age.

Answer Explanation

4 Detail Question

ⓒ The professor tells the students, "The center is called the umbra."

5 Understanding Organization Question

Ⓑ About the Carrington Event, the professor says, "They can cause powerful electromagnetic storms on the Earth. The Carrington Event in 1859 was one such storm."

6 Detail Question

1, 4 The professor remarks, "In addition, during the Little Ice Age, there were many large volcanic eruptions. Dust from these eruptions likely blocked solar radiation. The Earth's axis might have been tilted slightly more than normal as well. This means that winters were longer than usual in some places."

7 Understanding Function Question

Ⓓ The professor implies that sunspots can be several times larger than the Earth since some can be 150,000 kilometers in diameter while the Earth is only 13,000 kilometers in diameter.

| Vocabulary Review   p. 70

Answers

A
1 features   2 offspring   3 outlaw
4 partitioned   5 commodities

B
1 b   2 a   3 b   4 a   5 b
6 b   7 a   8 a   9 b

| Basic Practice

p. 73

Answers   A Ⓐ   B Ⓑ   C Ⓑ   D Ⓒ

| Script |

A

Listen to part of a conversation between a student and a student employment office employee.

W1 Student: Good morning. I'm here to pick up my weekly check. Here's my ID card.

W2 Student Employment Office Employee: Thank you very much . . . Here's your check. You know, uh . . . you might want to consider using direct deposit. Then, you won't have to come here to get paid every week.

W1: Hey, that sounds good to me. What do I need to do?

W2: Do you have your bankbook with you? If you have it, I can sign you up easily.

W1: Yeah, it's in my purse. Let me get it out.

Answer Explanation

Ⓐ When the employee asks the student if she has her bankbook, the student answers, "Yeah, it's in my purse. Let me get it out." So she will probably give the employee her bankbook next.

B

Listen to part of a lecture in an environmental science class.

W Professor: There are numerous spectacular waterfalls around the world. Among them are Victoria Falls in Africa, Niagara Falls in North America, and Angel Falls in South America. Some of these waterfalls have huge volumes of water flowing over them each second. Eventually, that will result in these waterfalls becoming smaller. Some might even disappear. Do you know why?

M Student: Erosion, right?

W: Correct. As water moves rapidly, it breaks away small parts of the riverbeds. In some cases, large chunks of rocks can be displaced. The result is that the waterfalls move. Some become lower to the ground until they are eventually level and disappear. Others move backward as rock gets eroded. For instance, the position of Niagara Falls has changed more than eleven kilometers in the past 12,000 years. It used to erode one or two meters each year. However, the rate of erosion has slowed to about 0.3 meters these days.

Answer Explanation

Ⓑ The professor states, "For instance, the position of Niagara Falls has changed more than eleven kilometers in the past 12,000 years. It used to erode one or two meters each year. However, the rate of erosion has slowed to about 0.3 meters these days." So it can be inferred that the position of Niagara Falls continues to change.

C

Listen to part of a lecture in a botany class.

W Professor: Much like humans and animals, plants can suffer from diseases. Many of them can wind up killing the plants they affect. Dutch elm disease, for instance, has killed countless elm trees throughout North America.

One common type of disease that affects plants is called a blight. Blights can be caused by bacteria or fungi. Plants with blight may have their leaves and branches suddenly stop growing. Then, they wither and die. Blight can affect farm crops such as tomatoes and potatoes, and it can affect trees, including apple, pear, and other varieties of fruit trees.

Rots are another common type of disease. As the name indicates, rots cause various parts of plants to decay. They can affect roots, stems, flowers, and fruits. They are normally caused by bacteria or fungi. Tubers, such as potatoes, and bulbs and fruits are particularly vulnerable to rots.

Answer Explanation

Ⓑ The professor mentions, "Plants with blight may have their leaves and branches suddenly stop growing," and, "As the name indicates, rots cause various parts of plants to decay. They can affect roots, stems, flowers, and fruits." Thus she implies that plant diseases can affect every part of a plant.

D

Listen to part of a lecture in a geology class.

M Professor: Most people think of Norway when they hear the word fjord. Yet Norway isn't the only country with fjords. Actually, they're found in places around the world. There are fjords in Canada, parts of the United States, Northern Europe, New Zealand, and several other countries.

All fjords share a few characteristics. First, they were formed by the actions of glaciers. In addition, they are located near the coast of an ocean or sea. They are deep, narrow, and surrounded by water on three sides. The longest fjord in the world stretches approximately 350 kilometers. Most others are not nearly that long though.

W Student: 🎧 How did glaciers form fjords?

M: **I was about to get to that**. It's simple. When some glaciers retreated, they carved out narrow valleys. Since they were close to the sea, water eventually poured into them. That's all there was to it. Of course, it took a long time to happen.

Answer Explanation

Ⓒ When the professor says, "I was about to get to that," in response to the student's question, he implies that he plans to discuss glacier formation in his lecture.

Practice with Short Passages
p. 74

A

Answers 1 Ⓐ 2 Ⓐ

| Script |

Listen to part of a conversation between a student and an Economics Department office secretary.

W Economics Department Office Secretary: Hello. Is there something I can do for you?

M Student: Good morning. I hope so. I wonder if you can tell me the requirements for Economics 18? Uh, that's Professor Nelson's class.

W: Sorry, but I have no idea. That's not something we in the office know. You ought to speak directly with Professor Nelson.

M: I tried to do that just now. But he's not in his office. According to the department's website, he's supposed to be having office hours now. Do you know where he is?

W: I haven't seen him today. Why don't you go back to his office and wait? He probably just stepped out for a moment.

M: Um, I guess I could do that. But I have to attend a class in twenty minutes. What should I do if he doesn't show up by then?

W: Email him. He's very good about responding to students that way.

M: Ah, I never even considered that. I suppose I can do that instead. Thanks for the advice.

W: My pleasure.

Answer Explanation

1 Ⓐ The woman says, "He probably just stepped out for a moment." So she implies that Professor Nelson is somewhere nearby.

2 Ⓐ Since the student has class soon, the woman suggests that he send Professor Nelson an email. The student responds by saying, "I suppose I can do that instead."

B

Answers 1 Ⓑ 2 Ⓓ

| Script |

Listen to part of a lecture in an education class.

M Professor: Before we begin our discussion of the Platonic dialogue you were assigned to read for homework, do you have any questions about it? Pamela, your hand is up. What's your question?

W Student: While I was reading, I noticed that a gymnasium was mentioned a couple of times. But, um, it didn't seem like they were talking about playing sports there. So what was an ancient Greek gymnasium?

M: You really read closely, Pamela. Well done. That's an outstanding question, class. Let me tell you a bit about the gymnasium in ancient Greece. There were gymnasia as early as the sixth century B.C. As the name implies, they were connected with sports. At first, the ancient Greeks used them as places to engage in athletic activities. Only men went to gymnasia. Women weren't allowed in them. The men would participate in various sports, such as throwing the discus and javelin and wrestling.

Over time, gymnasia changed. They became places for young men to train themselves to fight wars. They learned to fight with swords and spears and to wear armor while doing so. They continued to evolve over time though. They became places where men could improve themselves both physically and mentally. Essentially, men would visit gymnasia to study and to engage in philosophical discussions. They were places where people would give speeches while others would listen. In a way, they were like modern universities. Teachers would go to gymnasia, and students would study under them there. Other interested people could listen to the talks, too.

So that's what's being referred to in the dialogue of Plato. The gymnasia were places to improve oneself in a variety of ways. Now, any more questions? Yes, you in the back?

Answer Explanation

1 Ⓑ The professor mentions several uses for gymnasia in ancient Greece. So it can be inferred that people visited them for different reasons.

2 Ⓓ At the end of the lecture, the professor says, "Now, any more questions? Yes, you in the back?"

A

Answers

1 Ⓐ   2 Fact: ☑2, ☑3 Not a Fact: ☑1, ☑4 3 Ⓐ

| Script |

Listen to part of a conversation between a student and a professor.

W Student: Good morning, Professor Cheah. I read your email last night. You need to speak to me about something?

M Professor: Good morning, Julie. Thanks for coming so promptly. Yes, I have something to discuss with you. What are your plans for summer?

W: Hmm . . . That's a good question. I have stayed on campus and taken classes the previous two years. I'll probably do that again this summer. And I imagine I'll try to find a part-time job somewhere.

M: Excellent. How would you like to work for me?

W: That sounds great. But, um . . . doing what? Uh, wait a minute. You don't want me to teach a class, do you? I don't think I could do that.

M: Oh, no. It's not a teaching position. I need a research assistant for some work I'm doing this summer. You'd be working with me five days a week. You'll get a salary. I'm not sure exactly how much though. I'll have to check with the office. You'll also have to attend a conference in Toronto. But the school will pay for the entire trip. Several professors and students are going on it together.

W: Wow, it sounds great. Do I need to fill out an application form or anything?

M: Not at all. If you want the position, it's yours.

W: I want it. This is so cool. Oh . . . What kind of research do you want me to do?

M: You'll be reading documents in French. You'll have to summarize them, and you might have to translate a few. Sound interesting to you?

W: You bet.

Answer Explanation

1 Ⓐ The professor asks, "How would you like to work for me?"

2 Fact: ☑2, ☑3 Not a Fact: ☑1, ☑4
About the position, the professor says, "I need a research assistant for some work I'm doing this summer," and then adds, "Oh, you'll also have to attend a conference in Toronto." However, he says that the position pays a salary and that the student does not have to do any teaching.

3 Ⓐ The professor comments, "You'll be reading

documents in French. You'll have to summarize them, and you might have to translate a few." Since the student needs to translate documents in French, it can be inferred that she is fluent in a foreign language.

Dictation

M: Excellent. <u>How would you like</u> to work for me?

W: That <u>sounds great</u>. But, um . . . doing what? Uh, wait a minute. You don't want me to teach a class, <u>do you</u>? I don't think I <u>could do that</u>.

M: Oh, no. It's not a teaching position. I need a <u>research assistant</u> for some work I'm doing this summer.

B

Answers

1 Ⓐ   2 Ⓑ   3 Ⓐ

| Script |

Listen to part of a lecture in an astronomy class.

M Professor: There are billions of stars in the Milky Way Galaxy, and countless planets circle them. How many have life is, well, it's unknown. We also lack a complete list of what may or may not make a planet habitable. Regarding that, we can only look at our own situation. We know what makes life possible on the Earth. But we don't know if the same rules apply elsewhere.

Well, let's look at what makes our planet habitable and then see if any other planets fit this mold. First, life needs a constant energy source. Ours is the sun. Its energy allows life to evolve and survive. Astronomers have calculated that only certain types of stars make life possible. Most of them fall into the medium-sized class of stars, like the sun. These stars must last long enough for life to develop. That's at least a few billion years. They can't produce too much ultraviolet radiation either. That would kill off life. Finally, the stars must be hot enough so that nearby planets aren't frozen ice balls. But they can't be too hot, or liquid water can't exist on the planets.

W Student: Does all life need liquid water to survive?

M: The vast majority does. But this is a gray area for us. As far as we know, most life needs liquid water. Nevertheless, it's entirely possible that life forms on other planets don't need it. We have no way of knowing right now.

Okay, uh, back to the stars. Many stars have solar systems, so they have what we call a habitable zone. This is the region not too close and not too far from the star. In the zone, the temperatures and radiation levels are in perfect balance. So they can sustain life. Earth, of course, is in the habitable zone in our solar system.

In the past couple of decades, powerful telescopes have discovered many exoplanets in habitable zones around distant stars. Yet that doesn't necessarily mean that those planets have life. There are other factors. These include the masses of the planets, their orbits, and the presence of certain chemicals. The planets also need an atmosphere of some type. Let's look into these aspects in more detail.

Answer Explanation

1 Ⓐ The professor says, "Well, let's look at what makes our planet habitable and then see if any other planets fit this mold. First, life needs a constant energy source. Ours is the sun. Its energy allows life to evolve and survive."

2 Ⓑ Throughout the lecture, the professor talks as though life can exist on other planets if the conditions are correct.

3 Ⓐ At the end of the lecture, the professor remarks, "There are other factors. These include the masses of the planets, their orbits, and the presence of certain chemicals. The planets also need an atmosphere of some type. Let's look into these aspects in more detail."

Dictation

❶ We know what makes life possible on the Earth. But we don't know if the same rules apply elsewhere.

❷ As far as we know, most life needs liquid water. Nevertheless, it's entirely possible that life forms on other planets don't need it. We have no way of knowing right now.

❸ In the past couple of decades, powerful telescopes have discovered many exoplanets in habitable zones around distant stars. Yet that doesn't necessarily mean that those planets have life.

iBT Practice Test   p. 80

Answers

PART 1
1 Ⓓ   2 Ⓐ   3 Ⓑ   4 Ⓑ   5 Ⓐ
6 Fact: ②, ④ Not a Fact: ①, ③ 7 Ⓑ   8 Ⓐ
9 Ⓑ   10 Ⓒ
11 Fraternal Twins: ②, ④   Identical Twins: ①, ③

PART 2
1 Ⓐ   2 Ⓓ   3 Ⓒ   4 Ⓒ   5 Ⓒ
6 Fact: ①, ④ Not a Fact: ②, ③ 7 Ⓐ

PART 1

[1–3] Conversation

| Script |

Listen to part of a conversation between a student and a professor.

W Professor: Okay, Rafael, have you decided on a topic for your term paper yet?

M Student: Yes, ma'am. I have chosen one. I spent several hours in the library doing research during the past week. And I think I have found a good topic.

W: Excellent. Please go ahead and tell me about it.

M: Sure. You're familiar with the local Native American tribe here, right?

W: Yes, I am. In fact, I'm going to spend one of our classes lecturing about that tribe next week.

M: Oh, wow, that sounds awesome. Anyway, uh . . . One of my friends here at school belongs to that tribe. He has told me some interesting stories from its past, so I got interested in learning the tribe's history. That made me decide to do my research paper on it.

W: Okay. That's a good starting point. There should be plenty of information about the tribe since it's from around here. You can also probably speak with some tribe members if you have time. And, uh, maybe you could visit a dig site or two.

M: Yes, those thoughts occurred to me as well.

W: Very good. So what exactly do you want to write about concerning the tribe?

M: Well, this is the interesting part. You see, uh, my friend told me that the tribe's roots here go back about five hundred years. According to the tribe's mythology, they migrated from the east coast to this area around the year 1500. So I'd like to do some research on that.

W: Oh . . . There might be a slight problem with that. You didn't happen to read yesterday's local paper, did you?

M: The paper? No. Why?

W: Professor Red Eagle from Central University published a paper recently. According to him, there is research suggesting that the tribe has been in this area for more than 1,000 years. He has been working at a dig site outside the city. The evidence for his claim is pretty solid. You should probably read the article.

M: Okay, I will. And, uh, I guess I'll need a new topic, won't I?

W: Well, I don't think you need to change too much. Actually, it would be interesting to compare the stories with the reality.

M: Uh, what do you mean?

W: For example, the myths say they came here five hundred years ago. But the reality appears to be that they have been here for twice as long. Why don't you do some research to find out why the stories say one thing but the facts say another? I think that would be a fascinating topic. You might want to speak with Professor Red Eagle. I can introduce you to him if you want.

M: That would be perfect. Thanks so much, Professor Nightingale.

Answer Explanation

1 Understanding Function Question

Ⓓ First, the professor says, "Professor Red Eagle from Central University published a paper recently. According to him, there is research suggesting that the tribe has been in this area for more than 1,000 years. He has been working at a dig site outside the city. The evidence for his claim is pretty solid. You should probably read the article." Then, she adds, "Well, I don't think you need to change too much." So she wants the student to change the topic of his paper.

2 Understanding Attitude Question

Ⓐ The professor is very helpful toward the student and even offers to introduce him to a professor at another university. So she is eager to help him with his paper.

3 Making Inferences Question

Ⓑ The professor remarks, "You might want to speak with Professor Red Eagle. I can introduce you to him if you want." Since she is offering to introduce Professor Red Eagle, it can be inferred that she knows him personally.

[4–7] **Lecture #1**

| Script |

Listen to part of a lecture in a history class.

W Professor: Farming in ancient Greece was influenced by two main factors: the climate and the landscape. The biggest problem for Greek farmers was the lack of land good for farming. Greece is, uh, it's rather mountainous, so farmland was limited in availability. Only around, um, twenty percent of the land was good for farming. As a result, most farms were small and family run. By small, I mean they were merely a few acres in size. These small farms grew enough food for the family plus a small surplus they could sell. Of course, some wealthy individuals owned large farms. Managers ran them with paid laborers or slaves doing the work.

The main crops grown on Greek farms were olives, grapes, wheat, and barley. All four crops were suited to Greece's climate. It has hot, dry summers. Winters are very rainy but not particularly cold. Rain in Greece isn't evenly spaced throughout the year. Instead, little falls in summer while a lot falls in winter. Without a year-round source of rainfall, Greek farmers sometimes endured crop

failures. Because it rained more in winter, they planted grains such as wheat and barley in fall and harvested them in spring. Olives were picked in late fall and early winter. Grapes usually ripened in early fall. The Greeks sometimes practiced crop rotation. This wasn't universal since each farm had a limited amount of space to grow crops. The Greeks used localized irrigation systems for their farms. Basically, they dug ditches around their fields and orchards. They contained water that was used during drier periods.

Common tools were hoes, plows, and sickles. They were often made of wood and were sometimes tipped with iron or stone. Nearly all labor was done by hand. Wealthy farmers might have had a team of oxen to pull the plow though. The grain was threshed, and then the seeds were either cooked or ground into flour for bread. Grapes were trampled by people in vats and then made into wine. Olives were squeezed in stone presses to make olive oil. It was used for cooking and for lighting lamps.

The main food the Greeks ate was porridge made from barley or wheat as well as bread made from either grain. They supplemented that with olive oil, raw or dried olives, and grapes. They also drank wine. The Greeks typically added water to wine to make it weaker. They would mix one part wine with two parts water. Their diet also included fruits and vegetables. Many farms had small vegetable gardens as well as fruit trees. Beans, chickpeas, and lentils were common, and so were cucumbers, onions, and garlic. Common fruits were figs, apples, and pears, and they also cultivated nuts such as almonds and walnuts.

Greeks living in seaside areas consumed large amounts of fish since it was easy to catch. As for meat, there was little land available for grazing. So large herds of animals couldn't be raised in most places. Still, most small farms had some chickens, goats, and sheep as well as a cow or two. They were used for their meat, wool, and skin as well as for other products such as milk and eggs. Greek farmers often made cheese from cow and goat milk. They rarely just drank the milk. The Greeks also had some horses, mules, and donkeys, but they were used mainly to transport goods, not for farm labor.

Now, uh, let's look at some slides of Greek farm implements. I think you'll find them quite interesting to look at.

Answer Explanation

4 Gist-Content Question

Ⓑ The professor mostly discusses the crops grown and the animals raised on Greek farms.

5 Detail Question

Ⓐ The professor says, "The main food the Greeks ate was porridge made from barley or wheat as well as bread made from either grain."

6 Detail Question

Fact: ②, ④   Not a Fact: ①, ③

The professor states, "As a result, most farms were small and family run. By small, I mean they were merely a few acres in size," and, "Many farms had small vegetable gardens as well as fruit trees. Beans, chickpeas, and lentils were common, and so were cucumbers, onions, and garlic. Common fruits were figs, apples, and pears, and they also cultivated nuts such as almonds and walnuts" However, crop rotation was not practiced by all farmers as the professor says, "The Greeks sometimes practiced crop rotation. This wasn't universal since each farm had a limited amount of space to grow crops." And slave labor was not utilized by most farmers as the professor mentions, "Of course, some wealthy individuals owned large farms. Managers ran them with paid laborers or slaves doing the work."

7 Making Inferences Question

Ⓑ At the end of the lecture, the professor says, "Now, uh, let's look at some slides of Greek farm implements. I think you'll find them quite interesting to look at."

[8–11] Lecture #2

| Script |

Listen to part of a lecture in a physiology class.

M Professor: Sometimes a mother has two babies at the same time. We call these babies twins. There are two types of twins. Fraternal twins are one type while identical twins are the other. Their differences are the result of how they are conceived. Let me discuss that right now.

Fraternal twins occur when a mother produces two eggs at the same time. The eggs are released by the ovaries. Then, two separate sperm fertilize them. The fertilized eggs divide and grow, forming two zygotes. That's why we sometimes call this type of twins dizygotic. However, I think fraternal is a bit easier to say, so let's continue using that word. So, um, fraternal twins are just like two children born as single births from the same parents. There may be two boys, two girls, or one boy and one girl.

W Student: Do they share any similarities at all?

M: Certainly. Just like any brothers and sisters with the same parents, they share fifty percent of their DNA. They may look similar, but they won't be exactly the same. So they may have the same hair or eye color and similar facial features. But they won't be mirror images.

As for identical twins, these are children who are almost exactly alike in appearance. Identical twins form when one egg is fertilized by one sperm. The egg divides and grows, and then it becomes a zygote. But then the zygote divides into two separate embryos during the next stage of pregnancy. Why this happens has not yet been determined. Anyway, because the twins come from

a single zygote, we can call them monozygotic twins. Identical twins are almost always the same sex. So they're either two boys or two girls. Okay, uh, there are some very rare instances when this doesn't happen, but the number is incredibly tiny.

Now, uh, identical twins look exactly alike during their early childhood. But some noticeable differences may occur as they grow older. For example, um, one may become taller than the other. One twin might get a scar from an accident . . . A disease may alter one's appearance . . . One may get fatter or thinner than the other. Many things could cause them to look slightly different. Ah, one thing that's always different, even from birth, is their fingerprints. They are never the same for twins.

Many studies have been done on twins. Psychologists are particularly interested in their behavior. For the most part, twins don't act exactly alike. They usually develop a unique personality. They may have some common traits, but those are typically like those other siblings have.

However, when there are similarities, they're more common among identical twins than fraternal twins. Long-term studies on medical issues show that identical twins are more likely to get the same medical problems than fraternal twins. For instance, if one identical twin gets Alzheimer's disease, there's a fifty-percent chance the other will get it. Among fraternal twins, the chance is only twenty-five percent.

What about psychological troubles? Well, if one identical twin has mental issues, the other twin has a very strong possibility of having similar problems. This could be due to the fact that identical twins have nearly the same DNA. Because of that, both types of twins have been used extensively for testing theories on genes. Let me give you the results of some of these tests.

Answer Explanation

8   Gist-Content Question

Ⓐ The professor mainly talks about the differences between two types of twins in the lecture.

9   Detail Question

Ⓑ The professor remarks, "Ah, one thing that's always different, even from birth, is their fingerprints. They are never the same for twins."

10   Making Inferences Question

Ⓒ The professor says, "This could be due to the fact that identical twins have nearly the same DNA. Because of that, both types of twins have been used extensively for testing theories on genes." The professor therefore implies that the DNA of twins makes them valuable for scientific studies.

11   Connecting Content Question

Fraternal Twins: ②, ④   Identical Twins: ①, ③

About fraternal twins, the professor says, "Fraternal twins occur when a mother produces two eggs at the same time. The eggs are released by the ovaries. Then, two separate sperm fertilize them. The fertilized eggs divide and grow, forming two zygotes," and, "Just like any brothers and sisters with the same parents, they share fifty percent of their DNA." Regarding identical twins, the professor states, "Identical twins are almost always the same sex. So they're either two boys or two girls," and, "Long-term studies on medical issues show that identical twins are more likely to get the same medical problems than fraternal twins. For instance, if one identical twin gets Alzheimer's disease, there's a fifty-percent chance the other will get it."

PART 2

[1–3] Conversation

| Script |

Listen to part of a conversation between a student and a professor.

W Professor: It's time for you to start thinking about next semester's classes, Jeff. Have you decided which courses you're planning to take?

M Student: Yes, Professor Gamble. I've already chosen the ones I hope to sign up for. Here, uh, take a look at the list I made.

W: Okay, let me see . . . Two history classes. That's good. It's better to take multiple classes since that's your major.

M: Yes, that's what I thought. And I can't wait to take Professor Marbury's medieval history class.

W: He's quite a good lecturer. You'll love it. Everyone who takes it has great things to say about that class. Okay, what else . . . ? A biology class to fulfill your science requirement . . . That's fine . . . An English class on Renaissance literature. Sure, that makes sense. And a Latin class . . . A Latin class?

M: Well, I've always wanted to learn it. And I am planning to take a medieval history class next semester.

W: Okay, yeah, that's logical. It can only help. I approve of that.

M: Thanks. I'm looking forward to being in Professor Bernard's class. One of my friends told me that his language classes are really entertaining.

W: Professor Bernard? Oh, wait a minute. I hate to let you down, but there's a bit of a problem. You see, uh, Professor Bernard announced that he's moving to another university last week. This is his last semester here, so, unfortunately, you won't be able to take his class.

M: What a shame. I really wanted to study with him. Well, I guess I'll just have to take the class with another professor. It probably won't be as entertaining, but I still want to

learn the language.

W: Um . . . I just remembered . . . I'm not sure that your new plan is going to be possible either.

M: Huh? Why not?

W: I heard some news at this morning's faculty meeting. The school might not find a replacement for Professor Bernard. Apparently, the school is facing a bit of a financial crisis. So it's not planning to replace any professors when they leave or retire. And, uh, as far as I know, Professor Bernard is the only Latin teacher at the school.

M: Well, that just destroys my plans, doesn't it?

W: Hmm . . . Not exactly. We have an agreement with Lakeview College. Students here can take classes there and vice versa. The college has a very impressive Latin program with several teachers. Now, uh, it would take you thirty minutes to drive there. 🎧³ But if you really want to learn that subject, you can enroll in a class at Lakeview College. Would you like to know more about the program?

M: **I'll take you up on that offer.**

Answer Explanation

1 Gist-Content Question

Ⓐ The professor tells the student, "I hate to let you down, but there's a bit of a problem. You see, uh, Professor Bernard announced that he's moving to another university last week. This is his last semester here, so, unfortunately, you won't be able to take his class." Then, she mentions that the professor will not be replaced. So the student will not be able to take a class he is interested in.

2 Making Inferences Question

Ⓓ The professor remarks, "Two history classes. That's good. It's better to take multiple classes since that's your major." So she implies that History is the student's major.

3 Understanding Function Question

Ⓒ When the student says, "I'll take you up on that offer," he is indicating that he would like to know more about the program. So it can be inferred that he is interested in going to Lakeview College to take a class there.

[4–7] Lecture

| Script |

Listen to part of a lecture in an environmental science class.

W Professor: For a long time, scientists believed precipitation formed only in one way . . . Heat evaporates water in oceans, lakes, and rivers. Water vapor rises in the air until the temperature cools. Then, it condenses, leaving water droplets suspended in the air. These droplets join with particles of dust and minerals in the air. They further combine to form clouds. When the clouds get too heavy, they drop water in the form of rain, snow, or ice. This is the water cycle. Every child is taught this in elementary school.

But . . . we now know there's another way that precipitation forms. In the 1980s, American scientist David Sands had a theory. He believed bacteria were also responsible for creating precipitation. Well, his theory has since been proven correct. We call this bioprecipitation. Just so you know, the *bio* in bioprecipitation stands for biological. Let me explain how it works. Here, uh . . . would you all please look at this chart on the screen? It explains the bioprecipitation cycle.

First, bacteria forms in colonies found, uh, usually on plants. Then, blowing winds shake the bacteria off the plants and blow them into the atmosphere. As the bacteria rise, water droplets attach themselves to the bacteria. The ball of water that forms around the bacteria grows bigger as even more water molecules in the air clump onto it. Eventually, these growing water balls fall to the ground as rain or snow. The bacteria fall to the ground as well. If only a single bacterium lands on a plant, the cycle repeats itself. A new bacteria colony grows, gets blown into the air, and so on.

So, uh, what's so important about this . . . ? Well, as I just said, we once believed that water droplets only attached themselves to dust or various minerals in the air. However, it looks like water droplets can attach themselves to many kinds of bacteria. And here's something very interesting . . . In order for snow to fall, ice crystals must form around some kind of a nucleus. Well, certain bacteria allow ice crystals to form at warmer temperatures than dust and minerals require.

M Student: I'm sorry, but I'm a bit unsure about what you just said. Are you implying that bacteria let ice crystals form even when the temperature is not below freezing? Wouldn't that increase the amount of snow that can fall?

W: You inferred correctly, Thomas.

M: Can you give us an example of one bacterium that does this?

W: Sure. *Pseudomonas syringae* is one. Just so everyone knows, we normally call it *P. syringae*. Basically, it binds water molecules in a unique way that lets them form ice particles at temperatures above freezing. We find this bacterium everywhere, uh, on the ground, in the air, on plants . . . It is an important bacterium in the creation of bioprecipitation. It creates snow in places all over the world, especially in Antarctica.

I wonder if any of you can think of a drawback to bioprecipitation. I just mentioned that we can find *P. syringae* on plants. Thomas, what do you think?

M: Hmm . . . It lets ice form at temperatures above freezing . . . It's on plants . . . So, uh, wait a minute. I've got it. It can harm plants by causing them to freeze.

W: Well done. Many plants are vulnerable to frosts. Uh, you know, when the temperature drops below freezing. Because *P. syringae* can create ice at temperatures above freezing, plants that it's on can be harmed—or even killed—by its actions.

Of course, there are also benefits to bioprecipitation. Let me tell you how it can be helpful.

Answer Explanation

4 **Gist-Content Question**

Ⓒ The professor mostly talks about how bioprecipitation forms.

5 **Understanding Function Question**

Ⓒ The professor tells the students, "Here, uh . . . would you all please look at this chart on the screen? It explains the bioprecipitation cycle."

6 **Detail Question**

Fact: ① , ④   Not a Fact: ② , ③
First, the professor points out, "Basically, it binds water molecules in a unique way that lets them form ice particles at temperatures above freezing." Then, the professor notes, "Because *P. syringae* can create ice at temperatures above freezing, plants that it's on can be harmed—or even killed—by its actions."

7 **Making Inferences Question**

Ⓐ At the end of the lecture, the professor says, "Of course, there are also benefits to bioprecipitation. Let me tell you how it can be helpful." So the professor will probably continue lecturing on the topic.

Vocabulary Review

p. 90

Answers

A
1 harvest   2 personality
3 requirement   4 mentally   5 sustain
B
1 a   2 a   3 b   4 a   5 b
6 a   7 b   8 a   9 a

| Basic Practice | p. 93

Answers A Ⓒ   B Ⓒ   C Ⓑ   D Ⓐ

| Script |

A

Listen to part of a conversation between a student and a student activities office employee.

W Student: Hello. I'm here about the gaming club. There's a, um, small problem.

M Student Activities Office Employee: Is there? What's the matter?

W: Well, I had hoped to organize a gaming club on campus. But only seven people signed up for it. I'm pretty sure that all campus clubs need to have twelve or more members. So, uh, can we still have a club?

M: 🎧 It doesn't look like it. But you still have two more days to get more members.

W: Really? Okay, I'll see you again on Wednesday.

M: Good luck.

Answer Explanation

Ⓒ When the student says, "Okay, I'll see you again on Wednesday," she is implying that she will try to recruit more members.

B

Listen to part of a lecture in a zoology class.

M Professor: 🎧 Take a look at this insect. Does anyone know what it is?

W Student: It's a praying mantis, isn't it?

M: Well done, Jennifer. Look at its stance. It appears to be praying, doesn't it? That's where it gets its name from. There are roughly 2,000 species of the praying mantis. It's one of the insect world's most fearsome predators. As you can see in this picture, it's a very large insect. So its size helps it as a hunter.

It can also rotate its head 180 degrees. That, in addition to its enormous compound eyes, gives it an excellent range of vision. It uses camouflage as well. Notice how it's green in color. This lets it blend in with leaves and grass. When it gets close to its prey, it seizes the animal with those huge, powerful front arms. The praying mantis usually hunts crickets, moths, bees, and beetles. But it has been known to capture small reptiles and birds. On occasion, it captures small mammals.

Answer Explanation

Ⓒ When the professor says, "Well done, Jennifer," in response to her answer, he is indicating that her guess is correct.

C

Listen to part of a lecture in an art class.

W Professor: People have been making ceramics for thousands of years. Shards of pottery have been found at dig sites around the world. People in most ancient cultures learned to make ceramics. They used ceramics for various purposes. Among them were to act as containers and to cook food in.

We're going to make some ceramics in class today. But first, I want to tell you the steps involved in the process. The first, obviously, is to find the material. We'll use clay for our ceramics. Clay is basically an earthy material that becomes easy to manipulate when it gets wet.

Once you have your clay, you need to knead it like bread. You see, uh, clay has lots of air bubbles. And air bubbles can make ceramics crack. So you should roll the clay around and knead it until all the air bubbles get removed. This process usually takes a few minutes. Once the air bubbles are all gone, we can proceed to the next step.

Answer Explanation

Ⓑ The professor says, "Once you have your clay, you need to knead it like bread. You see, uh, clay has lots of air bubbles. And air bubbles can make ceramics crack. So you should roll the clay around and knead it until all the air bubbles get removed."

D

Listen to part of a lecture in a history class.

M Professor: The mid-1800s was an exciting time in the history of the United States. Millions of people were heading west across the Mississippi. In fact, large parts of the west weren't even settled then. However, there were plenty of people in California. Those people wanted to be connected to the rest of the country. They also wanted their mail.

Mail going to California could be sent by ship. That took several months to arrive. 🎧 Or the mail could go there by land in a stagecoach. That took twenty-five days. That just wasn't good enough. So in 1860, the Pony Express was established. It delivered mail in ten days or fewer.

Starting at St. Joseph, Missouri, Pony Express riders rode horses at fast speeds for seven to ten miles. Then, they switched horses and kept heading west. They did this for more than 1,800 miles all the way to Sacramento,

California. It was a brilliant idea. But it was a financial failure. The Pony Express lasted fewer than two years.

Answer Explanation

Ⓐ The professor says that sending mail by stagecoach took twenty-five days. Then, he adds, "That just wasn't good enough." He is implying that using stagecoaches to send mail was too slow.

Practice with Short Passages   p. 94

A

Answers   1 Ⓐ   2 Ⓒ

| Script |

Listen to part of a conversation between a student and a professor.

W Professor: Are you looking forward to this weekend's field trip to the national park, Stuart? You've never been there before, have you?

M Student: No, I haven't. I really want to see the rock layers. And I hope we get a chance to dig for fossils.

W: We will. There's a place we'll visit that has tons of small fossils. They're pretty easy to find.

M: Oh, that reminds me. What equipment do I need to bring? I mean, uh, we're hunting for fossils, right? So, uh . . . I should bring tools, shouldn't I?

W: It's good you're thinking like that, Stuart. But you don't need to worry about a thing.

M: I don't? Why not?

W: The department has everything we need. I'll be bringing enough equipment for everyone to use. 🎧² The tools are a bit heavy though . . . So if you'd like to assist me with them, I'd appreciate it.

M: My pleasure. **Shall I show up here an hour before we leave then?**

W: Half an hour early would be perfect. Thanks, Stuart.

Answer Explanation

1 Ⓐ The student asks, "What equipment do I need to bring?"

2 Ⓒ The professor asks the student for assistance. When he answers, "Shall I show up here an hour before we leave then?" it can be inferred that he is willing to help the professor.

B

Answers   1 Ⓑ   2 Ⓓ

| Script |

Listen to part of a lecture in an astronomy class.

M Professor: There are hundreds of billions of stars in the Milky Way Galaxy. There are countless others in all of the other billions of galaxies in the universe. Eventually, all of these stars will exhaust their energy. The largest of them will explode, causing supernovas. They will then transform into either black holes or neutron stars. The smaller stars, however, don't have enough energy to explode like that. Instead, they will become white dwarf stars.

Let's talk about our sun as an example. In a few billion years, it will expend most of its energy. At that time, it will turn into a red giant. It will increase in size a tremendous amount. It will become so large that it will engulf Mercury, Venus, and Earth. After some time, all of the sun's energy will be exhausted. Then, only the core of the red giant will remain. This is when it will turn into a white dwarf.

How big will this star be? It will be relatively tiny. It will have a diameter about the size of the Earth. But it will be very dense because it will contain the mass of the sun. This will cause its gravity to be extremely strong. Astronomers believe it will be 350,000 times the Earth's gravity. 🎧² What will happen to the sun at that time? Well, we're not completely positive. But it will most likely become a black dwarf star. However, that's not the case for all white dwarf stars. For example, one that belongs to a binary system could add mass from its partner star. When that happens, the additional mass could result in a supernova. Or it could cause it to become a neutron star.

Answer Explanation

1 Ⓑ The professor mentions the sun as an example of a star that will one day become a white dwarf.

2 Ⓓ When the professor says, "We're not completely positive," he is indicating that his next comment about what will happen to the sun is a guess.

Practice with Long Passages

A

Answers   1 ⓒ   2 Ⓐ   3 ⓒ

| Script |

Listen to part of a conversation between a student and a student center employee.

W Student: Hello. Are you in charge of reserving rooms for student activities?

M Student Center Employee: Yes, I am. But, uh, you don't come here to do that. You're supposed to do that online.

W: Er . . . Actually, I did make a reservation on the website. I did that, uh, three days ago. However, I never got an emailed confirmation. I've reserved rooms several times in the past, and I always got a confirmation email in my inbox. But that didn't happen this time.

M: Ah, I see. When did you say that you made the reservation?

W: Three days ago. So that would be, uh, Saturday night.

M: Okay, that explains it. The website was down for maintenance during parts of the weekend.

W: Yeah, I noticed that. It was pretty hard for me to log on. I even got kicked off the website a couple of times before I managed to make the booking.

M: That usually happens when work is being done on the site. Anyway, uh, pretty much no new information got saved over the weekend. And that's why you didn't get an email. Your request simply didn't get processed.

W: 🎧³ Oh . . . So I need to find a computer and make my booking online now?

M: Normally, yes, but **I'll make an exception in your case.**

W: Excellent. I really appreciate it. I've got to attend class in fifteen minutes, so I don't have time to go online.

M: All right. Then let's hurry up since you're in a rush. Why don't you fill out this form right here? You need to show me your student ID as well.

Answer Explanation

1 ⓒ The student states, "Actually, I did make a reservation on the website. I did that, uh, three days ago. However, I never got an emailed confirmation. I've reserved rooms several times in the past, and I always got a confirmation email in my inbox. But that didn't happen this time." So she is inquiring about a reservation.

2 Ⓐ The student complains that a website was not working well, so the man tells her about the website maintenance.

3 ⓒ When the man tells the student that he will make an exception for her, he means that she does not need to make an online booking.

Dictation

M: <u>When did you say</u> that you made the reservation?

W: Three days ago. So <u>that would be</u>, uh, Saturday night.

M: Okay, <u>that explains it</u>. The website was <u>down for maintenance</u> during parts of the weekend.

W: Yeah, I <u>noticed</u> that. It was pretty hard for me to log on. I even <u>got kicked off</u> the website a couple of times before I <u>managed to</u> make the booking.

B

Answers

1 ⓒ   2 *Le France*: ①, ④   Zeppelin: ②, ③
3 Ⓓ

| Script |

Listen to part of a lecture in a history of technology class.

M1 Professor: The airship was the first practical flying machine for long distances. It's also sometimes called the blimp, the dirigible, and the zeppelin. The airship is different from the balloon as it has engines and the ability to steer. The first airships were developed in France in the late eighteenth century. These early designs relied on human power for energy. They utilized propellers operated by hand or wings that flapped to propel the airship. As you can imagine, um, they weren't very practical.

Then, in 1852, French inventor Henri Giffard built the first airship with an engine. It had a small steam engine which generated three horsepower. 🎧³ It could fly about nine kilometers an hour.

M2 Student: That's not very fast.

M1: Compared to the speeds we can reach today, it was horribly slow. **However, for the time, it was quite an impressive achievement.** On one flight, Giffard flew twenty-seven kilometers. Unfortunately, he had problems controlling it when he was aloft. So it was ultimately a failure. Later, in 1884, two other French inventors built *Le France*. It was an airship made for the French army. It was the first airship that could take off, navigate, and return to land in the same spot.

Other inventors designed and constructed various airships in the late eighteenth century. Hungarian David Schwarz created a design for a rigid airship in 1895. It had a metal covering instead of fabric like most other airships. He died before it could be built though. His wife constructed it and flew it in Berlin in 1897. German soldier and inventor Count Ferdinand von Zeppelin was inspired by the design.

Zeppelin improved the design. In 1900, he flew his first airship, which he named after himself. Each zeppelin had a metal internal frame and many small gasbags inside a larger fabric all around it. Under the frame were cabins called gondolas. They were for the crew and passengers. Zeppelins took part in many bombing raids on England and France during World War One.

After the war, the Germans began to operate a transatlantic passenger service with zeppelins. But there were some accidents. The most famous was the crash of the zeppelin *Hindenburg* on May 6, 1937, in New Jersey. Thirty-six people died in the accident. After World War Two, airplanes replaced airships.

Answer Explanation

1 Ⓒ During his lecture, the professor talks about the inventions in chronological order.

2 *Le France*: [1], [4] Zeppelin: [2], [3]
About *Le France*, the professor says, "Later, in 1884, two other French inventors built *Le France*. It was an airship made for the French army. It was the first airship that could take off, navigate, and return to land in the same spot." Regarding the zeppelin, he notes, "Hungarian David Schwarz created a design for a rigid airship in 1895. It had a metal covering instead of fabric like most other airships. He died before it could be built though. His wife constructed it and flew it in Berlin in 1897. German soldier and inventor Count Ferdinand von Zeppelin was inspired by the design." Then, he adds, "Each zeppelin had a metal internal frame and many small gasbags inside a larger fabric all around it. Under the frame were cabins called gondolas."

3 Ⓓ When the professor responds to the student by saying, "However, for the time, it was quite an impressive achievement," he is disagreeing with the student's comment that the first airship was not very fast.

Dictation

❶ The first airships <u>were developed</u> in France in the late eighteenth century. These early designs <u>relied on</u> human power for energy.

❷ <u>Compared to</u> the speeds we can reach today, it was <u>horribly slow</u>. However, for the time, it was <u>quite an impressive</u> achievement.

❸ Zeppelin <u>improved</u> the design. In 1900, he flew his first airship, <u>which he named after</u> himself.

iBT Practice Test   p. 100

Answers

PART 1

1 [1], [3]   2 Ⓒ   3 Ⓓ   4 Ⓐ   5 Ⓒ
6 Ⓑ   7 ⒷⒹⒶⒸ   8 Ⓑ   9 Ⓓ
10 Ⓑ   11 Ⓓ

PART 2

1 Ⓓ   2 Ⓑ   3 Ⓒ   4 Ⓐ   5 Ⓒ
6 [1], [4]   7 Ⓑ

PART 1

[1-3] Conversation

| Script |

Listen to part of a conversation between a student and a professor.

W Student: Good afternoon, Professor Marlowe. Have you had a chance to look at my résumé yet? I'm curious to find out what you think of it.

M Professor: You have great timing, Maria. I just finished reviewing it about ten minutes ago. As you can see here, I'm typing an email to you to ask you to visit my office.

W: Oh, great. I'm glad I dropped by then. Uh . . . you, uh, don't mind talking to me now, do you? I hope I'm not imposing.

M: Not at all. Now is as good a time as any to go over your résumé. Why don't you sit down so that we can discuss it?

W: Excellent. Thank you. So . . . how is it? Do you think it's okay to send to some companies now?

M: Hmm . . . Overall, your instincts on how to write a résumé are good. You included pretty much all of the vital information you need. Let's see . . . Your contact information, your education, your job experience. They're all here. They look good, but . . . You made one huge mistake . . . It's too long.

W: Too long? But it's only a page and a half.

M: Right. And that extra half page has made it too long.

W: I don't understand. How can that be too long? I mean, uh, I write eight-page papers and ten-page papers all the time. And I don't consider them to be too long.

M: Ah, Maria, there's a difference between the academic world and the business world. Here at school, your professors want to test your knowledge of certain subjects. You know, uh, they want you to discuss topics in depth. So they want you to turn in long papers. That's one way they can determine your knowledge. But the business world . . . uh, you know, résumé writing . . . Well, that's something different. The people reading your résumé want brevity, not length.

W: Why is that?

M: There are a couple of reasons. First, think about how many applicants some of these jobs get. Hundreds of people may apply for a single position. Now, imagine you're the person who has to read every résumé.

W: Oh . . . I get it. I would probably ignore the long ones and look at the short ones. I would most likely throw anything over two pages into the trash. What's the other reason?

M: It's a test of your writing ability. 🎧3 Basically, uh, are you able to condense the relevant information into a single page? People who can do that show that they have good judgment and writing ability. **So, uh, let's figure out how we can shorten it.**

Answer Explanation

1 Detail Question

⒈, ⒊ About the student's résumé, the professor notes, "You included pretty much all of the vital information you need. Let's see . . . Your contact information, your education, your job experience."

2 Connecting Content Question

Ⓒ The professor states, "Ah, Maria, there's a difference between the academic world and the business world. Here at school, your professors want to test your knowledge of certain subjects. You know, uh, they want you to discuss topics in depth. So they want you to turn in long papers. That's one way they can test your knowledge. But the business world . . . uh, you know, résumé writing . . . Well, that's something different. The people reading your résumé want brevity, not length."

3 Understanding Function Question

Ⓓ When the professor says, "So, uh, let's figure out how we can shorten it," he is indicating his desire to look at the student's work to assist her.

[4–7] Lecture #1

| Script |

Listen to part of a lecture in a music class.

W Professor: Good morning, everyone. I believe I have received most of your papers. If you haven't turned them in yet, I suggest you do so by five o'clock today. Otherwise, your papers will be considered late.

Now, let's continue our look at some famous composers. The first one of the day is Franz Joseph Haydn of Austria. He's considered one of the most prominent composers of the eighteenth century. Haydn helped develop the classical form of music. He also played a major role in the formation of three forms of music: the sonata, the string

quartet, and the symphony. Among those who were influenced by him were Beethoven, Brahms, Schubert, and Mendelssohn. During his life, Haydn composed hundreds of works in various forms. Included among them are, uh, let's see . . . more than one hundred symphonies . . . almost one hundred works for string quartets . . . and dozens of piano sonatas. In short, classical music would be a lot different without him.

First, a bit about his life . . . Haydn was born in a small village in Austria in 1732 and died in Vienna in 1809. His parents were both musicians. Haydn was an excellent singer at a young age. His parents wanted him to learn more, so they sent him to live with a relative who was a choirmaster. There, Haydn learned to play several instruments, including the violin and harpsichord. Later, he moved to Vienna to sing with a choir at St. Stephen's Cathedral.

After his youth ended, Haydn became a freelance musician. But he struggled, finding little work. Finally, in 1752, Italian composer Nicola Porpora gave Haydn a position as an apprentice. Haydn would later say that was where he first learned to become a composer. One of the first well-known works was an opera he wrote in 1753. He soon got work as a court composer for various wealthy families. By 1761, he had been named the court composer for the wealthy Esterhazy family in Hungary. Haydn stayed with that family for the next thirty years.

M Student: Why did he stay with them? I mean, wasn't he famous?

W: He was famous, but at that time, there was no way for composers to acquire great wealth like today. There were no record sales or multimillion dollar concert tours. Nearly all the great musicians had patrons. These were wealthy people who paid musicians to work for them. So Haydn spent a lot of time writing music for the family and traveling with them.

During that time, Haydn constantly wrote music and performed it. As he worked, um, mainly in isolation, he developed new ideas. You see, as a court musician, he had little contact with other great composers. Some music historians think this is why he developed such a unique style. During one trip with his patron family, Haydn met Mozart in Vienna. The two became friends. He also traveled to other parts of Europe and was well received and respected.

In 1790, Haydn met Beethoven. Haydn recognized the talent in the young man and invited Beethoven to study with him. From 1792 to 1794, Beethoven was his student. By that time, Haydn was no longer a full-time court composer. He was married and had his own home in Vienna. From 1795, Haydn wrote a great deal of music for public performances. Most of these were liked by the public. Around 1803, he fell ill. From that time until his death in 1809, he composed little music. Now, that's enough about Haydn's life. Let's look more closely at the music he wrote.

4 Understanding Function Question

Ⓐ The professor encourages the students to submit their papers in saying, "I believe I have received most of your papers. If you haven't turned them in yet, I suggest you do so by five o'clock today. Otherwise, your papers will be considered late."

5 Understanding Attitude Question

Ⓒ The professor believes Haydn was an important person in classical music. She shows this when she lectures, "The first one of the day is Franz Joseph Haydn of Austria. He's considered one of the most prominent composers of the eighteenth century. Haydn helped develop the classical form of music. He also played a major role in the formation of three forms of music: the sonata, the string quartet, and the symphony. Among those who were influenced by him were Beethoven, Brahms, Schubert, and Mendelssohn. During his life, Haydn composed hundreds of works in various forms. Included among them are, uh, let's see . . . more than one hundred symphonies . . . almost one hundred works for string quartets . . . and dozens of piano sonatas. In short, classical music would be a lot different without him."

6 Detail Question

Ⓑ The professor remarks, "You see, as a court musician, he had little contact with other great composers. Some music historians think this is why he developed such a unique style."

7 Connecting Content Question

Ⓑ Ⓓ Ⓐ Ⓒ First, "Haydn was an excellent singer at a young age. His parents wanted him to learn more, so they sent him to live with a relative who was a choirmaster. There, Haydn learned to play several instruments, including the violin and harpsichord. Later, he moved to Vienna to sing with a choir at St. Stephen's Cathedral." Second, "By 1761, he had been named the court composer for the wealthy Esterhazy family in Hungary." Third, "During one trip with his patron family, Haydn met Mozart in Vienna. The two became friends." Fourth, "In 1790, Haydn met Beethoven. Haydn recognized the talent in the young man and invited Beethoven to study with him. From 1792 to 1794, Beethoven was his student."

[8 – 11] Lecture #2

| Script |

Listen to part of a lecture in an economics class.

M Professor: The objective of every company or business is to sell its products or services. People can be informed

about them through marketing. There are numerous marketing methods, some of which are currently being developed. Now, uh, to make this part of today's lecture simpler, I'll divide these techniques into older ones and newer ones.

First, let me cover some of the oldest marketing methods. I suppose the oldest is word of mouth. This means that people recommend a product or service to others. This method is great because it costs companies no money. But for it to work, a company needs to establish a reputation. So, uh, I suppose it indirectly costs money in the beginning. There's also a downside to it. If a product or service gets a bad reputation, no amount of marketing can prevent bad word of mouth from hurting sales.

Let's look at a few of the older ones. 🎧10 Any guesses?

W Student: How about TV, radio, and newspapers?

M: Certainly. All three are powerful and still important today. **However, the decline in newspaper readership makes it the weakest of the three.** TV remains a powerful way to market products and services. Unfortunately, producing ads and then airing them on TV costs quite a bit of money. And remember that lots of pay-for-view stations don't run any ads. So we may see TV marketing end soon or, at least, uh, decline greatly. Radio is also becoming less popular, so radio advertisements are in trouble as well. Oh, a few other older marketing methods are billboards, posters, mailings, free samples, and bumper stickers.

Now, what about some newer marketing methods? The most obvious one is the Internet. These days, virtually every website has ads at the top or on the sides. You can learn more simply by clicking on the ads. 🎧11 There are also popup ads that appear on your screen whether you want them to or not. Many people despise them, but they do work since they get people's attention. And that's the point of marketing. **Don't ever forget that.** Ah, one advantage Internet marketing has over TV ads is the price. Internet ads are much cheaper. An obvious disadvantage of Internet ads is that they may not reach as many people as TV ads. Many websites get few visitors, but millions of people may watch some TV programs.

Now, uh, what about social media? Perhaps the most widespread and effective marketing methods today are on social media. This includes Facebook, Twitter, and other places where people meet online. Ads on these platforms can reach millions of people in a short time, uh, especially if they go viral. By that I mean that the ads suddenly get spread far and wide. How that happens is hard to say. Most viral ads have something special about them that attracts or interests people. Many have to do with upcoming TV shows and movies. Production companies make short trailers. They may come out months before the movies do. But some trailers get millions of views on social media. That builds strong word of mouth for films.

Now, a bit of advice for you future marketers. Always

be aware of the next big thing. Things are changing rapidly these days. If you're not ready, you will lose big time. Marketing methods are constantly evolving. Soon, TV, radio, and print ads may be gone, and the future of marketing will almost certainly be online.

Answer Explanation

8 Gist-Content Question

ⓑ The professor's lecture focuses on the various types of marketing.

9 Understanding Organization Question

ⓓ When talking about word of mouth, the professor gives both positive and negative points about it.

10 Understanding Attitude Question

ⓑ In stating, "However, the decline in newspaper readership makes it the weakest of the three," the professor implies that he believes newspapers are less important than TV.

11 Understanding Function Question

ⓓ When the professor tells the students, "Don't ever forget that," he is emphasizing the point that he is making to the students.

PART 2

[1–3] Conversation

| Script |

Listen to part of a conversation between a student and a professor.

M Professor: Okay, Jessica, do you have any other questions?

W Student: Yes, sir. I hope, um, I hope you don't mind, but . . . um, today's lecture on airplanes was really difficult.

M: What didn't you understand?

W: Everything. First, I guess I'm just confused about how things so big and so heavy can achieve flight. But, um, of course, they can fly because we see them in the air all the time. Would you mind explaining the principles of flight one more time?

M: I've got a few minutes before my next class. So I suppose it won't be a problem. First, can you tell me the four basic aerodynamic forces involved in flight?

W: Yes, sir. They are, uh, lift, weight, thrust, and drag.

M: Perfect. What can you tell me about lift?

W: Let me see . . . Lift pushes the airplane up into the air. But I'm not exactly sure how. I think it has something to do with the wings. But I don't remember.

M: You're correct about the wings. An airplane gets lift due to the way the air moves around its wings. Airplane wings are designed to push air in an efficient manner to let airplanes achieve flight. Now, what about weight?

W: I think it's like gravity. I mean, uh, weight pulls the airplane back to the Earth. So I guess that lift and weight act as sort of opposing forces.

M: Yes, that's right. The force that pulls airplanes down toward the ground is weight. That's why airplanes are built in a way which spreads their weight out from the front to the back. This gives them more balance and reduces the effects of weight.

W: Okay. How about thrust? What is it?

M: You tell me.

W: Thrust, um . . . it comes from the engines. They provide the power that moves planes forward. So I guess that's what thrust is, isn't it? It's the force which propels planes in a forward direction. And as for drag, it's the opposing aerodynamic force to thrust. I guess it's like friction because it slows airplanes down a bit.

M: Bingo. Airplanes are designed to reduce the amount of drag that affects them. This lets the thrust produced by engines push planes forward at great speeds. So do you think you understand everything now?

W: Yes, sir. I do. I guess I know it better than I realized. Um, I just needed to talk it out with you. Thanks so much for helping me.

M: If you are still confused, check out the link to the video that's on our class webpage. It's an animated video showing how all four forces work together. After watching it, you shouldn't have any problem understanding the material.

W: Awesome. I'll check it out. Thanks again.

Answer Explanation

1 Gist-Purpose Question

ⓓ The student tells the professor, "Today's lecture on airplanes was really difficult." Then, she asks, "Would you mind explaining the principles of flight one more time?"

2 Detail Question

ⓑ The professor remarks, "An airplane gets lift due to the way the air moves around its wings. Airplane wings are designed to push air in an efficient manner to let airplanes achieve flight."

3 Understanding Function Question

ⓒ The professor tells the student, "If you are still confused, check out the link to the video that's on our class webpage. It's an animated video showing how all four forces work together. After watching it, you shouldn't have any problem understanding the material."

| Script |

Listen to part of a lecture in a zoology class.

W Professor: Living in large colonies, ants are among the most social insects. The goal of the ants in a colony is to survive by gathering food, reproducing, and protecting the colony. In order to accomplish these tasks, ants have a highly organized system of behavior. This organization gives them an advantage over most other insects. Proving how successful they are, ants today live almost everywhere on the planet, and their numbers are increasing.

Ant colonies are usually located underground but may be formed as a large mound of dirt. Some are also inside trees, in leaf piles, and under large rocks. Different species of ants form different types of colonies. Some colonies may have just a few ants while others may be home to millions. Each colony is specifically designed for its environment. There are always a way in and a way out of the colony. It also has a ventilation system to let air in and out. Every colony has a special place to raise new ants, too. Known as the brood chamber, it is where the queen lays her eggs. Then, they become larvae and eventually mature into adult ants. By cooperating, ants are able to build colonies and to survive for the long term.

There are three types of ants. No matter how many ants there are or what type of colony it is, there's always a queen ant. She's the leader of the colony and produces all of the new ants. There are some males, which are used only for mating with the queen. Most of the other ants are female worker ants. Each one has a specific function. For instance, some gather food while others guard the colony from invaders. The youngest worker ants typically remain in the colony, protect it, and raise new ants.

M Student: What about the queen? Does she decide which ants do certain tasks?

W: Not at all. She has very little to do with how the colony is organized or runs. 🎧7 For the most part, the queen ant spends her days feeding and laying eggs. That's her role in the colony. How the rest of the ants work together was a mystery for some time. But we now know that they communicate by using chemical signals we call pheromones. The signal for each activity is different. For instance, uh . . . ants have a pheromone for gathering food. Say that one ant finds a nice source of food. As it returns to the colony, it releases pheromones, creating a trail. Then, ants can follow the trail back to the food source to get supplies for the colony. Have you ever seen a line of ants marching somewhere? Sure, you have. That's what they were doing.

Other pheromones indicate when danger is approaching so that the ants can gather to defend the colony. Ants are extremely aggressive when attacked. But they'll also attack other insects, especially if they're near the colony.

Most species of ants have powerful stings when they bite. They can therefore disable large insects and carry them back to the colony to consume. Ants may also go to war with other ants. If two colonies are located close together, they'll fight over the resources in the area.

Now, uh, what about some unusual behavior of individual ant species? Let me see . . . Oh, army ants and fire ants behave in rather interesting ways. Let me tell you about what they do right now . . .

Answer Explanation

4 Detail Question

Ⓐ The professor says, "Every colony has a special place to raise new ants, too. Known as the brood chamber, it is where the queen lays her eggs."

5 Understanding Organization Question

Ⓒ The professor tells the students about the duties of all three types of ants.

6 Detail Question

1️⃣, 4️⃣ The professor says, "For instance, uh . . . ants have a pheromone for gathering food. Say that one ant finds a nice source of food. As it returns to the colony, it releases pheromones, creating a trail. Then, ants can follow the trail back to the food source to get supplies for the colony," and, "Other pheromones indicate when danger is approaching so that the ants can gather to defend the colony."

7 Understanding Function Question

Ⓑ In stating, "How the rest of the ants work together was a mystery for some time," the professor implies that scientists now know how ants work together.

| Vocabulary Review   p. 110

Answers

A

1 influenced	2 released	3 propel
4 fossils	5 colonies	

B

1 b	2 b	3 a	4 b	5 a
6 b	7 a	8 b	9 a	

| Basic Practice | p. 113

Answers   A (A)   B (B)   C (B)   D (A)

| Script |

A

Listen to part of a conversation between a student and a Registrar's office employee.

W1 Student: Hello. I'd like to get an extra copy of my diploma, please. Here's the form.

W2 Registrar's Office Employee: Okay, let me take a look at it . . . Uh, you forgot to put the year you graduated on the form. When did you do that?

W1: Actually, um, I haven't graduated yet. I'm going to finish school next month.

W2: In that case, I have to refuse your request. You can't receive a second diploma until you actually have one. That's a rule here.

W1: Oh, that's kind of silly. I was hoping you could just send me two later on. Anyway, thanks.

Answer Explanation

(A) The student says, "Oh, that's kind of silly," about the rule. So she dislikes it.

B

Listen to part of a conversation between a student and a professor.

M Student: Professor Featherstone, I'm a bit unclear about the assignment. We're supposed to make a video, right? But, uh, what kind of video?

W Professor: It's pretty simple, Boris. You need to interview three random people on the street. And be sure to record your interviews with them.

M: Uh, okay. What kinds of questions am I supposed to ask?

W: 🎧 That's up to you. Just make sure they're related to the topics we have studied in class.

M: Okay. I suppose I can figure this out. I'll do my best.

Answer Explanation

(B) When the student says, "I suppose I can figure this out," he is implying that he is still not sure what to do.

C

Listen to part of a lecture in a chemistry class.

W Professor: When people have surgery these days, it's a fairly straightforward process. They get prepared for the surgery, are given anesthesia, and then undergo the process. Thanks to anesthesia, they don't feel a thing while the operation is underway.

However, anesthesia was not successfully introduced in public until 1846. That was when William T.G. Morton became the first person to use ether anesthesia during a publicly observed surgery. A year earlier, Dr. Horace Wells had used nitrous oxide to extract a tooth. But people doubted that his method was effective.

Morton's work, however, was widely praised. Other doctors soon began using his method, so it spread widely. Of course, other more effective methods were later developed. But it was Morton who showed people how to use it first. It's actually a shame that his name isn't better known to people. After all, his contribution to the field of medicine was quite impressive.

Answer Explanation

(B) The professor says, "But it was Morton who showed people how to use it first. It's actually a shame that his name isn't better known to people. After all, his contribution to the field of medicine was quite impressive."

D

Listen to part of a lecture in a music class.

M Professor: 🎧 Take a look at this musical instrument I'm holding. Can anyone tell me what it is?

W Student: It looks like an oud.

M: **That's a very good guess.** Would anyone else like to try . . . ? Okay, this is a lute from the Renaissance. It actually evolved from the oud, so Cathy almost got it right.

During the European Renaissance, the lute was the most popular musical instrument. As you can see, it's a stringed instrument. At first, it had six courses. A course is either a single string or a double string played together. The top course for the Renaissance lute was always a single string. The remaining courses were double strings. Later, there would be more courses added to the lute. By the end of the Renaissance, there were some with ten courses.

What did it sound like? Well, I happen to be trained in this instrument, so listen for a moment as I play it.

Answer Explanation

(A) When the professor says, "That's a very good guess," he means that the student gave an incorrect answer.

A

Answers	1 Ⓐ	2 Ⓑ

| Script |

Listen to part of a conversation between a student and a study abroad office employee.

W Student: 🎧1 I'm sorry, but do you have a moment? I have a couple of questions about studying abroad.

M Study Abroad Office Employee: That's what I'm here for.

W: Great. Thanks. Um . . . Basically, here's the deal. I would love to study in France for an entire year. I know the school has a study abroad program in Paris. But, uh, how competitive is it?

M: Competitive? Do you mean the classes you'll be taking there?

W: No, not that. I'm talking about the application process. Uh . . . You see, my grades aren't the best. And I'm not exactly fluent in French, so . . .

M: Ah, you're wondering if you'll get accepted or not. Is that correct?

W: Yeah, totally. My GPA is only a 2.9. Is that too low?

M: I'm afraid so. The cutoff is 3.0. 🎧2 But why don't you apply anyway? After all, if you do well this semester, your GPA will go up, right? Then, you'll be accepted to the program.

W: That's not a bad idea. Oh, and what about speaking French fluently?

M: Don't worry. Most students who go there don't know much. They learn it in France.

Answer Explanation

1 Ⓐ The student says that she has some questions for the man. He says, "That's what I'm here for." In saying that, he means that he can answer the student's questions.

2 Ⓑ The man suggest that the student apply to the program and gives a reason why. The student responds by saying, "That's not a bad idea." She is therefore implying that she intends to apply to the program.

B

Answers	1 Ⓒ	2 Ⓒ

| Script |

Listen to part of a lecture in a marine biology class.

M Professor: When many people visit the beach, they're constantly looking for sharks. That's understandable,

especially around this time of the year. We had two shark attacks in this area three years ago. Well, in some parts of the world, sharks aren't the only dangerous animals in the water. People also need to be on the lookout for sea snakes.

Sea snakes live all around the world. They're particularly common in the warm waters of the Indian and Pacific oceans. Yet they can be found elsewhere, including the eastern and western Atlantic Ocean, the Caribbean Sea, and the Red Sea. While they typically live in shallow water, some have been found swimming more than 160 kilometers away from shore.

Sea snakes should be avoided because they're extremely venomous. There are around sixty species of them, and a few are highly aggressive. So, uh, you definitely don't want to provoke them. A tiny amount of the venom of several sea snakes can be lethal to humans.

They are usually between one and two meters long, but some can grow to be three meters in length. Most of these snakes live their entire lives in the water. A couple go onto land to lay eggs, but they're exceptions. Despite living in the water, sea snakes don't have gills. As a result, they have to come to the surface to breathe. Some of these snakes can dive around ninety meters beneath the surface and stay submerged for hours. They may dive to hunt for fish, eels, or other prey. Or they may go beneath the surface when they are pursued by a predator or suddenly startled.

Answer Explanation

1 Ⓒ The professor states, "Well, in some parts of the world, sharks aren't the only dangerous animals in the water. People also need to be on the lookout for sea snakes."

2 Ⓒ The professor remarks, "There are around sixty species of them, and a few are highly aggressive. So, uh, you definitely don't want to provoke them. A tiny amount of the venom of several sea snakes can be lethal to humans." The professor therefore implies that sea snakes will attack people that bother them.

A

Answers	1 Ⓑ	2 Ⓐ	3 Ⓓ

Listen to part of a conversation between a student and a professor.

M1 Student: Professor Caldwell, do you have a moment to talk to me about my grade? I'm, uh, I'm not doing very well in your class.

M2 Professor: Your name is, hmm . . . You're Brian Dawson, right?

M1: Yes, sir. That's me.

M2: Ah, right. I was just looking at the class grades this afternoon. You did all right on the first test. But your homework hasn't been that good. And your recent test was . . . uh, what happened? You got a sixty-seven on it.

M1: Honestly, I forgot about it and didn't study for the test. I got back at my dorm room from my part-time job late the night before the test, so I went to bed immediately. The next day, I woke up and suddenly remembered we had a test that day.

M2: 🎧³ It sounds like you need to keep a calendar.

M1: **I went out and bought one the next day.** But, uh, it didn't do me any good on the test. So, uh, anyway . . . I was wondering if there was something I could do to improve my grade.

M2: Well, studying harder and doing better on your homework are two options.

M1: Right. But how about writing an essay for extra credit? Do you permit that?

M2: Sorry, Brian, but I don't allow that. However, don't get down. There are still two more tests in this class. If you do well on them, you can pull your grade up. And start focusing on your homework. You're losing easy points due to careless mistakes.

M1: Yes, sir. I'll do my best from now on. I really like this class, so it bothers me that I'm doing poorly in it.

Answer Explanation

1 Ⓑ The student comments, "I'm, uh, I'm not doing very well in your class." The professor adds, "But your homework hasn't been that good. And your recent test was . . . uh, what happened? You got a sixty-seven on it."

2 Ⓐ The student asks the professor, "But how about writing an essay for extra credit?"

3 Ⓓ The professor advises the student to get a calendar. Then, the student responds, "I went out and bought one the next day." It can therefore be inferred that the student agrees with the professor's advice.

Dictation

M1: So, uh, anyway . . . I was wondering if there was something I could do to improve my grade.

M2: Well, studying harder and doing better on your

homework are two options.

M1: Right. But how about writing an essay for extra credit? Do you permit that?

M2: Sorry, Brian, but I don't allow that. However, don't get down. There are still two more tests in this class. If you do well on them, you can pull your grade up. And start focusing on your homework. You're losing easy points due to careless mistakes.

B

Answers   1 Ⓓ   2 Ⓐ   3 Ⓑ

| Script |

Listen to part of a lecture in an anthropology class.

W Professor: Another interesting aspect of the Inuit people of the Arctic is their stone statues. Take a look at this statue here . . . We call that an *inuksuk*. Spell it I-N-U-K-S-U-K. Just so you know, it's an Inuit word.

The Inuit build *inuksuit* . . . er, that's the plural form . . . mainly from flat stones they pile on top of one another. The stones tend to be large and heavy. So it can require many people to make one. Sometimes the stones are in straight, upright positions. Others resemble human figures with legs as a base and arms outstretched like a statue.

M Student: You know, um, they don't look like statues to me.

W: Well, they certainly don't resemble most Western art. I suppose that many people would just call them cairns. Those are piles of stones stacked by humans. All across the Arctic, uh, from Alaska to Greenland, you can find these stone piles. Some are alone while others are found in large groups.

M: Why do the Inuit make them?

W: Good question. We believe they've been making them for centuries for a couple of reasons. First, centuries ago, the Inuit lacked compasses and other mechanical means of navigation. In the barren Arctic lands, there are few landmarks. The *inuksuit* therefore serve this purpose. They show travelers waypoints so that they don't get lost on their journeys. 🎧³ The stones that appear to have arms may be pointing to a path, to the site of a nearby village, or, uh, to a good hunting or fishing place. **This is, uh, speculation for the most part.** But anthropologists are pretty sure this is an accurate guess.

A second purpose of *inuksuit* is more spiritual. The Inuit people say that *inuksuit* provide a glimpse into the human spirit. Each one is built with care. Knowledge of how to build them has been passed down from generation to generation. The human spirit of those who came before is said to be built into each one. Sometimes the Inuit gather at an *inuksuk* to have important meetings, to make decisions, and to worship their ancestors. Some say the *inuksuit* are places for deep thinking. In this regard, the stone statues help the Inuit navigate their way through life.

Answer Explanation

1 (D) In response to a student's comment, the professor says, "Well, they certainly don't resemble most Western art. I suppose that many people would just call them cairns."

2 (A) The professor focuses on one of the purposes of *inuksuit* in saying, "A second purpose of *inuksuit* is more spiritual. The Inuit people say that *inuksuit* provide a glimpse into the human spirit. Each one is built with care. Knowledge of how to build them has been passed down from generation to generation. The human spirit of those who came before is said to be built into each one. Sometimes the Inuit gather at an *inuksuk to* have important meetings, to make decisions, and to worship their ancestors. Some say the *inuksuit* are places for deep thinking. In this regard, the stone statues help the Inuit navigate their way through life."

3 (B) In stating, "This is, uh, speculation for the most part," the professor means that nobody knows for sure, so her analysis may be incorrect.

Dictation

❶ Take a look at this statue here . . . We call that an *inuksuk*. Spell it I-N-U-K-S-U-K. Just so you know, it's an Inuit word.

❷ The *inuksuit* therefore serve this purpose. They show travelers waypoints so that they don't get lost on their journeys.

❸ The Inuit people say that *inuksuit* provide a glimpse into the human spirit.

---

iBT Practice Test

p. 120

Answers

PART 1

1 (D)		2 (B)		3 (C)		4 (B)		5 (C)	
6 *Voyager 1*: [2], [3]		*Voyager 2*: [1], [4]				7 (D)			
8 (D)		9 [2], [3]		10 (A)		11 (B)			

PART 2

1 (C)	2 (C)	3 (A)	4 (C)	5 (D)
6 (A)	7 (B)			

PART 1

[1–3] Conversation

| Script |

Listen to part of a conversation between a student and a Chemistry Department office secretary.

W1 Student: Uh, hello. You work in this office, don't you?

W2 Chemistry Department Office Secretary: I sure do. Can I assist you with something?

W1: I hope so. Uh, I'm a transfer student here, and I'm a bit confused. I'm trying to figure out how I can get credit for the chemistry classes I took when I attended Lakeside University. Could you give me some assistance, please?

W2: That's no problem. What you need to do is fairly simple. Do you happen to have a copy of the course catalog from your previous school?

W1: Yes, I do. I've got it right here.

W2: Great. And you've got a course catalog from our school, right?

W1: Er . . . No, I don't have that yet.

W2: Okay, you need to acquire one from the Registrar's office. I think they cost three dollars, um, just so you know. But in the meantime, let me give you something . . . Hold on a second . . . Aha, here you go . . . This brochure contains a complete course description of all the classes taught in the Chemistry Department here.

W1: Thanks. So, um . . . what am I supposed to do with this?

W2: Take a look at the descriptions of the courses you took. Then, compare them with the descriptions of the courses taught here. You might have a bit of a problem for the high-level courses. But the low-level classes, uh, you know, the introductory classes . . . should be pretty easy.

W1: I took eight courses at Lakeside.

W2: You must be a junior then, right?

W1: Yes, I am. I decided to transfer here because I need to be closer to my family. Lakeside is just too far away from home.

W2: I can understand that. Anyway, uh, find the classes that match the ones you took. Then, find the professor who's listed as the instructor of the course. Show him or her the course descriptions. If the professor agrees they are basically the same, you can get the paper signed. Turn that in to the Registrar's office, and you'll receive transfer credit.

W1: Okay, that sounds straightforward enough. Oh, wait a minute. I have to get a paper signed? What paper?

W2: It's a transfer credit form. You can go to the Registrar's office to pick one up. Uh, since you're a junior, I suppose you need to pick up a bunch of them. Good luck.

W1: Thanks so much for your help. I appreciate it. I guess I know where I need to head to next.

1 Understanding Attitude Question

Ⓓ The employee gives complete explanations to the student's questions during the conversation.

2 Detail Question

Ⓑ The employee says, "Aha, here you go . . . This brochure contains a complete course description of all the classes taught in the Chemistry Department here."

3 Making Inferences Question

Ⓒ The employee says, "You can go to the Registrar's office to pick one up." Then, the student responds by saying, "I guess I know where I need to head to next."

[4–7] **Lecture #1**

| Script |

Listen to part of a lecture in an astronomy class.

M Professor: Last week, someone asked about the *Voyager* missions. So I thought I'd start today's class by talking about them for a bit. The *Voyager* program was one of the most ambitious space missions in history. The plan was to send two probes through the solar system and then beyond it while recording as much information as possible. Thanks to the *Voyager* probes, we have greatly expanded our knowledge of the universe. In fact, right now, the *Voyager* probes are the two most distant manmade objects from Earth. Isn't that fascinating?

So, uh, the plan began in the 1970s. Astronomers knew that in the late 1970s and early 1980s, Jupiter, Saturn, Uranus, and Neptune would be lined up. Uh, by that, I mean that their orbits would take them close together. By using the gravity field of each planet that they passed, the probes could get an extra boost to travel to the next one. This provided NASA with a chance to send space probes to explore these planets up close. A decision was made to send two of them.

Each *Voyager* probe was small and light, weighing fewer than 800 kilograms. Take a look at *Voyager 1* up on the screen. Notice the large antenna used to send information back here. Most of the rest of the equipment is scientific instruments and cameras for collecting data. The probe was designed incredibly well, uh, especially considering the technology of the time.

W Student: I don't see any solar panels on it. How does it get power?

M: There aren't any. Each probe has a plutonium core. And, uh, it's not like the plutonium used in nuclear bombs. It's contained in a special reactor which generates about thirty volts of electricity. That's enough for the probe's functions. As the plutonium decays, the power decreases. But that's a slow process, so there's enough plutonium to create power for at least fifty years.

Each probe was given a different flight path. *Voyager 1* would fly by Jupiter, Saturn, and Titan, Saturn's largest moon. *Voyager 2* would fly by Jupiter, Saturn, Uranus, and Neptune. They had different launch windows as well. *Voyager 2* launched first on August 20, 1977. *Voyager 1* was launched on September 5, 1977. Both were sent up on top of a Titan-Centaur rocket. In space, distances between objects are great, so it took time to reach the planets. *Voyager 1* reached Jupiter in March 1979, and *Voyager 2* got there in July 1979. They both arrived at Saturn in the early 1980s, and *Voyager 2* made it to Uranus in 1986 and Neptune in 1989.

What they discovered, well . . . It changed how we view the solar system. The probes took some of the first closeup photographs of these planets. They discovered many moons around the gas giants. And they learned that some moons weren't frozen rocks. For example, Io, one of Jupiter's moons, has extensive volcanic activity. Other moons show signs of surface activity. The probes also discovered that all four outer planets have ring systems more complex and extensive than anyone had imagined. Further data gathered dealt with the planets' orbits, atmospheric compositions, magnetic fields, and radiation.

After completing their primary missions, the probes continued moving through space. Right now, they're beyond the known edge of the solar system. So we can say that they're in interstellar space. They continue sending data, too. Much of the data we're receiving has to do with magnetic fields and cosmic rays. While the crafts will eventually lose power, they'll continue moving toward the distant stars.

Answer Explanation

4 Understanding Organization Question

Ⓑ The professor says, "Last week, someone asked about the *Voyager* missions. So I thought I'd start today's class by talking about them for a bit."

5 Understanding Attitude Question

Ⓒ The professor remarks, "Take a look at *Voyager 1* up on the screen. Notice the large antenna used to send information back here. Most of the rest of the equipment is scientific instruments and cameras for collecting data. The probe was designed incredibly well, uh, especially considering the technology of the time."

6 Connecting Content Question

Voyager 1: ②, ③   *Voyager 2*: ①, ④

About *Voyager 1*, the professor says, "*Voyager 1* would fly by Jupiter, Saturn, and Titan, Saturn's largest moon," and, "*Voyager 1* reached Jupiter in March 1979, and *Voyager 2* got there in July 1979." Regarding *Voyager 2*, the professor comments, "*Voyager 2* would fly by Jupiter, Saturn, Uranus, and Neptune. They had different launch windows as well. *Voyager 2* launched first on August 20,

1977."

7 Detail Question

Ⓓ The professor states, "Right now, they're beyond the known edge of the solar system. So we can say that they're in interstellar space."

[8–11] Lecture #2

| Script |

Listen to part of a lecture in an environmental science class.

W Professor: 🎧11 Forest fires are good things . . . **Shocked I said that?** Sure, you are. You're probably amazed because forest fires can cause great amounts of damage and kill people and animals. They destroy the habitats of countless animals as well. But there are several reasons forest fires are beneficial. Let me name four of them for you now . . . They clear the forest floor. They create new habitats. They kill insects and diseases. And they allow for new generations of growth.

Now, let me explain these benefits one by one. First is, uh, clearing the forest floor. What does that mean? Well, as a forest grows, the spaces between larger trees fill up with smaller trees, brush, dead branches, and dead trees. Over time, this builds up a great amount. If there are no fires for a long time, this brush can create an enormous fire when one does occur. That can result in a forest fire burning out of control. Essentially, everything on the floor is like fuel that makes a fire bigger and more dangerous. Luckily, forest fires occur at regular intervals. These fires kill undergrowth, provide space for new growth, and nourish the soil with nutrients from the burned undergrowth. And remember that many trees have thick bark. So they're protected from fire and don't die during small forest fires.

M Student: If that's true, then, uh, then why do we even fight forest fires? I mean, um . . . shouldn't we just let them burn?

W: We mostly fight them to prevent them from spreading too far. Today, we sometimes let them burn as long as they aren't anywhere near residential areas. In the past, we tended to extinguish them as quickly as possible. But we slowly learned that this method permitted the buildup of too much undergrowth. As a result, when fires happened, they became too big and got out of control. Nowadays, smaller, more controllable burns are preferred.

Now, another benefit is that forest fires provide new habitats. Removing heavy undergrowth makes room for grasses and other plants to grow. This, in turn, provides new food sources for forest animals. Burning heavy undergrowth also increases a forest's water supply. How? Well, fewer plants are using water, so the runoff makes streams fuller. This, in turn, allows more plant growth and attracts more animals.

A third benefit is that they kill diseases and insects. Trees suffer from diseases just like people do. In fact, more trees die from diseases than are burned in fires each year. Many diseases are caused by fungi. Some fungi tree diseases are aspen cankers, beech bark disease, and Dutch elm disease. Insects also pose serious threats to some trees. One of them is the emerald ash borer. It bores into trees and weakens them until they die. Forest fires kill insects as well as infected trees. This helps stop the spread of diseases and insects to other trees.

The fourth major benefit is that forest fires help with the growth of new generations of plants. You see, uh, some plants need fire to reproduce. The chaparral family of plants is like this. These plants are common in California and thrive in its hot, dry climate. Many species of chaparral require the presence of high temperatures caused by fire for their seeds to germinate in the soil. Some cone-bearing trees also need fire for their cones to open and to drop their seeds. Interestingly, some trees assist in this process. They have resins in their leaves which catch fire easily and help it spread.

Answer Explanation

8 Gist-Purpose Question

Ⓓ The professor is describing a benefit of forest fires by explaining how they clear the forest floor.

9 Detail Question

② , ③ The professor states, "A third benefit is that they kill diseases and insects," and, "Burning heavy undergrowth also increases a forest's water supply. How? Well, fewer plants are using water, so the runoff makes streams fuller."

10 Making Inferences Question

Ⓐ The professor states, "Many species of chaparral require the presence of high temperatures caused by fire for their seeds to germinate in the soil." She therefore implies that its seeds germinate after forest fires end.

11 Understanding Attitude Question

Ⓑ When the professor says, "Shocked I said that?" it can be inferred that she expected her statement to surprise the students.

PART 2

[1–3] Conversation

| Script |

Listen to part of a conversation between a student and a professor.

W Student: Excuse me, Professor Wren. I'm Andrea Salzburg. I was enrolled in your introduction to archaeology class which finished last week. I wonder if you have a moment to chat.

M Professor: Of course, Andrea. I was just grading the final exams in your class. I'll be posting the grades soon. You'll be happy to know that you got an A.

W: I did? Wow! That's great news. And, uh, you remember me?

M: Sure. You did stellar work all semester. You spoke up in class, and your paper was well researched. You were easily one of the top students in the class. You don't happen to be an Archaeology major, do you?

W: No, sir. I'm majoring in International Relations, but, uh, I came here to ask about the possibility of majoring in Archaeology.

M: Do you mean you'd like to change majors?

W: I don't believe so. I really enjoy the classes I take in my current major. I also think I can probably have a good career in diplomacy in the future. However, I loved your class. So I wonder if it would be possible to double-major. I mean, uh, it wouldn't be too much of a burden on me, would it?

M: Hmm . . . Let me see . . . You're a sophomore, right?

W: Yes, sir.

M: So you've just finished your third semester here. You have five more to go. Uh, I'm assuming, of course, that you plan to graduate in four years. Now, to major in Archaeology, you need to take a minimum of eight classes in this department. You must also take two classes in a related field. Most students do that in History or Anthropology. So you'd have to enroll in one Archaeology class every semester until you graduate. And you'd need to enroll in two during two semesters.

W: Or I could do summer school, right?

M: That's correct. This department always offers classes during the summer. So to answer your question . . . Yes, you could easily double-major.

W: That's great news. But . . . I don't just want to take classes. I'd like to do some fieldwork as well. You know, go on a dig or something. How easy is that to do?

M: You're in luck. I plan to lead some students on a dig during summer break after next semester ends. My specialty is Incan archaeology. So my group will be visiting Peru. We'll be digging close to Machu Picchu for six weeks.

W: That sounds incredible. How do I sign up for it?

M: I'm not accepting applications until the spring semester begins. But I'll inform you as soon as that happens. Just so you know, the cost will be around $4,500. Will that be a problem?

W: It shouldn't be. But I'll need to check with my parents first.

1 Gist-Purpose Question

Ⓒ The student asks the professor, "So I wonder if it would be possible to double-major. I mean, uh, it wouldn't be too much of a burden on me, would it?"

2 Understanding Attitude Question

Ⓒ The professor tells the student, "You were easily one of the top students in the class."

3 Detail Question

Ⓐ The professor says, "You're in luck. I plan to lead some students on a dig during summer break after next semester ends. My specialty is Incan archaeology. So my group will be visiting Peru. We'll be digging close to Machu Picchu for six weeks."

[4–7] Lecture

| Script |

Listen to part of a lecture in an education class.

M Professor: I'd like to cover the education reforms which happened in the United States in the nineteenth century now. First, let me discuss some of the education methods used then. Education differed in the various states after the American Revolution ended. In the northern states, there were both private and public schools. In general, wealthy families sent their children to private schools. They normally paid high tuition to do so. Some families also had private tutors teach their children at their homes. These children often proceeded to study at universities such as Harvard or Yale.

Yet most children attended public schools. This was particularly true of those living in rural areas. The majority of these schools were one-room buildings with a single teacher. All the students studied together no matter how old they were. Older students helped the teacher instruct the younger ones. These schools were supported by local taxes. But there was usually barely enough money for a teacher and supplies. Children didn't attend school all year. Attendance depended upon the season. Most children lived on farms, so they did farm work to help their families. During the planting and harvesting seasons, they wouldn't attend school. When they did attend school, most of what they learned was basic reading, writing, and math. Back then, many people were deeply religious, so schools taught morality and enforced strict discipline. So, uh . . . yes? You with your hand up?

W Student: You mentioned the northern states, but what about the South?

M: Education was different there. Few rural areas had any schools. There were some large private schools in towns and cities. But the southern states had fewer public schools than the northern ones. There were, however, many private teachers. They would travel from place to place seeking work with those who could pay them. And like in the North, many southern children worked on family farms. Most of what they learned came from their families.

This changed in the middle of the nineteenth century though. Most of the changes were thanks to the efforts of Horace Mann, a politician from Massachusetts. Mann was a strong believer in education reform and, in my opinion, one of the most influential educators in history. He had studied the education system in Prussia, a German state. He was impressed with its education system and wanted to use it as a model of reform in the U.S.

First, Mann believed children should be grouped in classes according to their ages. They should then progress together from grade to grade. Students would therefore start together in elementary school and then move on to secondary school. They would graduate upon finishing the last grade and receive a certificate of achievement. Now, uh, this is normal to us. But at that time, most children didn't study much beyond elementary school. Second, Mann wanted schools to be supported by more public funds. These were raised by increasing property taxes. Third, Mann believed that schools should have no religious connections. He also disagreed with using harsh discipline. Finally, he knew that more teachers were needed, so he initiated a program to train high school graduates as teachers.

Mann became the Secretary of Education in Massachusetts in 1837. He promptly enacted his reform ideas. He also wrote about his beliefs on education. He argued that school reform would improve literacy rates and make children more disciplined. His ideas quickly spread to other states. By 1870, every American state offered free elementary education. And by the early twentieth century, most states had passed laws making school attendance mandatory.

Answer Explanation

4 Detail Question

ⓒ The professor comments, "Children didn't attend school all year. Attendance depended upon the season. Most children lived on farms, so they did farm work to help their families. During the planting and harvesting seasons, they wouldn't attend school."

5 Gist-Purpose Question

ⓓ The professor compares the education system in the southern American states with those in the northern states.

6 Understand Attitude Question

Ⓐ The professor says, "Mann was a strong believer in education reform and, in my opinion, one of the most influential educators in history."

7 Connecting Content Question

Ⓑ First, the professor states, "First, Mann believed children should be grouped in classes according to their ages. They should then progress together from grade to grade. Students would therefore start together in elementary school and then move on to secondary school." Then, the professor comments, "Mann became the Secretary of Education in Massachusetts in 1837. He promptly enacted his reform ideas." So it is likely that Massachusetts students were grouped according to their age after Horace Mann became the Secretary of Education in that state.

| Vocabulary Review

p. 130

Answers

A
1	generates	2	equipment	3	glimpse
4	occur	5	methods		

B
1	a	2	b	3	a	4	b	5	a
6	b	7	a	8	b	9	a		

Basic Practice

p. 133

Answers   A Ⓐ   B Ⓑ   C Ⓐ   D Ⓒ

Script

A

Listen to part of a lecture in a history of technology class.

W Professor: Look at this picture here . . . Recognize it . . . ? It's the Electrical Numerical Integrator and Calculator. Okay, perhaps you've heard of ENIAC? Yes, now I see some heads nodding. ENIAC is widely considered one of the first computers.

As you can see from the picture, it was enormous. How big was it? Well, it had more than 17,000 vacuum tubes and 70,000 resistors. It took up 167 square meters of space and weighed thirty tons.

It was developed in 1946 and was intended to do many things, including making calculations for the design of the hydrogen bomb and predicting the weather. It was state-of-the-art technology when it was created. It could do 5,000 addition problems, 357 multiplication problems, or thirty-eight division problems in one second. Of course, the mobile phones you carry in your pockets are much more powerful than ENIAC was. But for the next decade, it would be just about the most powerful computer in existence.

Answer Explanation

Ⓐ The professor says, "It was developed in 1946 and was intended to do many things, including making calculations for the design of the hydrogen bomb and predicting the weather. It was state-of-the-art technology when it was created. It could do 5,000 addition problems, 357 multiplication problems, or thirty-eight division problems in one second." So she mostly discusses ENIAC to talk about its capabilities.

B

Listen to part of a lecture in an astronomy class.

M Professor: In 1997, the *Cassini* space probe blasted off from the Earth. Seven years later, it arrived at its destination: the planet Saturn. For the next thirteen years, it provided a wealth of data on Saturn, its ring system, and some of its moons.

One of its greatest feats was sending the lander *Huygens* to Titan, Saturn's biggest moon. *Huygens* transmitted pictures of Titan's surface as well as other information back to Earth. We astronomers are interested in Titan since it may have the conditions necessary for life on it.

But that wasn't all *Cassini* did. It discovered new moons orbiting Saturn. It learned about the rings of Saturn. It investigated some other moons of Saturn, including Enceladus. That moon is another prime candidate for alien life. I want to look at some of the pictures *Cassini* sent back. And I'll tell you just why they're so important as we look at them.

Answer Explanation

Ⓑ The professor focuses on the accomplishments of *Cassini* while talking about it.

C

Listen to part of a lecture in an art class.

M Professor: Here's a question for you: Is photography art? It's an interesting question because people are so divided about it. My guess is that about half of you think it's art while the other half disagree.

Photography has been around since the mid-1800s. The first photographers actually didn't believe their work was art. In fact, they strongly argued against being considered artists. But that began to change in the early 1900s. One of the reasons for this was Ansel Adams. I'm sure you all know about him. He took many beautiful photographs of nature. His pictures of Yosemite National Park brought him great fame. He and other photographers he associated with wanted their work to be considered art.

Not everyone was convinced though. For instance, look at the photographs that are featured in newspapers and magazines. Those are surely not works of art. But what about other works? Look at this one . . . and this one here . . . and this one . . . Would you say that they're art?

Answer Explanation

Ⓐ The professor discusses the events in the lecture in chronological order.

D

Listen to part of a lecture in an urban design class.

W Professor: In recent times, there has been a major trend among urban designers. They are adding green spaces to cities. As you should be well aware, urban designers these days try to be environmentally conscious. Making cities greener is one highly effective way.

I suppose the most famous urban green space in the world is Central Park. It's located in the borough of Manhattan in New York City. It's a huge park that takes up several blocks of valuable real estate. There are, of course, parks in virtually every other urban area in the world. And more are being added these days.

Why is that? There are several reasons. One is that these

parks provide places for people to spend their leisure time in. They can go for walks in them or relax. Parks can also help fight urban heat island. We talked about that in last Friday's class. Can anyone tell me how they are useful in that regard? Brian, what do you think?

Answer Explanation

Ⓒ About Central Park, the professor states, "I suppose the most famous urban green space in the world is Central Park."

Practice with Short Passages
p. 134

A

| Answers | 1 Ⓑ | 2 Ⓓ |

| Script |

Listen to part of a lecture in an architecture class.

W Professor: Let's continue last week's talk about architecture in medieval times. Last week, we got to the year 1000. We discussed Carolingian and Ottonian architecture. These styles were prominent from around 800 to 1000. They are also known by the name Pre-Romanesque architecture.

Right now, I'd like to go over Romanesque architecture. It lasted in Europe from around the year 1000 to 1170. We usually divide it into two periods: Early Romanesque and Mature Romanesque. Let's look at some pictures on the screen as I talk. As you can see here . . . and here . . . and here . . . there are elements of Roman, Byzantine, and Islamic architecture in Romanesque works.

When we think of Romanesque architecture, three types of buildings come to mind: cathedrals . . . monasteries . . . and castles . . . Impressive, aren't they? Romanesque architecture first developed in parts of northern Italy, France, and Spain. Structures built in this style shared several characteristics. Let's see . . . First, they had very thick walls. Look at this . . . and this . . . The walls had few openings. And any windows the buildings had were quite small. They also use semicircular arches. See here . . . Arcades were popular too. Ah, an arcade is a row of arches . . . like this . . . Towers were another popular feature. They could be square . . . circular . . . or even octagonal . . . As for the roofs, some were made of wood while others were made of stone.

Look at this picture of Ripoll Monastery. It's a Benedictine monastery in the town of Ripoll. That's in Catalonia in Spain. Notice the thick walls here . . . the high tower . . . and the arcade. This is a perfect example of an Early Romanesque structure. Now look at this. It's St. Andrew's Church in Krakow, Poland. Again, you can see the typical

features of a Romanesque structure. I love this one, so let's look at it carefully.

Answer Explanation

1 Ⓑ During the lecture, the professor describes the characteristics of Romanesque architecture and shows some examples of it to the students.

2 Ⓓ The professor says, "Look at this picture of Ripoll Monastery. It's a Benedictine monastery in the town of Ripoll. That's in Catalonia in Spain. Notice the thick walls here . . . the high tower . . . and the arcade. This is a perfect example of an Early Romanesque structure."

B

| Answers | 1 Ⓒ | 2 Ⓐ |

| Script |

Listen to part of a lecture in an education class.

W1 Professor: We have a test coming up next week. I imagine some of you have already started studying. Before the test, I assume all of you will study. How will you study? Most of you will read your notes and your textbook. You'll read them over and over again as you try to memorize everything we've learned. Can anybody tell me what kind of learning method this is? Martina, your hand is up.

W2 Student: It's rote learning, isn't it, Professor Herbert?

W1: That's correct. Thank you. The memorizing of information by constantly repeating it is rote learning. This is one of the most common learning methods. It's one that all of you used in the past and likely continue to use today. For instance, how did you learn the alphabet when you were younger? In all likelihood, your parents and teachers made you repeat it again and again until you knew it perfectly. You did the same thing with numbers. That's how I taught my children to count from one to ten. I made them repeat the numbers until they had memorized them.

As you can see, rote learning is effective. It can let people learn crucial information they will need in the future. It also has some drawbacks. For instance, as soon as the test ends next week, many of you will forget most of the information you learned. That's a big problem with rote learning. If you don't keep practicing it, you're likely to forget certain information. In addition, rote learning doesn't teach critical thinking skills. So you can learn information, but you don't learn analysis. You don't learn to think on your own.

1 ⓒ During the lecture, the professor gives several examples to the students to prove her point.

2 ⒶThe professor says, "In addition, rote learning doesn't teach critical thinking skills. So you can learn information, but you don't learn analysis. You don't learn to think on your own."

Practice with Long Passages

p. 136

A

Answers	1 ⒹD	2 ⒶA	3 ⒸC

| Script |

Listen to part of a lecture in a meteorology class.

W Professor: Some of the most dangerous, yet incredibly beautiful, storms are thunderstorms. They feature heavy rain, high winds, and plenty of lightning and thunder. Let me talk about them with you for a few moments.

For a thunderstorm to form, there needs to be lots of moisture in the air. Second, warm air must rise above cooler air. This can happen in three ways. First is when warm air hits a mountain chain and is forced upward. The second way is when a warm front and a cold front collide. The less dense warm air rises above the denser cold air. The third way happens on very hot sunny days. Air close to the ground heats up from the sun's hot rays striking the Earth's surface. The air then begins to rise above the cooler air on top of it.

M Student: Can the third way happen anywhere? I mean, uh, can it happen over the ocean?

W: It's possible. But it normally happens over large areas of open land, uh, such as farmland. These types of places get a more even amount of direct sunlight than cities or forests do. And note that oceans absorb lots of heat, too. However, as long as there is enough heat, the third way can happen anywhere. Now, uh, as the air rises, it forms cumulus clouds. These are small puffy white clouds . . . you know, like the ones we can see in the sky today. The air cools as it rises. Then, the moisture in the air condenses into clouds. As more air rises and cools, the cumulus clouds become dark, towering thunderstorm clouds. We call them cumulonimbus clouds.

The clouds get darker and heavier with condensed raindrops. Soon, rain falls, and lightning and thunder start. If the air is unstable with fast-rising warm air and falling cold air, there are high winds. These can form powerful downdrafts in the center of the storm. If these cause many clouds to combine, a large thunderstorm,

called a super cell, forms. These usually form where warm and cold fronts meet.

After some time, the rain stops, the lightning and thunder end, and the storm goes away. This happens when the downdrafts of cool air are more powerful than the updrafts of warm air. So no new raindrops can form into clouds. Slowly, the storm disappears from the bottom to the top.

1 Ⓓ In discussing how warm air rises above cooler air, the professor is explaining a condition necessary for thunderstorms to occur.

2 Ⓐ The professor comments, "But it normally happens over large areas of open land, uh, such as farmland. These types of places get a more even amount of direct sunlight than cities or forests do."

3 Ⓒ The professor says, "The clouds get darker and heavier with condensed raindrops. Soon, rain falls, and lightning and thunder start. If the air is unstable with fast-rising warm air and falling cold air, there are high winds. These can form powerful downdrafts in the center of the storm. If these cause many clouds to combine, a large thunderstorm, called a super cell, forms."

❶ For a thunderstorm to form, there needs to be lots of moisture in the air.

❷ It's possible. But it normally happens over large areas of open land, uh, such as farmland.

❸ This happens when the downdrafts of cool air are more powerful than the updrafts of warm air. So no new raindrops can form into clouds.

B

Answers	1 ⒹD	2 ⒷB	3 ⒶA

| Script |

Listen to part of a lecture in a geology class.

M Professor: The North and South poles are covered by ice caps. Both formed in similar ways and have similar features. But they have some differences. I'd like to compare the two before we finish for the day.

Both poles formed due to their location in relation to the sun. At the poles, the amount of heat and sunlight are less than anywhere else on the Earth's surface. At times, there's virtually no sunlight for months. This has created a harsh environment of extreme cold. As a result, there are permanent ice caps at both places.

W Student: Permanent? Are you sure? Couldn't they melt

completely someday?

M: I consider that highly unlikely. While there's some melting during summer, the ice caps are too large to melt entirely. They're more likely to expand. For example, during past ice ages, they grew so much that they covered large portions of the world.

Now, uh, what about their differences? Well, the main ones are their compositions, sizes, and the thickness of the ice. The northern ice cap is frozen sea water floating on top of more water. The southern one consists of freshwater ice sitting on a landmass. The northern ice cap is about twelve million square kilometers at its greatest size. The southern one is a bit larger. It's slightly smaller than fourteen million square kilometers. Of course, these numbers fluctuate with the seasons.

As for the thickness, the southern ice cap is much thicker. ∩2 The northern one is rarely more than three or four meters thick. The southern one averages more than one and a half kilometers in thickness. Yes, I said kilometers. Much of this ice formed from snowfall that didn't melt. Over time, it transformed into ice. The southern ice cap is so big and thick that it holds around seventy percent of the world's fresh water.

What about life on the ice caps? Well, neither place has any plant life. As for animal life, most is in or near the oceans surrounding them. In the north are polar bears and many species of fish, seals, whales, and birds. In the south are penguins as well as various fish, seals, whales, and other birds. These animals are all carnivores since there's no vegetation to consume.

∩3 **Okay, now, I need to inform you about the term papers you have to write.** This is important. So please listen carefully.

Answer Explanation

1 Ⓓ During his lecture, the professor compares and contrasts the two ice caps.

2 Ⓑ When the professor says, "Yes, I said kilometers," he is indicating to the students that he spoke correctly.

3 Ⓐ In saying, "Okay, now, I need to inform you about the term papers you have to write," it can be inferred that the professor will no longer lecture to the class. Instead, he will discuss an assignment.

Dictation

❶ Both poles formed due to their location in relation to the sun.

❷ I consider that highly unlikely. While there's some melting during summer, the ice caps are too large to melt entirely. They're more likely to expand.

❸ The northern ice cap is frozen sea water floating on top of more water. The southern one consists of freshwater ice sitting on a landmass.

iBT Practice Test
p. 140

Answers

PART 1

1 Ⓑ	2 Ⓐ	3 Ⓑ	4 Ⓒ	5 Ⓐ
6 Ⓑ	7 Ⓑ	8 Ⓒ	9 Ⓑ	10 Ⓑ

11 ②, ③

PART 2

1 Ⓑ	2 Ⓒ	3 Ⓐ	4 Ⓓ	5 Ⓐ
6 ③, ④	7 Ⓒ			

PART 1

[1–3] Conversation

| Script |

Listen to part of a conversation between a student and a professor.

W Student: Professor Gamble, I'm having a hard time with my senior thesis.

M Professor: What's the matter with it, Andrea? You aren't having difficulty finding source material, are you?

W: No, that's not it. It's just that, well . . . I don't really like my topic.

M: Can you explain a bit more, please? What exactly do you dislike about it?

W: Everything, to be honest. I mean, uh, we came up with this topic a few months ago back in spring. I was excited about it at first. I spent all my free time in the school's library doing research this past summer. But, uh, the more research I did, um . . . Well, I actually became less interested in the topic.

M: I see. So what do you propose doing?

W: Is it possible just to stop writing my thesis?

M: Hmm . . . You could do that. I mean, the deadline for dropping a class hasn't passed yet. However, there are two big disadvantages to doing that. First, if you drop the thesis now, you'll get a W on your transcript.

W: A W? What does that mean?

M: It means that you signed up for the class but then withdrew from it. That W will be on your permanent transcript. There's no way to get rid of it. Therefore, any future employers you send your transcript to will see it. To be frank, um, I don't think they'll be impressed if they see that.

W: Oh, yeah. You're right . . . That would be less than ideal.

M: You can say that again. And here's the second disadvantage of quitting. As I recall, you want to attend graduate school to get a PhD. ∩3 In that case, you'd better write a senior thesis then. That's one of the things graduate schools look for. They want to know that you're capable of doing a big independent research project.

W: **Okay, you've convinced me.**

M: That's great.

W: But the topic is still boring. Isn't there any way I can, uh, change the topic?

M: It would be a shame to waste all of the research you have done. But perhaps you can come up with an alternative point of view. That might be a better way to write your thesis. Do you happen to have the outline of your thesis with you?

W: I sure do. It's on my USB stick here. I always carry it around with me.

M: Let's take a look at it. Maybe we can figure out another way to do your paper. I just need to see your outline first. Then, perhaps I can make a suggestion or two.

Answer Explanation

1 **Gist-Content Question**
   Ⓑ About her thesis, the student says, "But, uh, the more research I did, um . . . Well, I actually became less interested in the topic."

2 **Understanding Function Question**
   Ⓐ The professor discusses getting a W on a transcript to tell the student a result of her not doing her thesis.

3 **Understanding Function Question**
   Ⓑ When the student says, "Okay, you've convinced me," she is implying that she will continue to write her thesis.

[4–7] Lecture #1

| Script |

Listen to part of a lecture in a history class.

M Professor: The last landmass on the planet which explorers discovered was Antarctica. For centuries, Europeans believed an enormous continent existed in the southern latitudes. Some thought it was connected to the tips of Africa or South America. However, in the fifteenth and sixteenth centuries, ships sailed south around both continents. So this theory was proved to be wrong.

Nevertheless, the belief in a southern continent persisted. Several ships sailed southward and sighted islands. They also found enormous colonies of seals and many whales. In fact, for the longest time, most explorations in the area were done by sealers and whalers. But none sailed far enough south to see Antarctica.

Between 1772 and 1775, famed British explorer James Cook sailed through the region. He ventured as far as, uh, seventy-one degrees south latitude. He saw no land, so he turned back. Yes, you have a question?

W Student: 🎧7 Yes, sir. Why did he stop there? Why didn't he continue southward to Antarctica?

M: There were two main reasons: heavy drifting ice and bad weather. **Those reasons apply not only to Cook but also to others.** You see, uh, the southern seas have some of the world's most violent storms. And remember that they were sailing in small wooden ships. It was, simply put, dangerous. In fact, Cook's voyage was the last to sail that far south for decades. Interestingly, he sailed completely around Antarctica despite never seeing it.

Antarctica wasn't found until almost fifty years later. During the year 1820, three expeditions sighted Antarctica. They were from Russia, Britain, and the United States. The Russian team first saw Antarctica on January 28, 1820. They were led by Admiral Fabian Bellingshausen. Yet none of the teams landed on the continent. That would be accomplished the following year. Now, uh, there's a bit of controversy regarding who was first. John Davis, an American sealer, claimed he landed there in February 1821. But there's no actual proof of his claim.

During the next few decades, various explorers, sealers, and whalers discovered more islands. Many also sighted Antarctica. Then, in the early 1840s, two important expeditions began. Charles Wilkes led an American team while James Ross led a British one. Wilkes discovered the area now named Wilkes Land. It's near the Indian Ocean. Ross explored the areas called the Ross Ice Shelf and Ross Island. He also discovered Mount Erebus, a volcano on Ross Island. Ross tried to find the south magnetic pole. He seemed to have worked out where it was, but he wasn't able to travel far enough inland to reach it.

Reaching the south magnetic pole and the south geographic pole became goals of future explorers. However, interest in Antarctica disappeared for some time. Why? Well, many people felt it wasn't worth the trouble. They believed they could never penetrate the continent's interior. Then, in the 1890s, there was a revival of interest in Antarctica. Part of the reason was the lack of places to explore. After all, most of the world had been discovered. The interior of Antarctica was among the last unknown places.

Explorers once again determined to find the magnetic and geographic south poles. The initial attempts all failed. Then, in December 1911, a Norwegian team led by Roald Amundsen reached the geographic South Pole. They beat a British team led by Robert Scott by a few weeks. Tragically, the entire British team died while returning to the coast. Let me tell you that story in detail now.

Answer Explanation

4 **Understanding Organization Question**
   Ⓒ During the lecture, the professor talks about various

events in chronological order.

5 Making Inferences Question

Ⓐ The professor states, "Now, uh, there's a bit of controversy regarding who was first. John Davis, an American sealer, claimed he landed there in February 1821. But there's no actual proof of his claim."

6 Detail Question

Ⓑ The professor says, "Then, in the early 1840s, two important expeditions began. Charles Wilkes led an American team while James Ross led a British one. Wilkes discovered the area now named Wilkes Land. It's near the Indian Ocean. Ross explored the areas called the Ross Ice Shelf and Ross Island. He also discovered Mount Erebus, a volcano on Ross Island. Ross tried to find the south magnetic pole. He seemed to have worked out where it was, but he wasn't able to travel far enough inland to reach it."

7 Understanding Function Question

Ⓑ The professor mentions bad weather as causing problems near Antarctica. When he says, "Those reasons apply not only to Cook but also to others," he implies that bad weather affected many ships near Antarctica.

[8–11] Lecture #2

| Script |

Listen to part of a lecture in a zoology class.

W Professor: The hottest and driest place in the United States is Death Valley in California. It gets approximately six centimeters of rain each year. That's it. It's also extremely hot. The hottest recorded temperature there was, um, fifty-six degrees Celsius. The average high in summer is forty-six degrees Celsius. In winter, the temperature can drop below freezing, but that doesn't happen very often. Now, uh, you may think that due to these extreme temperatures, there's little life in Death Valley. After all, even its name suggests a lack of life. However . . . more than 400 species of animals and 1,000 species of plants live there.

Among the common mammals in Death Valley are bats, gophers, rats, squirrels, foxes, bighorn sheep, bobcats, mountain lions, jackrabbits, and coyotes. There are numerous insects, including many species of butterflies. Spiders are plentiful. There are around, um, fifty species of tarantulas living there. Some are venomous, so visitors must be wary around these hairy spiders. As for amphibians, there are several species of frogs and toads. Reptiles such as tortoises, lizards, and snakes, including rattlesnakes, are plentiful.

There are birds as well, but most species are temporary visitors. They stop in the valley in spring for short periods while migrating to and from their winter nesting grounds.

Many of the permanent bird residents live high in the mountains at the edge of the valley. Up there, it's cooler, so there's more water. There's also more vegetation, and nesting sites are found in abundance. Finally, you may be surprised to learn that fish—yes, fish—live in Death Valley. There are only a few species though. The small pupfish is the most common fish. It lives in hot springs, which are often underground. The pupfish is a great example of how animals have adapted to live in Death Valley. It can survive in both very hot and very salty water. It was once part of a larger ecosystem of many fish species. They lived in a large lake that existed before the last ice age. After it ended, the lake dried up, and most of the fish died. Uh, but the pupfish survived.

Now, let's see if you can come up with any other ways the animals I mentioned have adapted to Death Valley. Craig?

M Student: Many are nocturnal, right? And some live underground.

W: Well done. It looks like you did the assigned reading, Craig. Many animals are active at night, when it's cooler. Most snakes hunt at night. So do coyotes. Even prey animals are nocturnal. Coyotes, for example, hunt jackrabbits. These big-eared rabbits can run faster when it's cooler at night. So they can more easily acquire food and avoid coyotes and other predators. In addition, the extreme heat during the day can literally kill animals. So many animals find shade to get out of the sun or burrow underground.

The tortoise is a burrowing animal. It digs a hole underground and becomes inactive during the day. It can also enter a state of dormancy during the hottest part of summer. That lets it save energy and conserve water. Other animals have adapted to the lack of water. Let's see . . . The bighorn sheep can live without water for several days. It loses lots of weight during that time but regains that lost weight when it drinks water again. It can also drink a large amount of water at one time. That helps it survive in case water becomes scarce again. Other animals, such as the kangaroo rat and jackrabbit, don't drink water. They get water from the plants they consume.

Answer Explanation

8 Understanding Organization Question

Ⓒ Throughout the lecture, the professor focuses on the animals that live in Death Valley.

9 Gist-Purpose Question

Ⓑ The professor states, "The small pupfish is the most common fish. It lives in hot springs, which are often underground. The pupfish is a great example of how animals have adapted to live in Death Valley."

10 Understanding Attitude Question

Ⓑ The professor is clearly pleased when she tells the student, "Well done. It looks like you did the assigned reading, Craig."

11 Detail Question

2, 3 About the tortoise, the professor remarks, "The tortoise is a burrowing animal. It digs a hole underground and becomes inactive during the day. It can also enter a state of dormancy during the hottest part of summer. That lets it save energy and conserve water."

PART 2

[1–3] Conversation

| Script |

Listen to part of a conversation between a student and a professor.

M Student: Good afternoon, Professor Hunter. I'm here to apply for a position doing fieldwork with you.

W Professor: Hi, Matt. Um . . . you're a bit late, aren't you? I announced I was accepting applicants more than a month ago.

M: Yeah, I know. I'm really sorry. I wasn't sure about my work schedule until now. I had to talk to my boss at the clothing store I work part time at. I told him that I might not be able to work weekends if I get the position with you. He didn't give me a response until this morning. He said it would be all right since another worker would be able to do my shift. So, uh, that's why I had to wait so long.

W: I see . . . Well, you're definitely qualified for the position, Matt. I remember you told me about how you worked on your family farm in the past. So I know you won't have any problems doing fieldwork in the swamp near the school.

M: That's great. Thanks.

W: However, there were eight available positions when I made the announcement. And I've already filled six of them.

M: Oh . . . What about the other two?

W: There are twenty-six other students who applied. So I need to look over their applications. Do you have your complete application?

M: Right here . . .

W: Okay. Now, um, I need to mention something important. Every student in the Biology Department is required to do fieldwork in order to graduate. You're only a sophomore. There might be some seniors who have applied to work with me. If that is the case, I will have no choice. I'll have to take on the seniors. Otherwise, they won't be able to graduate.

M: Sure. That makes sense. I understand.

W: I know you really want to do fieldwork, so you should probably consider some other options.

M: Such as?

W: Don't just apply for a position with me. Talk to one of the other professors in the department. Professors Jenkins, Watson, and Caldwell are all doing fieldwork projects.

M: I didn't know that. 🎧3 But, um, I haven't taken classes with any of them.

W: That doesn't matter. Tell me who you're applying to work with. Then, I'll put in a good word for you. But just remember . . . I still might accept you for my work. If I don't have to take a senior, you're my top choice. I'll let you know what's going on by tomorrow afternoon. That's the best I can do. How does that sound?

M: That's fine with me, Professor Hunter. Thanks so much.

Answer Explanation

1 Gist-Content Question

Ⓑ The speakers spend most of the conversation talking about the student applying to do some fieldwork with the professor or someone else.

2 Detail Question

Ⓒ The professor says, "Now, um, I need to mention something important. Every student in the Biology Department is required to do fieldwork in order to graduate. You're only a sophomore. There might be some seniors who have applied to work with me. If that is the case, I will have no choice. I'll have to take on the seniors. Otherwise, they won't be able to graduate."

3 Understanding Attitude Question

Ⓐ When the professor says, "Then, I'll put in a good word for you," she means that she will recommend the student to another professor. When a person "puts in a good word" for another individual, it means that the person says good things about the other person.

[4–7] Lecture

| Script |

Listen to part of a lecture in an urban design class.

W Professor: As you know, skyscrapers are tall buildings and are common throughout the world. For a long time, we couldn't build skyscrapers. Then, in the middle of the nineteenth century, several inventions allowed them to be constructed. For instance, strong yet lightweight steel and reinforced concrete were developed. Elevators that could reach high floors were invented. Electrical systems to illuminate the buildings were created. And improved water pumps and systems for plumbing were made.

The world's first skyscraper was the Home Insurance Building in Chicago, Illinois. It was finished in 1885. It was only ten stories high, which is tiny compared to today's skyscrapers. Soon, more appeared in major cities. They were large buildings used mainly as office space. As companies expanded, many built their own skyscrapers. Companies frequently competed to build bigger and higher buildings. In the early twentieth century, New York City saw the greatest growth of skyscrapers, resulting in a skyline of tall buildings.

Not everyone liked this. Many tall buildings on one street created a canyon effect. Basically, some parts of the street and nearby buildings got little or no sunlight. People who once had nice views suddenly could only see concrete walls. As a result, many urban dwellers wanted laws enacted to limit the heights of skyscrapers. Unfortunately for them, several of their attempts failed. Then, in 1913, the Equitable Building in Manhattan was completed. It was a concrete monolith that dominated the nearby buildings and neighborhood. Here's a picture of it on the screen . . . Big, huh . . . ? Well, many people disliked it, so this new skyscraper—and several others—led directly to the reform of New York City's zoning laws in 1916.

The new zoning law didn't limit building heights. However, buildings couldn't be erected with continuous straight walls. Instead, they had to be built with setbacks. Do you know that term . . . ? Hmm . . . Maybe not. Well, a setback is like a series of steps. Essentially, the building is wide at the bottom and narrower at the top. You can see what I mean here in this picture of Manhattan today. Note the many buildings with setbacks here . . . here . . . and here . . . The city was divided into zones. Those zones determined how high the initial wall could be. In some zones, it could only be as high as the street below was wide. In other zones, it could be one and a half, two, or two and a half times as high. The wider the street, the higher the initial wall. Some building walls could be up to 200 feet high. That's around sixty meters. Any further height had to be built as setbacks. The main purpose of this law was to permit more sunlight to reach street level.

M Student: Did other cities follow New York's example with regard to height limits?

W: Good question, Peter. The answer is yes, many did. In addition, setbacks spread around the world in the 1920s even in places without height laws. Setbacks inspired a generation of architects to make wonderful buildings. The Art Deco style is noted for using setbacks. Two noted examples are the Empire State Building and the Chrysler Building in New York City.

Some cities had actually already limited heights before 1916. Baltimore had done so due to a fear of fires. In 1904, Los Angeles passed a law limiting building heights to 150 feet, uh, around forty-six meters. This law was later changed in 1968. Today, L.A. has plenty of skyscrapers. Some have setbacks, but there's no law requiring them.

Answer Explanation

4 Gist-Content Question

Ⓓ The professor mostly focuses on how laws changed

the way skyscrapers were made in her lecture.

5 Understanding Organization Question

Ⓐ About the Equitable Building, the professor points out, "Well, many people disliked it, so this new skyscraper—and several others—led directly to the reform of New York City's zoning laws in 1916."

6 Detail Question

③, ④ First, the professor states, "Buildings couldn't be erected with continuous straight walls. Instead, they had to be built with setbacks." Then, the professor notes, "The main purpose of this law was to permit more sunlight to reach street level."

7 Making Inferences Question

Ⓒ The professor lectures, "The Art Deco style is noted for using setbacks. Two noted examples are the Empire State Building and the Chrysler Building in New York City." So it can be inferred that the Empire State Building was designed in the Art Deco style.

| Vocabulary Review   p. 150

Answers

A
1 dense   2 prominent   3 construct
4 harsh   5 voyage

B
1 b   2 a   3 b   4 a   5 a
6 a   7 a   8 b   9 b

Basic Practice

p. 153

Answers

A Ⓑ   B Ⓐ

C Sigmund Freud: ②   Carl Jung: ①, ③   D Ⓒ

| Script |

A

Listen to part of a conversation between a student and a professor.

M Student: Professor Beale, you're teaching a seminar on Egyptian archaeology next fall?

W Professor: Yes, I am, Nate. Are you interested in taking it?

M: Totally. But, uh, I don't know if I'm qualified.

W: Have you taken Archaeology 47 yet? You can't enroll in the seminar without it.

M: Oh, no. I haven't. Is it being offered this summer?

W: As a matter of fact, I'm going to be teaching it during the first session. I know you are staying here this summer. So you might want to register for it.

Answer Explanation

Ⓑ The professor mentions she will teach a class during summer school. It is required to take a seminar. So if the student attends summer school, he will probably take a seminar in the fall.

B

Listen to part of a lecture in an anthropology class.

M Professor: Humans discovered agriculture sometime between 10,000 and 12,000 years ago. Over time, ancient farmers noticed that their fields produced fewer and fewer crops. Sometimes once-fertile land simply stopped producing crops. The main reason was that the crops were removing nutrients from the soil. And new nutrients weren't being put into the soil. Farmers needed a method to improve the quality of the soil so that they could grow more crops.

It was around 6,000 years ago that farmers learned about crop rotation. There is evidence that farmers in Mesopotamia used it. Basically, each year, farmers planted different crops in their fields. On occasion, they didn't plant any crops at all. Instead, they left some fields fallow. Ancient farmers preferred the three-field method. They would plant something like corn or wheat in one field and legumes such as peas in another. They would plant nothing in the third. Each year, they would rotate the fields they planted crops in and left fallow. This kept the

soil fertile and helped replace lost nutrients.

Answer Explanation

Ⓐ The professor states, "Over time, ancient farmers noticed that their fields produced fewer and fewer crops. Sometimes once-fertile land simply stopped producing crops. The main reason was that the crops were removing nutrients from the soil. And new nutrients weren't being put into the soil. Farmers needed a method to improve the quality of the soil so that they could grow more crops." Then, the professor discusses the benefits of crop rotation. So the likely result of ancient farmers practicing crop rotation is that their fields produced more crops.

C

Listen to part of a lecture in a psychology class.

W Professor: Two of the biggest names in psychology were Sigmund Freud and Carl Jung. The two psychologists knew each other and were initially friends. However, they had a fallout mainly due to their disagreements on psychological theory.

M Student: Like what?

W: Well, I plan to go into detail on both of them today. But, um, I suppose I can tell you a couple of differences now. First, they differed regarding the human mind. Freud believed it was based upon the id, the ego, and the superego. I'll define these terms later, so don't ask now. Jung, however, divided the mind into the ego, the personal unconscious, and the collective unconscious. Jung's thoughts, in case you're curious, were inspired by his studies of Buddhism and Hinduism.

The men also disagreed about dreams. Freud believed studying dreams could tell a lot about a person. He thought a person's deepest desires were reflected in that individual's dreams. Jung, however, focused on the symbolic imagery of dreams. He thought dreams could have a variety of meanings.

Answer Explanation

Sigmund Freud: ②   Carl Jung: ①, ③

About Sigmund Freud, the professor comments, "First, they differed regarding the human mind. Freud believed it was based upon the id, the ego, and the superego." Regarding Carl Jung, the professor notes, "Jung's thoughts, in case you're curious, were inspired by his studies of Buddhism and Hinduism," and, "Jung, however, focused on the symbolic imagery of dreams. He thought dreams could have a variety of meanings."

D

Listen to part of a lecture in an environmental science class.

M Professor: In April 1815, the volcano Mount Tambora erupted in Indonesia. It was the most powerful volcanic eruption in more than 1,000 years. It killed at least 70,000 people and cast vast amounts of rock and dust into the air.

The following year, spring came as it normally did. But then the weather turned cold in summer. In Spain, the weather never rose above fifteen degrees Celsius the entire year. In the United States, the temperature dropped below freezing in June. It snowed in parts of Northern Europe throughout summer. 1816 became known as "The Year without Summer."

Basically, the dust cloud from Tambora obstructed light from the sun. This caused global temperatures to plummet in the Northern Hemisphere. Countries such as Ireland got much more rain than normal in summer. There were crop failures in Europe and North America. People in both places starved to death. This would affect society in a variety of ways.

Answer Explanation

Ⓒ The professor says, "In the United States, the temperature dropped below freezing in June," and, "Countries such as Ireland got much more rain than normal in summer."

Practice with Short Passages   p. 154

A

Answers

1 Ⓑ   2 Day School: ② Night School: ①, ③, ④

| Script |

Listen to part of a conversation between a student and a professor.

M1 Professor: You understand what I was talking about now, right, Jeff?

M2 Student: I sure do, Professor Malone. Thanks for explaining everything to me. Now, uh, before I go . . . I have one more question. Do you mind?

M1: Please go ahead.

M2: Thanks. As you know, I work full time in addition to attending school. Well, uh, my boss wants me to work during the day. So I have to start attending night school. What do you think of that?

M1: Hmm . . . Not every class is offered at night. So you might not get to take the classes you want.

M2: Okay. What about the quality of the lectures? How good are they?

M1: Quite good. There's no difference between day and night school in that regard. But, uh, attendance in night classes is often lower than in day classes. That can actually give you an advantage. In smaller classes, you'll get more opportunities to speak up. And the professors can give you more individual attention.

M2: Huh, I never thought of that. I guess I'll tell my boss I can change shifts once the semester ends. Thanks for the information, sir.

Answer Explanation

1 Ⓑ The professor tells the student, "There's no difference between day and night school in that regard. But, uh, attendance in night classes is often lower than in day classes. That can actually give you an advantage. In smaller classes, you'll get more opportunities to speak up. And the professors can give you more individual attention." So he explains about the quality of both classes.

2 Day School: ② Night School: ①, ③, ④
About day school, the professor states, "Attendance in night classes is often lower than in day classes." Regarding night school, the professor remarks, "Not every class is offered at night," and, "In smaller classes, you'll get more opportunities to speak up. And the professors can give you more individual attention."

B

Answers

1 Ⓓ   2 Dune: ②, ③ Wadi: ①, ④

| Script |

Listen to part of a lecture in a geology class.

W Professor: Okay, so now you know how deserts form. We should cover some of the landforms that are found in deserts now. You might be surprised to learn that there are a wide variety of them.

Sand is the most prominent feature of the majority of deserts. When the wind blows, the sand in deserts can move. In many instances, it forms dunes. These are essentially large formations of sand that take on various shapes. There are, for instance, crescent dunes, which are the most common types of dunes in the world. There are also linear dunes, which form straight lines. Dunes do not remain constant. Look at some place in the desert and then look at it again a month later. If the wind has been blowing, it will appear different. Dunes can move and change their shapes relatively quickly.

Now, uh, what about wadis? These are another type of desert landform. A wadi is a dry riverbed in a desert.

Remember that many deserts were once fertile lands with rivers and streams. When they became deserts, the waterways dried up. But the remains of these rivers can still be seen. Oh, some of you from the southwestern part of the country may know these as arroyos. That's simply another name for a wadi. You probably also know that wadis can be very dangerous when it rains. Deserts are very dry, so water tends to remain on the surface rather than getting absorbed into the soil. When it rains, flashfloods can happen quickly. A wadi is about the worst place you can possibly be during a desert rainstorm. Even just a centimeter or two of rainfall can create a raging flood in one of them.

Answer Explanation

1 Ⓓ First, the professor says, "Sand is the most prominent feature of the majority of deserts." Then, she adds, "Remember that many deserts were once fertile lands with rivers and streams." The professor therefore implies that the sand in most deserts used to be fertile soil.

2 Dune: ②, ③   Wadi: ①, ④
About dunes, the professor says, "When the wind blows, the sand in deserts can move. In many instances, it forms dunes. These are essentially large formations of sand that take on various shapes," and, "Dunes do not remain constant. Look at some place in the desert and then look at it again a month later. If the wind has been blowing, it will appear different. Dunes can move and change their shapes relatively quickly." Regarding wadis, the professor notes, "Oh, some of you from the southwestern part of the country may know these as arroyos. That's simply another name for a wadi," and, "A wadi is about the worst place you can possibly be during a desert rainstorm. Even just a centimeter or two of rainfall can create a raging flood in one of them."

Practice with Long Passages   p. 156

A

Answers

1 Ⓒ   2 Ⓓ
3 *Oliver Twist*: ③, ④   *A Christmas Carol*: ①, ②

| Script |

Listen to part of a lecture in a literature class.

W Professor: Charles Dickens was the most famous British writer of the nineteenth century. Many works of his are considered masterpieces of literature. Dickens lived from 1812 to 1870. He wrote fifteen novels and hundreds of short stories. Among his most famous works are *Oliver*

Twist, Great Expectations, David Copperfield, A Christmas Carol, and *A Tale of Two Cities*. I'm sure everybody has read at least one or two of them.

Dickens was a self-made man. He grew up in poor circumstances and had little formal education. Many of his writings deal with poverty and the rough side of life in the nineteenth century. This is especially true of *Oliver Twist*, his second novel. It's the story of a young orphan boy who falls in with a gang of thieves. Much of the novel centers on the plight of orphans and other social problems of the day. Dickens also goes into great detail about criminal life in Britain. Like many of his stories, *Oliver Twist* was serialized in a magazine from 1837 to 1839. As a result, readers had to wait for the next magazine issue to find out what happened next. I suppose that's much like how we wait for new TV shows today.

M Student: Why didn't he publish it as a book?

W: Back then, serialization was cheaper and safer than printing a book that might not sell. In addition, when a serialized story was successful, it was typically published in book form later.

Another of Dickens's famous works was not serialized. It was *A Christmas Carol*. It's a small novella which was first published in book form in 1843. It has been made into numerous movies and TV shows. They often air around Christmas.

The story is about Ebenezer Scrooge, a rich businessman with an empty heart. In the story, Scrooge's employee Bob Cratchit serves as the common everyman. He works hard but receives little pay. So he struggles to support his family. The themes from this book come from Dickens's own life as well as the lives of many others living in Britain then. You know the story, right? On Christmas Eve, Scrooge is visited by the ghost of his dead business partner, Jacob Marley, and three other ghosts. They convince him to change his ways and to open his heart. Basically, um, it's a story about redemption.

Answer Explanation

1 Ⓒ During the lecture, the professor discusses the works of Charles Dickens.

2 Ⓓ The professor says, "This is especially true of *Oliver Twist*, his second novel. It's the story of a young orphan boy who falls in with a gang of thieves. Much of the novel centers on the plight of orphans and other social problems of the day. Dickens also goes into great detail about criminal life in Britain. Like many of his stories, *Oliver Twist* was serialized in a magazine from 1837 to 1839." Then, she adds, "Back then, serialization was cheaper and safer than printing a book that might not sell. In addition, when a serialized story was successful, it was typically published in book form later." Since she calls it a novel, it can be inferred that *Oliver Twist* was later published as a book.

3 *Oliver Twist*: ③, ④   *A Christmas Carol*: ①, ②

About *Oliver Twist*, the professor remarks, "This is especially true of *Oliver Twist*, his second novel. It's the story of a young orphan boy who falls in with a gang of thieves. Much of the novel centers on the plight of orphans and other social problems of the day. Dickens also goes into great detail about criminal life in Britain. Like many of his stories, Oliver Twist was serialized in a magazine from 1837 to 1839." Regarding *A Christmas Carol*, she states, "Another of Dickens's famous works was not serialized. It was *A Christmas Carol*. It's a small novella which was first published in book form in 1843." Then, she adds, "On Christmas Eve, Scrooge is visited by the ghost of his dead business partner, Jacob Marley, and three other ghosts.

Dictation

❶ Charles Dickens was <u>the most famous</u> British writer of the nineteenth century. Many works of his <u>are considered</u> <u>masterpieces</u> of literature.

❷ Much of the novel <u>centers on</u> the plight of orphans and other social problems <u>of the day</u>. Dickens also <u>goes into</u> <u>great detail</u> about criminal life in Britain.

❸ <u>Back then</u>, serialization was <u>cheaper</u> and <u>safer</u> than printing a book that might not sell. <u>In addition</u>, when a serialized story was successful, it was <u>typically</u> published in book form later.

B

Answers

1 Ⓑ   2 Cause: ①, ②, ④   Effect: ③   3 Ⓐ

| Script |

Listen to part of a lecture in an economics class.

M Professor: In the first century A.D., Rome was an enormous empire. Events in one place often influenced faraway places. This was never more obvious than during the financial crisis of 33 A.D. Failed business ventures in the Middle East sent shockwaves throughout the entire Roman financial world.

The crisis started in Egypt. A large merchant house there lost three ships in a storm. The ships were carrying valuable spices. The same merchants also had some trouble with land caravans from Ethiopia. Soon, there were rumors that the merchants would go bankrupt. At the same time, another famous merchant house in Tyre in Phoenicia went bankrupt. This happened when its workers went on strike and one of its managers stole some money. Both merchant houses had borrowed lots of money from a famous Roman bank.

W Student: Were Roman banks like modern banks?

M: To some extent, yes. For instance, they loaned money to businessmen and stored depositors' money. 🎧3 The most famous Roman banks in 33 A.D. were located on one street. It was called the Via Sacra. **I guess you could say it was the Wall Street of its time.** Well, when word of these business failures got back to Rome, there was a panic on Via Sacra. People began demanding their deposits back. Unfortunately, several banks didn't have enough money on hand to pay their depositors. You see, they had loaned it to others. They called in those loans, but many borrowers couldn't repay them. So, um, the banks closed down.

The crisis was worsened by a new agriculture law. Emperor Tiberius said that all senators had to invest one-third of their wealth in land in Italy. Tiberius set a time limit of eighteen months to do this. Time was almost up, but many still hadn't invested in land. The senators needed cash to buy land. They called in their loans, which caused more financial strain. More people demanded their deposits back. And, uh, more banks closed down. Soon, the panic spread to every corner of the empire.

Tiberius finally stepped in to stop the panic. He loaned the most reliable banks one hundred million sesterces. Oh, a sesterce was a silver coin commonly used by the Romans. So, ah, these were interest-free loans for three years. The banks, in turn, gave this money to their depositors. In a short time, the crises eased as confidence was restored.

Answer Explanation

1 Ⓑ About the financial crisis, the professor comments, "In the first century A.D., Rome was an enormous empire. Events in one place often influenced faraway places. This was never more obvious than during the financial crisis of 33 A.D. Failed business ventures in the Middle East sent shockwaves throughout the entire Roman financial world." He therefore believes it was a major problem for the Roman Empire.

2 Cause: ①, ②, ④   Effect: ③

About the causes of the financial crisis, the professor notes, "The crisis started in Egypt. A large merchant house there lost three ships in a storm. The ships were carrying valuable spices. The same merchants also had some trouble with land caravans from Ethiopia. Soon, there were rumors that the merchants would go bankrupt. At the same time, another famous merchant house in Tyre in Phoenicia went bankrupt. This happened when its workers went on strike and one of its managers stole some money. Both merchant houses had borrowed lots of money from a famous Roman bank." He also mentions, "The crisis was worsened by a new agriculture law. Emperor Tiberius said that all senators had to invest one-third of their wealth in land in Italy. Tiberius set a time limit of eighteen months to do this. Time was almost up, but many still hadn't invested in land. The senators needed cash to buy land." As for the effects, the professor states, "Tiberius finally stepped in to stop the panic. He loaned the most reliable banks one hundred million sesterces."

3 (A) When the professor calls the Via Sacra "the Wall Street of its time," he is making a comparison.

Dictation

❶ Events in one place <u>often influenced</u> faraway places. This was <u>never more obvious than</u> during the financial crisis of 33 A.D.

❷ The crisis <u>was worsened by</u> a new agriculture law.

❸ Tiberius finally <u>stepped in</u> to stop the panic. He <u>loaned</u> the most <u>reliable</u> banks one hundred million sesterces.

---

iBT Practice Test   p. 160

Answers

PART 1

1 [2], [4]	2 (A)	3 (B)	4 (A)	5 (A)
6 Ur: [2], [3] Lagash: [1], [4]		7 (D)	8 [2], [4]	
9 (A)	10 (C)	11 (A)		

PART 2

| 1 (A) | 2 (A) | 3 (D) | 4 (D) | 5 (B) |
| 6 (D) | 7 (C) | | | |

PART 1

[1–3] Conversation

| Script |

Listen to part of a conversation between a student and a dormitory manager.

W Dormitory Manager: Hi, Jason. I heard you want to talk to me about something. What's going on?

M Student: Hello, Ms. Stanton. Yes, I'm so glad you're in. I really have got to talk to you. I, uh, need to get a new room as soon as possible.

W: Why? What's the matter?

M: It's my roommate Joe. We just don't get along. Honestly, uh, I don't think I can stay in that room with him another day.

W: Okay, okay. Slow down a bit and tell me exactly what's going on.

M: All right. Let me see. Well, first of all, we're complete opposites. I like having a quiet room, but he's always

making noise. He listens to music loudly and plays his guitar in the room late at night. He's always got friends over throughout the day. As a result, I can't study in my own room. And I don't enjoy studying at the library. I prefer to study in my room.

W: Is that all?

M: Oh, no. Not by a longshot. There's more. I like having a neat room, but he's a complete slob. He never cleans, so the room looks awful. He even eats the food I have in my fridge. Can you believe that?

W: Have you tried talking to him?

M: Yes, I have. I've asked him to stop being so noisy. And I've told him that he shouldn't steal my food. But he just ignores me. I think he enjoys making me feel uncomfortable.

W: Okay, that doesn't sound very good. Unfortunately, the date for changing dorm rooms has already passed. It was last Friday.

M: Seriously? That's the worst news I've heard in a long time.

W: However . . . When there are serious situations, students are permitted to move any time in a semester. This typically happens once or twice a year. From what you just said, I think you qualify. Now, uh, there's a process we have to follow. It involves going to the student housing office. I need to accompany you there to explain the situation and to give my approval. The entire process should only take an hour or so. How does that sound to you?

M: Wonderful. When do you think we can do this?

W: How about right now? If you don't have class, we can go there at once.

M: Well, I've got a class in fifteen minutes, but it only lasts an hour. Can I meet you at the student housing office after my class finishes? How does meeting at a quarter after three sound?

W: That's fine with me. And I think I'm going to have a chat with Joe now to find out what he has to say.

Answer Explanation

1 Detail Question

[2], [4] About his roommate, the student says, "He listens to music loudly and plays his guitar in the room late at night." Then, he adds, "He even eats the food I have in my fridge."

2 Connecting Content Question

(A) The woman tells the student about the process for changing rooms. She mentions that they need to go to the student housing office to do that. So if the student goes to the student housing office, he will likely get a new dormitory room.

3 Making Inferences Question

The woman remarks, "When there are serious situations, students are permitted to move any time in a semester. This typically happens once or twice a year. From what you just said, I think you qualify." In saying this, she implies that she dealt with similar problems in the past.

[4–7] Lecture #1

| Script |

Listen to part of a lecture in an archaeology class.

M Professor: One of the world's oldest civilizations was Sumer. We call it the Sumerian civilization. It was located in the area where the country of Iraq is today. It was near the Tigris and Euphrates rivers. The region's hot, dry climate has preserved many ancient Sumerian sites. Unfortunately, that same climate also hinders archaeologists from examining them. Many places are buried beneath shifting sands, making it difficult to find and excavate them.

Nevertheless, archaeologists have done lots of work on ancient Sumer. Right now, I'd like to look at two sites. They're the ancient cities of Ur and Lagash. First, let's look at Ur. That's spelled U-R, um, by the way. It's widely considered the oldest city in the world. It rose around 6,000 years ago and reached its peak 3,000 years ago before it declined. The site of Ur was first examined in detail by a British team in 1853. It was led by John George Taylor and was sponsored by the British Museum. He found the famous Ziggurat of Ur. This massive structure was a temple of the Sumerian people. It was built in a square shape with different layers in a stepped style. It's about thirty meters high. Taylor only uncovered the top part since, uh, most of it was buried in the sand. His team also uncovered more of the city's top layers and found numerous stones with inscriptions.

Sadly, this expedition had a bad aftermath. After Taylor's team departed in 1854, the site lay exposed for decades. 🎧7 Locals stole many relics from the site. They even took stones for their own building projects. **This is a constant problem in archaeology.** Basically, unguarded sites attract thieves. It's sad, but that's just what happens. Now, uh, no more work was done on Ur until 1922. By then, very much had been lost.

The next team was a joint British-American effort led by Sir Charles Leonard Woolley. His team uncovered most of the city and the Ziggurat of Ur over the next decade. They found many structures made of sunbaked bricks joined together by bitumen. That's a tarlike substance found near oil deposits. Taylor's team also found burial tombs, pottery shards, and many ancient artifacts that hadn't been disturbed.

A more modern Sumerian site is the city of Lagash, which is in the same region as Ur. It was founded 4,000 years ago, making it younger than Ur. It was first excavated by a German team in 1877. Since then, work has been done in a stop-and-start fashion by various groups. It's a large site that covers around 600 hectares. The area is covered in sand, so excavation work is difficult. About five percent of the city had been uncovered when work stopped during the Iran-Iraq War in the 1980s. More recently, a French team worked there in 2015 and 2016.

Many surprising finds have been made. These include what may be the earliest examples of cuneiform writing and some examples of art. There are also some artifacts showing the development of the pottery wheel and the origins of schools. Unfortunately, the site is now exposed to thieves like Ur once was.

W Student: Why can't they protect it?

M: For the most part, it's too big. There are some guards, but they aren't enough. More extensive security, such as fences, would be too costly. So once more, important artifacts may be lost. With luck, more excavations can be done. Then, invaluable relics can be taken to museums, where they belong.

Answer Explanation

4 Gist-Content Question

Ⓐ The professor mostly talks about the excavation work done on some Sumerian cities.

5 Making Inferences Question

Ⓐ The professor says, "His team uncovered most of the city and the Ziggurat of Ur over the next decade. They found many structures made of sunbaked bricks joined together by bitumen. That's a tarlike substance found near oil deposits." It can therefore be inferred that Ur was located near some oilfields.

6 Connecting Content Question

Ur: ②, ③   Lagash: ①, ④

About Ur, the professor says, "First, let's look at Ur. That's spelled U-R, um, by the way. It's widely considered the oldest city in the world. It rose around 6,000 years ago and reached its peak 3,000 years ago before it declined. The site of Ur was first examined in detail by a British team in 1853. It was led by John George Taylor and was sponsored by the British Museum. He found the famous Ziggurat of Ur." Regarding Lagash, the professor states, "These include what may be the earliest examples of cuneiform writing and some examples of art," and, "There are some guards, but they aren't enough."

7 Understanding Attitude Question

Ⓓ When the professor states, "This is a constant problem in archaeology," he means that dig sites often get robbed.

| Script |

Listen to part of a lecture in a musicology class.

W1 Professor: Before modern times, music composers in Europe didn't make much money. They only earned money when they performed. Now, uh, some worked for the church, but most didn't. Instead, they had to find patrons. Patrons were wealthy people who sponsored composers. Most patrons in the past were nobles and other wealthy individuals in Europe.

W2 Student: Exactly what time period are you referring to?

W1: The Baroque and Classical periods of music. Basically, uh, from around the sixteenth to nineteenth centuries. During that time, there were many famous composers. Among them were Bach, Mozart, Beethoven, Brahms, Haydn, and Wagner. Most of those men had patrons. There were two kinds of patrons then. In some cases, the composer lived with the patron. In other cases, the composer didn't live with his patron. Instead, the patron merely supported the composer with funds. The first type of patron provided more security whereas the second type gave the composer more independence.

There were both positive and negative aspects of both types of patrons. What were some good points? Well, financial security, of course. The patron provided money and often food, clothing, and shelter. This freed the composer from having to seek paying work. The major negative point was that it stifled creativity. You see, uh, the composer was basically the patron's employee. He had to write music to be performed for the family. This often left the composer isolated, so he didn't know other composers or even musical trends in other places. However, this also resulted in some rather unique musical pieces. So there were both good and bad points, uh, I suppose.

A composer who lived with his patron didn't merely write music. He also taught music to the family members, particularly the children. He was in charge of the court musicians and the music library and had to maintain the musical instruments. When the family traveled, the composer and some musicians often accompanied them. So, uh, as you can see, it wasn't an easy position. Oh, yes, the composer gave the patron one more thing: prestige. Basically, having a famous composer in one's court was considered necessary for most of Europe's royal and wealthy families.

Wolfgang Amadeus Mozart is an example of someone who both needed yet hated having patrons. In the late 1770s, he worked at the court in Salzburg, Austria. Interestingly, his father had been employed there as well. Mozart's patron was Prince Colloredo. Unfortunately, the two men quarreled often. Mozart wanted more freedom to travel and work outside Salzburg. But the prince refused. Mozart finally quit working for Colloredo and moved to Vienna in 1781. For many years, he was a successful independent composer. But hard times plus a marriage and children forced him to seek new patrons. Before his premature death, he worked part time for the king of Austria, Joseph II, and he also had some wealthy noble patrons.

King Ludwig II of Bavaria was another famous patron of composers. The most famous composer he supported was Richard Wagner. Ludwig was way too lavish with his money though. He gave Wagner enormous sums of money and helped him construct a large house. In the end, Ludwig's family and the Bavarian government took action to stop his overspending.

Yet another famous patron of music was the wealthy Russian Nadezhda von Meck. She supported the famous composer Peter Tchaikovsky for more than a decade. She had one rule: The two could never meet. Despite this, they often wrote to each other, so we know quite a lot about their relationship.

Answer Explanation

8 **Detail Question**

[2], [4] The professor lectures, "The major negative point was that it stifled creativity. You see, uh, the composer was basically the patron's employee. He had to write music to be performed for the family. This often left the composer isolated, so he didn't know other composers or even musical trends in other places."

9 **Making Inferences Question**

Ⓐ The professor says, "Mozart's patron was Prince Colloredo. Unfortunately, the two men quarreled often. Mozart wanted more freedom to travel and work outside Salzburg. But the prince refused." The professor therefore implies that Mozart and the prince did not get along well.

10 **Understanding Function Question**

Ⓒ The professor describes how King Ludwig II supported Richard Wagner when he was Wagner's patron.

11 **Connecting Content Question**

Ⓐ The professor tells the class, "Yet another famous patron of music was the wealthy Russian Nadezhda von Meck. She supported the famous composer Peter Tchaikovsky for more than a decade. She had one rule: The two could never meet." Since they never met, it can be inferred that she only supported Peter Tchaikovsky with funds.

PART 2

[1–3] Conversation

| Script |

Listen to part of a conversation between a student and an audio-visual services office employee.

M Audio-Visual Services Office Employee: Good morning. Is there something I can help you with? Are you here to watch a video for a class?

W Student: Good morning. No, actually, I called about thirty minutes ago.

M: Ah, you're here to pick up the video camera.

W: That's correct. It's all ready, isn't it? I'm really looking forward to using it.

M: Yes, I've got the camera, the tripod, the battery pack, and the recharger all here for you. Do you know how to use this camera? It's the latest model, and it's a bit hard for beginners to use.

W: I've used the Profile 2500 several times in the past. However, I haven't had the opportunity to use the Profile 3500 yet. Is it a lot different than the 2500?

M: Not really. However, there are a few things which might confuse you. Here, uh . . . take the user's manual with you. The primary changes are covered in chapter three. If you read it, you'll have absolutely no problems using the camera.

W: That's great news. Thanks a lot.

M: Sure thing. Out of curiosity . . . what are you planning to use it for? You're the first person to borrow this particular camera. Photography and filming are kind of hobbies of mine. So it's nice to see someone request a top-of-the-line camera.

W: I work as a photographer for the *Falcon* . . . uh, you know, the student-run monthly magazine. I need the best camera to take good pictures. The editor is probably going to put one of my pictures on the front cover next month. So I need to make sure the pictures I take come out well.

M: You don't have a thing to worry about with this camera then. What do you intend to take pictures of?

W: You know the new building that just opened on campus? Deacon Hall. It's the new engineering building. I love how it looks, so I'm taking pictures of it and writing an article on it.

M: The engineering building? You like it?

W: Sure, I love its Brutalist elements.

M: Seriously?

W: Hey, uh, I know that not everyone likes Brutalism, but I appreciate it. Let me guess . . . You prefer Neoclassical architecture.

M: You got that right. I like anything from ancient Greece as well as the Italian Renaissance. I would love to see the school erect more buildings like Maxwell Hall. Now that's a beautiful building.

W: You got that right. It does look nice.

M: Anyway, I'd better stop chatting because it looks like a student over there needs some help. I need to see your ID card to check this stuff out. Then, I can give you everything.

W: Sure thing. Here you are.

Answer Explanation

1 Gist-Purpose Question

Ⓐ The employee says, "Ah, you're here to pick up the video camera." So the student visits the office to borrow some equipment.

2 Detail Question

Ⓐ The employee tells the student, "Here, uh . . . take the user's manual with you."

3 Making Inferences Question

Ⓓ The student says, "You prefer Neoclassical architecture," while talking to the employee. Then, he responds, "You got that right. I like anything from ancient Greece as well as the Italian Renaissance. I would love to see the school erect more buildings like Maxwell Hall. Now that's a beautiful building." So it can be inferred that Maxwell Hall is a work of Neoclassical architecture.

[4–7] Lecture

| Script |

Listen to part of a lecture in an engineering class.

M Professor: When we build things, we know they won't last forever. Materials such as wood, concrete, stone, plastic, and metal all eventually suffer from damage, erosion, and sometimes even total failure. This may begin as small holes or, um, cracks in the material. They grow bigger over time, so the result is a great amount of damage. At times, catastrophic failure occurs. Examples of this are when an airplane crashes and when a building collapses. However, there's a new generation of materials that may solve these problems. We call them self-healing materials.

A self-healing material is one that can heal itself. I guess this is kind of like, uh, how when you get a cut or scratch on your body, it heals over time. Well, uh, some scientists wondered why this couldn't happen with building materials. So they started doing research. In the past twenty years, four main kinds of self-healing materials have been developed. Some have embedded healing agents. Others have internal vascular systems, which are like blood vessels. Shape-memory materials are another type. And last of all are reversible polymers. Let me talk about each one now.

Let's see . . . Embedded healing agents . . . Well, they're placed inside materials which are prone to cracking. The healing agent is made by mixing two chemicals. They are put into two separate capsules. When a crack forms, both capsules break open, and the liquids inside them combine. This forms a strong bonding agent, uh, like glue. This, in turn, repairs the crack. Another type uses a polymer material. The polymer is one agent while a chemical in a capsule is another agent. Again, a crack forms, and the capsule breaks. The chemical inside the capsule reacts with the original polymer material and creates more of the original material. This repairs the crack.

W Student: Are the capsules big or small?

M: The latter. If they're big, they'll weaken the material. And that's something which we as engineers want to avoid.

Now, the second type: vascular systems. They have very thin tubes—uh, thinner than human hair—inside the building material. The tubes connect to small pressurized containers which contain healing agents. If there's a crack, the container opens. Then, pressure inside the containers pumps the healing agent to various parts of the material through the tubes. Unfortunately, this method is pretty slow. So whenever a crack becomes too big rather quickly, this method is ineffective.

Shape-memory materials are the third type. These are materials which can reform their original shape if they are damaged. But they need an outside heat source to do that. So this system is sort of like the vascular system. A series of thin tubes are placed in the material. When it suffers damage, laser light is used to pump heat through the tubes. Then, the material returns to its original shape. This is really incredible technology that's quite advanced. But if there's a big crack which forms quickly, it could break the tubes, so the laser light will be ineffective.

Now, uh, the last self-healing material is reversible polymers. Whenever the material is damaged, the polymer's molecules actively seek to rejoin other molecules. This action basically repairs the damage. Again, however, a source of heat is required to start the reaction.

So as we can see, none of these systems is perfect. Some are still in the research phase. But scientists are improving them all the time. Hopefully, in the near future, we'll be able to make structures with materials that can easily repair any damage they suffer.

Answer Explanation

4 **Gist-Content Question**

ⓓ The professor talks about self-healing materials, which are materials that can repair themselves.

5 **Connecting Content Question**

ⓑ The professor states, "So whenever a crack becomes

too big rather quickly, this method is ineffective." So the likely result of a crack developing quickly is that the crack will not be repaired.

6 **Understanding Attitude Question**

ⓓ When talking about shape-memory materials, the professor remarks, "This is really incredible technology that's quite advanced."

7 **Detail Question**

ⓒ About reversible polymers, the professor says, "Now, uh, the last self-healing material is reversible polymers. Whenever the material is damaged, the polymer's molecules actively seek to rejoin other molecules. This action basically repairs the damage. Again, however, a source of heat is required to start the reaction."

Vocabulary Review   p. 170

Answers

A
1 materials   2 caravan   3 dry up
4 article   5 panic

B
1 a   2 b   3 a   4 a   5 b
6 a   7 a   8 b   9 a

Actual Test

Answers

PART 1

1	Ⓓ	2	Ⓐ	3	Ⓐ	4	Ⓑ	5	Ⓑ
6	Ⓒ	7	1, 3	8	Ⓓ	9	Ⓐ	10	Ⓒ
11	Ⓐ	12	Ⓐ	13	Ⓒ	14	Ⓓ	15	Ⓐ

16 Guilds in Europe: 2, 3
Guilds in the American Colonies: 1, 4   17 Ⓐ

PART 2

1	1, 3	2	Fact: 1, 3 Not a Fact: 2, 4	3	Ⓒ	
4	Ⓓ	5	Ⓑ	6	Ⓐ	7 Ⓑ 8 Ⓓ
9	Fact: 1, 2 Not a Fact: 3, 4	10	Ⓓ	11	Ⓐ	

PART 1 Conversation   p. 173

| Script |

Listen to part of a conversation between a student and a professor.

W1 Student: Good afternoon, Professor Caine. How are you doing today? You wanted to see me about something?

W2 Professor: Hello, Emily. I'm doing fine. Thanks for asking. Why don't you have a seat? I need to talk to you for a bit.

W1: Sure. What's going on?

W2: I received a call from the dean of students. He informed me that several of your professors are, um . . . alarmed by your performance this semester. So, uh, as your academic advisor, he wants me to speak with you. So . . . what's going on?

W1: Well, I don't think my grades are that bad.

W2: On the contrary, Emily, they are. Apparently, you failed two midterms. And the highest grade you have in your other three classes is a C-. Until this semester, you've been an outstanding student. I mean, uh, you made the dean's list three times in five semesters. That's great. And your overall GPA is 3.43. So I'd say your grades are most definitely bad right now.

W1: Yeah . . . I guess you're right.

W2: Okay. Talk to me. I can't help you if I don't know what's going on. Do you have family or personal problems? Are you working too much? What's wrong?

W1: Um . . . I have a, um, family issue going on right now. Uh . . . I don't really want to talk about it though. It's kind of personal. But I have been spending lots of time at home this semester. So I've missed several classes. I haven't done much homework, and I haven't studied much either.

W2: Okay. I don't want to invade your privacy. But I do want

to help you. So let me ask you this . . . Is this something that's going to continue throughout the semester?

W1: Hmm . . . Yes, probably. Is that important?

W2: Okay, uh, you might want to consider taking a leave of absence from the school.

W1: What does that mean?

W2: It means you would drop out of school temporarily until you solve your personal issues. This actually has a number of benefits. Let me see . . . First, it sounds like your grades won't get better if this problem is going to continue. Well, if you take a leave of absence, you won't get any grades on your transcript this semester. In addition, you'll be eligible for a small refund on your tuition. So you'd get some money back from the school. And you will be allowed to return to continue your studies anytime within the next two years.

W1: You know, uh, that sounds appealing. I'll have to talk to my parents about it. But I think they'll agree that I should drop out for a semester or two.

W2: There is one thing though.

W1: Yes?

W2: You'll need to explain your problem in detail to someone in the school administration. It doesn't have to be me. But it does have to be someone like the dean of students. You are, of course, free to confide in me. Then, I can help you deal with the dean.

W1: 🎧5 Um . . . Let me discuss this with my parents tonight. If they agree that I should drop out, I'll come back here tomorrow and tell you everything.

W2: **Fair enough.** I'll be here in my office between two and five. You can come anytime then. Good luck, Emily.

Answer Explanation

1 **Gist-Purpose Question**

Ⓓ The professor tells the student, "I received a call from the dean of students. He informed me that several of your professors are, um . . . alarmed by your performance this semester. So, uh, as your academic advisor, he wants me to speak with you." Then, she mentions how low the student's grades are and asks why.

2 **Detail Question**

Ⓐ The student remarks, "I have a, um, a family issue going on right now. Uh . . . I don't really want to talk about it though. It's kind of personal."

3 **Understanding Function Question**

Ⓐ The professor suggests a solution to the student's problem when she tells her about a leave of absence.

4 **Making Inferences Question**

(B) The professor is interested in the student's well-being. She tries to find out what the problem is and then suggests a way to help the student solve her problem.

5 **Understanding Attitude Question**

(B) When the professor says, "Fair enough," she means that she is satisfied with the student's comment on how she is going to deal with her problem.

PART 1 Lecture #1   p. 176

| Script |

Listen to part of a lecture in an environmental science class.

W Professor: The modern-day Sahara Desert looks nothing like it did in the past. Around 10,000 years ago, it was a lush land full of vegetation. Gradually, the land changed to its present state: a dry, barren landscape of shifting sand dunes and brutal heat. There are two main reasons this happened. The first is that slight periodic changes in the Earth's orbit resulted in the climate changing around the world. This caused the Sahara to, um, at times, receive varying amounts of rainfall. In addition, approximately 10,000 years ago, humans moved into the area. Their activities caused the environment to change permanently.

There's a theory that the creation of the Sahara Desert was caused in part by the shifting winds in the region. There's a boundary line in North Africa called the Intertropical Convergence Zone. That is where winds from the Northern Hemisphere meet winds from the Southern Hemisphere. Where they come together is, interestingly enough, the southern boundary of the Sahara Desert. The dry northern winds push down the humid tropical winds from Central Africa. This prevents humid air from moving north. That, in turn, stops it from raining in the north. We know that the line has shifted southward over time. For instance, a long time ago, it was nearly at the coast of the Mediterranean Sea. At that time, North Africa was a green land with plenty of water. But every so often, the line moved south due to changes in the Earth's orbit. This caused the desert to increase in size. Then, uh, the Earth's orbit changed again, the rains came back, and the desert shrank. But, well, about 10,000 years ago, the line began moving south again and hasn't returned north since then. That resulted in the Sahara Desert becoming enormous in size.

One reason the change has become permanent has to do with the invasion of humans into North Africa. It's connected with farming and raising animals. More than 10,000 years ago, people began settling in the Nile River Valley. They grew crops and domesticated animals, including goats. Gradually, they pushed westward across North Africa. They brought their herds of goats with them, too. Have any of you ever seen goats eat . . . ? Well,

in case you don't know, they'll devour virtually anything. They especially love plants. Over thousands of years, as people and goats spread, the goats consumed lots of vegetation in the area.

This created a, uh, a feedback loop. As the vegetation disappeared, the ground became more exposed. Dry, exposed ground reflects lots of heat while vegetation absorbs it. Basically, more heat was going into the air. There was less moisture, so the climate slowly became drier. Fewer plants grew, and those that did were smaller than the ones before them. The topsoil became loose. Then, the wind picked it up and blew it around. Over time, that once-fertile soil became sand, and then the entire region became a desert. Basically, the people and their goats would consume the vegetation in an area, watch it turn to desert, and then leave. In their new place, the same thing would happen. By around 4000 B.C., the entire region had become the desert we are familiar with today. This also caused the Intertropical Convergence Zone to shift southward. Why? 🎧11 Well, the lack of vegetation in the northern zone made the air much drier. This kept the humid southern air from returning.

M: **Excuse me, but how do we know the desert actually formed the way you are describing it?** I mean, uh, do we have written records?

W: No, Vlad, we don't. And I understand how you feel. I mean, uh, there's actually only a bit of evidence to support this theory. In fact, most of the support for it comes from knowledge we've gained in modern times. We know from our experiences on North America's plains and in parts of China and Mongolia that animals can quickly eat all the vegetation in an area. If the area is already dry, this can make a bad situation worse. Nowadays, some parts of the world are changing in the manner I described. That's why we think the Sahara changed this way, too.

In addition, there's evidence that it once had a wetter climate. We know there were once rivers and lakes in the Sahara. We've found dry riverbeds and lakebeds. Some studies have been done, but we need to do more. For instance, we have to dig into the lakebeds and pull up soil samples from long ago. We can often find the remains of vegetation in soil samples. By examining them, we can determine what plants grew there and when. That will also teach us about the people who lived there. For instance, we can learn if the plants were wild or domesticated. That will teach us plenty about the climate as well.

Answer Explanation

6 **Gist-Content Question**

(C) The professor mainly discusses the creation of the Sahara Desert in the past.

7 **Detail Question**

1, 3 The professor says, "There are two main reasons

this happened. The first is that slight periodic changes in the Earth's orbit resulted in the climate changing around the world. This caused the Sahara to, um, at times, receive varying amounts of rainfall. In addition, approximately 10,000 years ago, humans moved into the area. Their activities caused the environment to change permanently."

8 **Connecting Content Question**

Ⓓ In talking about the Intertropical Convergence Zone, the professor lectures, "We know that the line has shifted southward over time. For instance, a long time ago, it was nearly at the coast of the Mediterranean Sea. At that time, North Africa was a green land with plenty of water. But every so often, the line moved south due to changes in the Earth's orbit. This caused the desert to increase in size. Then, uh, the Earth's orbit changed again, the rains came back, and the desert shrank. But, well, about 10,000 years ago, the line began moving south again and hasn't returned north since then. That resulted in the Sahara Desert becoming enormous in size." So it is likely that if the line moves to the north, the Sahara Desert will become smaller.

9 **Understanding Organization Question**

Ⓐ The professor discusses how the Sahara Desert became larger through the actions of humans and goats in discussing a feedback loop.

10 **Making Inferences Question**

Ⓒ While talking about how deserts form, the professor comments, "We know from our experiences on North America's plains and in parts of China and Mongolia that animals can quickly eat all the vegetation in an area." So the professor implies that there are places in China and Mongolia that have become deserts.

11 **Understanding Attitude Question**

Ⓐ When the student says, "Excuse me, but how do we know the desert actually formed the way you are describing it"? it can be inferred that he is skeptical of the professor's explanation.

PART 1 Lecture #2   p. 179

| Script |

Listen to part of a lecture in an economics class.

M Professor: A guild is an organization of workers. They band together for various reasons. The primary one is to set up rules which its members must follow. These rules do many things. For example, uh . . . they keep the quality of work high . . . set fair prices and wages . . . and make sure there's no outside competition. In Europe, guilds arose during the Middle Ages. There were guilds in almost every

city and town, and they covered all kinds of occupations. Over time, they became a vital part of the European economy. The guilds essentially trained future workers. Many guild members started their lives as apprentices when they were children. During their apprenticeships, they were trained by master members of the guild.

I'm sure most of you have heard about guilds in Europe. However, fewer people are aware that there were guilds in the United States. But if you think about it, it was natural for Europeans to bring guilds to the New World when they settled in it. At first, the colonists tried to run things the same way they had in Europe. As towns and cities developed, guilds in certain trades were established. There were guilds for carpenters, metalsmiths, tailors, printers, shoemakers, weavers, stone masons, and merchants. In the American colonies, most of the guilds were in big cities like New York, Boston, and Philadelphia. However, there were few guilds in some of the colonies. Virginia was one of these places. Actually, guilds didn't last too long in the American colonies. This had to do with the economic situation there.

To understand what happened, we need to look back at Europe. There, guilds ruled certain parts of the economy with an iron fist. Every guild in a town had a monopoly on its particular trade. To join a guild, a person first had to be an apprentice for a certain number of years. Then, the person became a journeyman. That meant he was skilled but not quite a full member yet. After a while, the guild masters would approve the journeyman becoming a master himself. This process could take years. After all, the masters didn't want too much competition for work. In many cases, a journeyman had to wait for a master to die before being given master status. This was stifling for both young workers and the economy as a whole. Prices and wages stagnated, and there were few opportunities. That's why numerous Europeans decided to settle in the New World.

Most of those going to the American colonies were from Britain. In the 1700s, guilds were dying out in Britain. At that time, the notion of free trade was growing in Britain. Guilds were an obstruction to free trade, so they went into decline. Nevertheless, the colonists tried setting up guilds. But they encountered various problems. For one thing, labor was scarce in the colonies. That meant there were many chances for workers to go wherever they wanted and to do the work they wanted. They didn't have to wait for years under the thumb of a master before they set up their own shop. Suddenly, master craftsmen had trouble getting and keeping apprentices.

In addition, laws were passed to help apprentices. They were based on British laws. The idea was to provide orphans with apprenticeships. Other laws gave courts the right to take children from their parents if they couldn't raise them properly. The Virginia Poor Law in the late 1600s did that. So, uh, there were both masters and apprentices. But the guilds were loosely organized compared to European ones. Many masters complained that they would train apprentices only to see them set up shops in the same towns and become competitors. And the masters were powerless to stop them. While this was bad for the masters, it was good for the economy. More competition meant no monopolies. People had more options for the products and services they required.

By the 1700s, all of these factors led to guilds disappearing from the big cities in the northern colonies. In the southern American colonies, the guilds never really took root. Slavery had a lot to do with that. Slaves provided the south with a cheap and permanent supply of labor. They were trained in the skills that were needed. So a system with masters and apprentices never became established in the south. As for the north, the guilds there gradually changed into workers' associations. They became more like, uh, like clubs. They were places where workers could meet to discuss issues. They also raised money for injured workers or for the families of deceased workers.

W Student: 🎧 17 It sounds like they were labor unions.

M: Well, they were the basis for modern labor unions. But I'm not ready to talk about that. **You'll have to wait until a bit later in my lecture to hear about them.**

Answer Explanation

12 Gist-Content Question

Ⓐ The professor mostly talks about the early history of guilds in America in his lecture.

13 Detail Question

Ⓒ The professor says, "To join a guild, a person first had to be an apprentice for a certain number of years. Then, the person became a journeyman. That meant he was skilled but not quite a full member yet."

14 Making Inferences Question

Ⓓ The professor states, "After a while, the guild masters would approve the journeyman becoming a master himself. This could take years. After all, the masters didn't want too much competition for work. In many cases, a journeyman had to wait for a master to die before being given master status. This was stifling for both young workers and the economy as a whole. Prices and wages stagnated, and there were few opportunities. That's why numerous Europeans decided to settle in the New World." It can therefore be inferred that guilds harmed the economy in Europe.

15 Gist-Purpose Question

Ⓐ The professor comments, "In the southern American colonies, the guilds never really took root. Slavery had a lot to do with that. Slaves provided the south with a cheap and permanent supply of labor. They were trained in the skills that were needed. So a system with masters and apprentices never became established in the south."

16 Connecting Content Question

Guilds in Europe: ②, ③
Guilds in the American Colonies: ①, ④
About guilds in Europe, the professor says, "In Europe, guilds arose during the Middle Ages. There were guilds in almost every city and town, and they covered all kinds of occupations. Over time, they became a vital part of the European economy." Regarding guilds in the American colonies, the professor notes, "But the guilds were loosely organized compared to European ones," and, "As for the north, the guilds there gradually changed into workers' associations."

17 Understanding Function Question

Ⓐ When the professor tells the student, "You'll have to wait until a bit later in my lecture to hear about them, he is indicated that he will discuss a topic soon."

PART 2 Conversation

| Script |

Listen to part of a conversation between a student and a radio station manager.

M Student: Hi. You're the manager here, right? Could I have a brief word with you?

W Radio Station Manager: Hello. I'm Tina. Yes, I'm the manager. What can I do for you?

M: Ah, yes. My name is Mark Soroka. I'm a big fan of the radio station at school. In fact, uh, I pretty much listen to it constantly.

W: Wonderful. It's always nice to hear from a fan. Our ratings aren't that high, so I'm glad to hear you listen to us.

M: Yes, well, actually . . . I might be listening to you a bit less in the future. You see, um, I'm here because of that new radio program which airs from eight to ten every weeknight. You know the one I'm talking about, don't you?

W: Sure. You're talking about the program hosted by Ken O'Brien. He mostly plays music and also does a few interviews. You don't like the show?

M: Not at all. It's simply awful. First, the music selections are terrible. The show he replaced had much better music. I really enjoyed listening to the pop songs on the previous show. But the songs Ken plays just, uh . . . those oldies . . . Well, they just aren't appealing. And, uh, the interviews . . . He's not good at interviewing his guests. So the interviews are a waste of time for the most part.

W: Okay, um . . . you know, between you and me, we've gotten several comments like that ever since the program started. 🎧 5 I don't know what to do though. We have to air a program at that time. But we can't find anyone else to host a show.

M: **Well, it just so happens that I'm available during that time.** And I happen to have some experience on radio. I worked part time at my local radio station during high school. I also did an internship at WPLL here in town last summer.

W: Seriously? You could do every day of the week?

M: Well, I don't particularly want to, but I could do that if it's necessary.

W: Hmm . . . How about if Ken does a one-hour program and then you do a one-hour program? He might improve if he's only on the air for an hour. And maybe you could, uh, give him some pointers.

M: Yeah, that sounds like a good solution.

W: Excellent. Oh, there's one thing. I need you to take a short test. That way I can make sure you know your way around a radio studio.

M: That's not a problem. When do you want me to do that?

W: How about in a couple of minutes? I'm due to go on the air from eleven to noon. But you could do the first ten minutes of the show. I normally talk about a few news items on campus. And then I play a song or two. Do you think you can handle it?

M: Totally. But I can't stay too long. I've got a class to attend at 11:30. Oh, if I pass the test, when will I have my first show?

W: If all goes well, you'll be on the air tonight if that fits your schedule.

M: My evenings are always free. Don't worry about that.

Answer Explanation

1 Gist-Purpose Question

①, ③ First, the student says, "You see, um, I'm here because of that new radio program which airs from eight to ten every weeknight," and then he complains about the quality of a radio program. Next, he comments, "Well, it just so happens that I'm available during that time," so he is applying for a position.

2 Detail Question

Fact: ①, ③ Not a Fact: ②, ④
About Ken O'Brien's radio program, the student says, "You see, um, I'm here because of that new radio program which airs from eight to ten every weeknight," and the employee states, "He mostly plays music and also does a few interviews." However, it is not true that the show features pop music. Instead, the student says, "But the songs Ken plays just, uh . . . those oldies." It is also not true that the show has been on the air for two years. It is a new show.

3 Detail Question

ⓒ The student tells the employee, "I also did an internship at WPLL here in town last summer."

4 Making Inferences Question

ⓓ The employee says, "How about in a couple of minutes? I'm due to go on the air from eleven to noon. But you could do the first ten minutes of the show. I normally talk about a few news items on campus. And then I play a song or two. Do you think you can handle it?" The student agrees to her request.

5 Understanding Function Question

ⓑ When the student says, "Well, it just so happens that I'm available during that time," it can be inferred that he is willing to host a radio show.

PART 2 Lecture   p. 185

| Script |

Listen to part of a lecture in a history class.

M1 Professor: Thousands of years ago during the period of ancient Greece, Athens was the most dominant city-state. In fact, it held a position of power in the eastern Mediterranean world for several centuries. Thanks to its dominance, Greek ideas and culture spread far and wide. Right now, I'd like to take a few moments to explain how Athens became so powerful.

The site where Athens sits has been occupied by people for around 5,000 years. The dominant feature of Athens is the hill called the Acropolis. Early Athenians built a fort on it, and their town spread out from the hill. Eventually, they built walls around the town to provide protection. Athens then grew into a major trading center on the Mediterranean Sea. Then, uh, around 1200 B.C., a major disaster struck much of this world. Invaders attacked civilized areas in the eastern Mediterranean. Some came from the sea while others came overland. Athens was hit by a people that later historians would call the Dorians. Now, uh, we aren't sure who the Dorians were or where they came from.

But we do know that on account of their highly successful attacks, Athens declined for a couple of hundred years. Then, around 900 B.C., a group of powerful families began to rule Athens. Over the next several centuries, the beginnings of democracy took hold there. This began Athens's dramatic rise in power. This wasn't the only factor though. There were several. One was actually the lack of fertile land in the area around Athens, which is called Attica. This absence of good land led Athens to seek wealth elsewhere. The Athenians found it in trade. While the city isn't located directly on the sea, it's very close to it. A nearby harbor provided a base for Athenian trade and naval ships. Trade brought the riches of the Mediterranean world to Athens. This helped it grow into a powerful, wealthy city-state. Gradually, Athens started dominating the other towns and villages in Attica, eventually uniting them all under its control.

M2 Student: Didn't all of these factors exist even before the Dorian invasions?

M1: Yes, and that should make us ask why Athens didn't become powerful even earlier. The answer is that something else was necessary for Athens to become the leader of the Greek world. It, uh, it had to prove its power in war. The rise of Athens was directly related to its leadership in several wars Greece fought against Persia. Oh, uh, when I say Greece, I mean the collection of city-states which ruled parts of Greece at that time. Several Greek colonies were located near the Persian Empire. The two sides came into conflict, and the Persians invaded Greece in 492 B.C. At first, they were successful. Then, in 490 B.C., an Athenian-led army defeated the Persians at the Battle of Marathon.

The fighting against the Persians didn't end there. The Persians returned a decade later. After their large army landed in Greece, a fleet of Athenian warships defeated the Persian fleet at the Battle of Salamis in 480 B.C. Then, the famed 300 Spartan warriors slowed down the Persian army at the Battle of Thermopylae. That gave the rest of the Spartans, Athenians, and other city-states time to raise a large army. In 479 B.C., they defeated the Persians at the Battle of Plataea. After these battles, Athens emerged as the leader of Greece. After all, um, the Athenian army and navy had been prominent in the victories over the Persians. The Greek city-states decided to form a league for defense against possible future Persian invasions. It was called the Delian League after the island of Delos, where it was formed. The Spartans, however, were unimpressed and refused to join the alliance.

The members of the Delian League all contributed ships and men to a common fleet and army. But most of the city-states found this bothersome after a while. The Athenians then said that they would provide the bulk of the military force. However, the others had to pay them to do so. Initially, this seemed like a good idea for the smaller city-states. But it naturally gave Athens complete control over the Delian League. Athens acquired both money and power. As its army and navy increased in size, the other city-states' forces shrank as they gave their money for defense to Athens. The payments to the league took on the form of tribute. In effect, Athens was saying that the city-states had to pay up, or they would be attacked with the soldiers and ships they were paying for. This state of affairs endured for several decades. As you can no doubt imagine, many city-states were unhappy with the arrangement. Meanwhile, Sparta formed its own league, which would soon clash with Athens for control of Greece. Let's cover that now.

6   Understanding Organization Question

ⓐ The professor describes the events in the lecture in chronological order.

7   Understanding Attitude Question

ⓑ The professor says, "Invaders attacked civilized areas in the eastern Mediterranean. Some came from the sea while others came overland. Athens was hit by a people that later historians would call the Dorians. Now, uh, we aren't sure who the Dorians were or where they came from. But we do know that on account of their highly successful attacks, Athens declined for a couple of hundred years."

8   Detail Question

ⓓ The professor tells the students, "This absence of good land led Athens to seek wealth elsewhere. The Athenians found it in trade. While the city isn't located directly on the sea, it's very close to it. A nearby harbor provided a base for Athenian trade and naval ships. Trade brought the riches of the Mediterranean world to Athens. This helped it grow into a powerful, wealthy city-state."

9   Detail Question

Fact: ⊡1, ⊡2   Not a Fact: ⊡3, ⊡4

The professor says, "The two sides came into conflict, and the Persians invaded Greece in 492 B.C. At first, they were successful. Then, in 490 B.C., an Athenian-led army defeated the Persians at the Battle of Marathon. The fighting against the Persians didn't end there. The Persians returned a decade later. After their large army landed in Greece, a fleet of Athenian warships defeated the Persian fleet at the Battle of Salamis in 480 B.C. Then, the famed 300 Spartan warriors slowed down the Persian army at the Battle of Thermopylae. That gave the rest of the Spartans, Athenians, and other city-states time to raise a large army. In 479 B.C., they defeated the Persians at the Battle of Plataea." It is not true that the Persians defeated the Greeks in the Delian League. It formed after the Persian invasion ended. And the Greeks won the Battle of Plataea.

10   Understanding Function Question

ⓓ While talking about the Delian League, the professor explains how Athens used it to gain power over the other city-states.

11   Making Inferences Question

ⓐ At the end of the lecture, the professor says, "Meanwhile, Sparta formed its own league, which would soon clash with Athens for control of Greece. Let's cover that now."